A BOY & A GIRL

by Jamie S. Rich & Natalie Nourigat

JAN 0 8 2014

A BOY & A GIRL

Written by: Jamie S. Rich

Illustrated by: Natalie Nourigat

Lettered by: Ed Brisson

Edited by: Jill Beaton

Designed by: Jason Storey & Keith Wood

Oni Press, Inc.

Publisher: **Joe Nozemack**

Editor In Chief: **James Lucas Jones**

Art Director: **Keith Wood**

Director of Publicity: **John Schork**

Director of Sales: **Cheyenne Allott**

Editor: **Jill Beaton**

Editor: **Charlie Chu**

Digital Prepress Lead: **Troy Look**

Graphic Designer: **Jason Storey**

Administrative Assistant: **Robin Herrera**

Oni Press, Inc
1305 SE Martin Luther King Jr. Blvd.
Suite A
Portland, OR 97214

www.onipress.com
facebook.com/onipress : twitter.com/onipress : onipress.tumblr.com

First Edition: November 2013

1 2 3 4 5 6 7 8 9 10

Printed in China.

Library of Congress Cataloging-in-Publication Data
Rich, Jamie S.
A boy and a girl / written by Jamie S. Rich ; illustrated by Natalie Nourigat ; lettered by Ed Brisson ;
edited by Jill Beaton ; designed by Jason Storey. -- First edition.
pages cm
ISBN-13: 978-1-62010-089-9
ISBN-10: 1-62010-089-4
1. Graphic novels. I. Nourigat, Natalie, ill. II. Title.
PN6728.B648R54 2011
741.5--dc23
2013021724

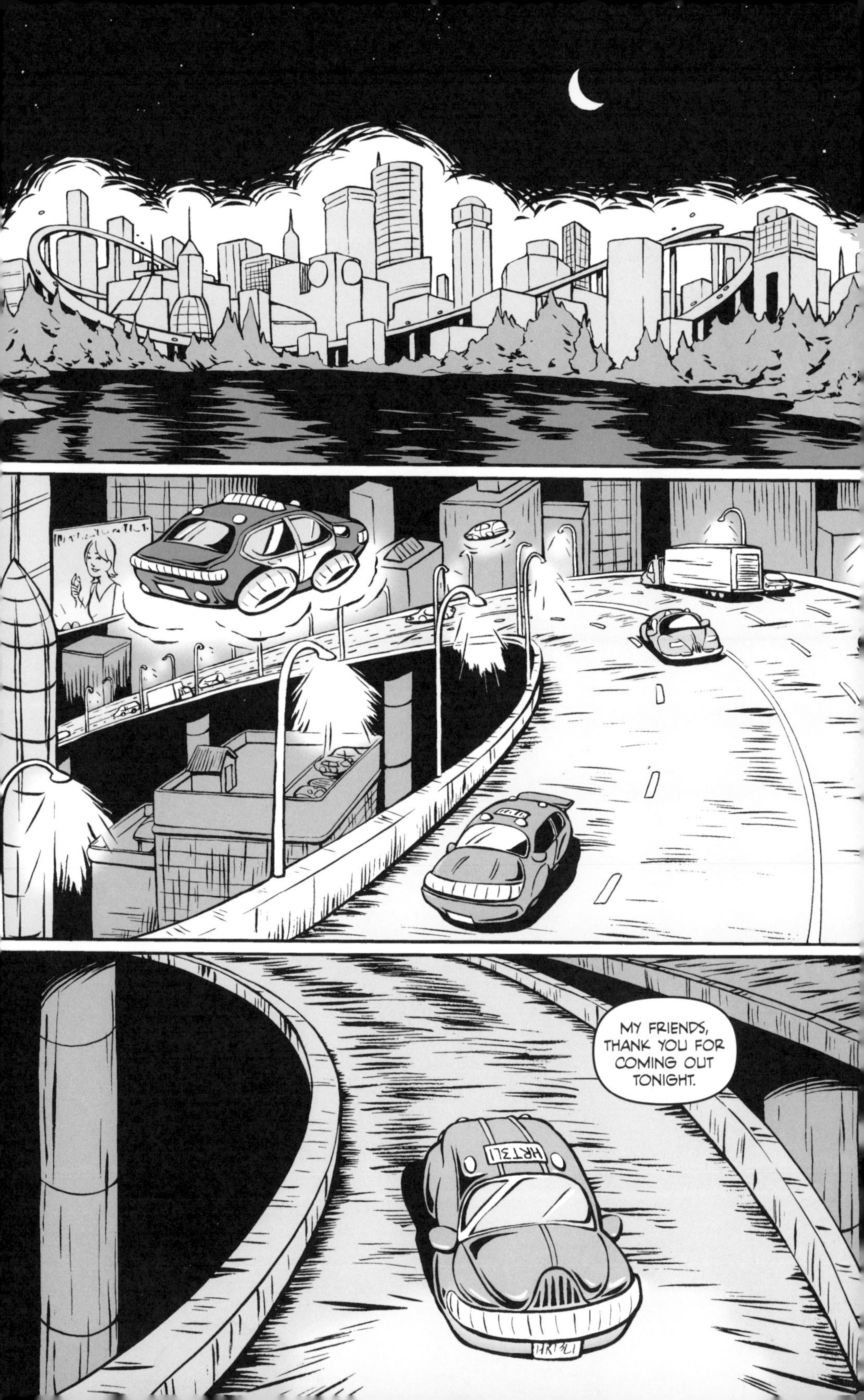
MY FRIENDS, THANK YOU FOR COMING OUT TONIGHT.

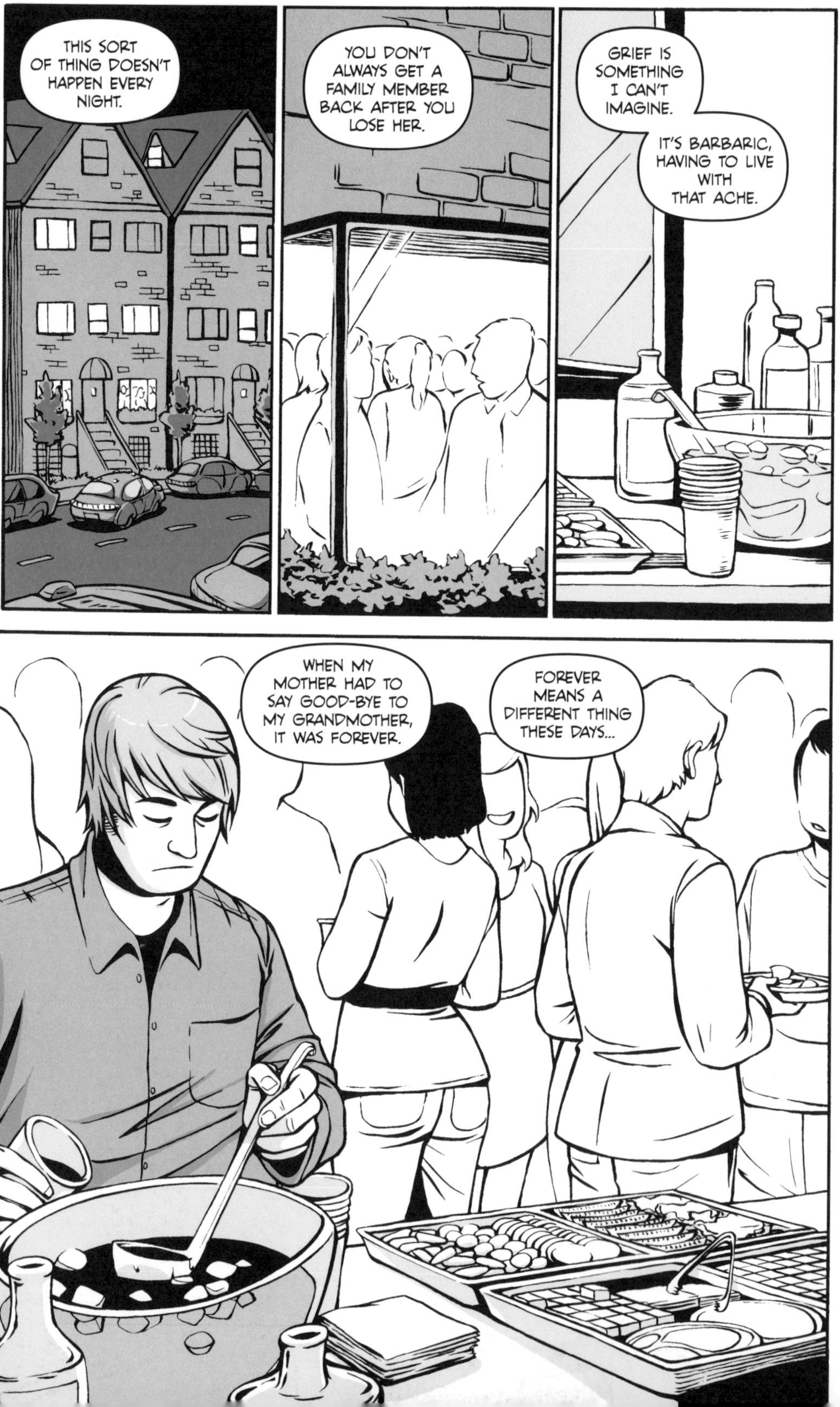
THIS SORT OF THING DOESN'T HAPPEN EVERY NIGHT.
YOU DON'T ALWAYS GET A FAMILY MEMBER BACK AFTER YOU LOSE HER.
GRIEF IS SOMETHING I CAN'T IMAGINE.
IT'S BARBARIC, HAVING TO LIVE WITH THAT ACHE.
WHEN MY MOTHER HAD TO SAY GOOD-BYE TO MY GRANDMOTHER, IT WAS FOREVER.
FOREVER MEANS A DIFFERENT THING THESE DAYS...

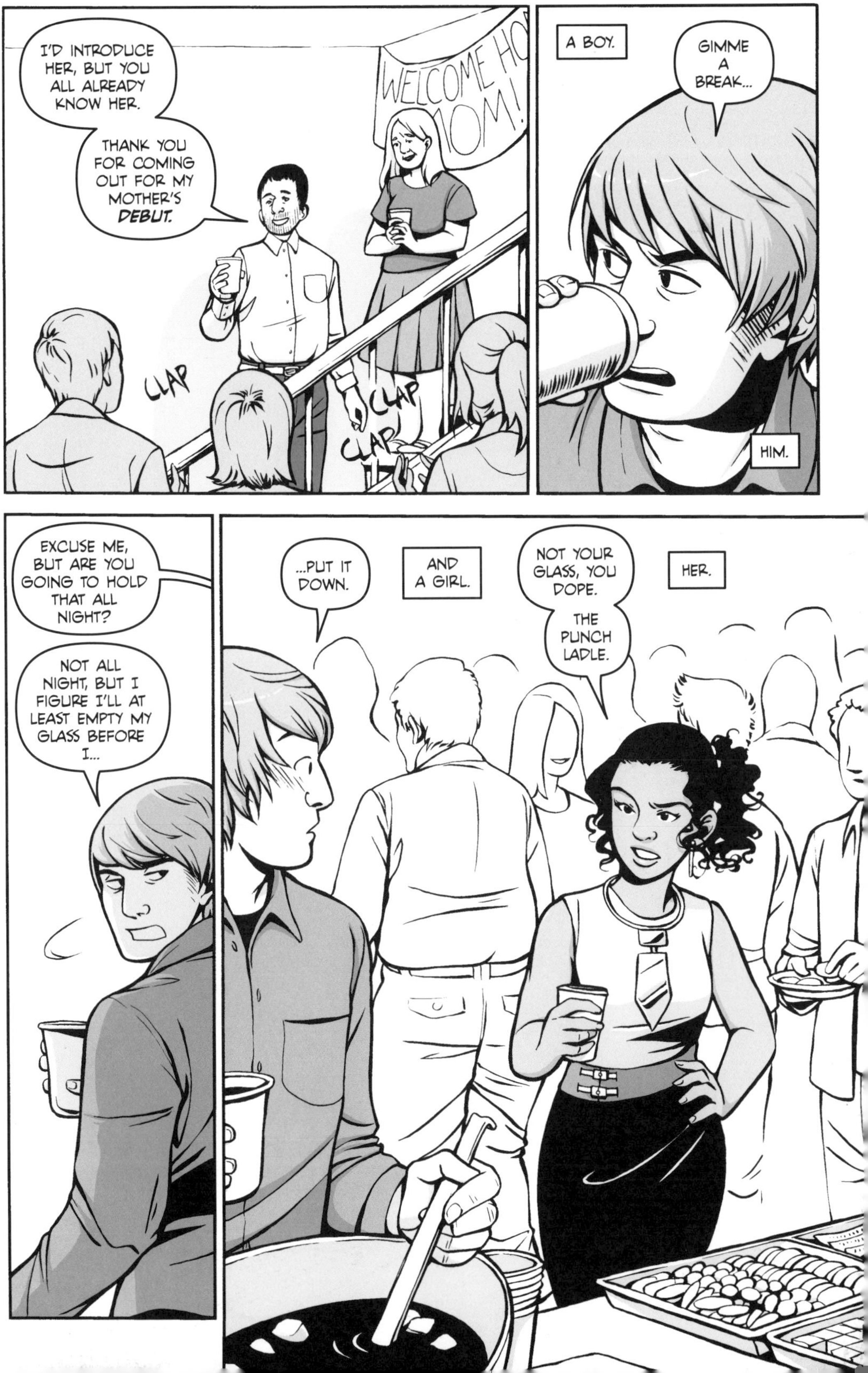
I'D INTRODUCE HER, BUT YOU ALL ALREADY KNOW HER.
THANK YOU FOR COMING OUT FOR MY MOTHER'S *DEBUT.*
WELCOME HO MOM!
CLAP
CLAP
CLAP
A BOY.
GIMME A BREAK...
HIM.
EXCUSE ME, BUT ARE YOU GOING TO HOLD THAT ALL NIGHT?
NOT ALL NIGHT, BUT I FIGURE I'LL AT LEAST EMPTY MY GLASS BEFORE I...
...PUT IT DOWN.
AND A GIRL.
NOT YOUR GLASS, YOU DOPE.
THE PUNCH LADLE.
HER.

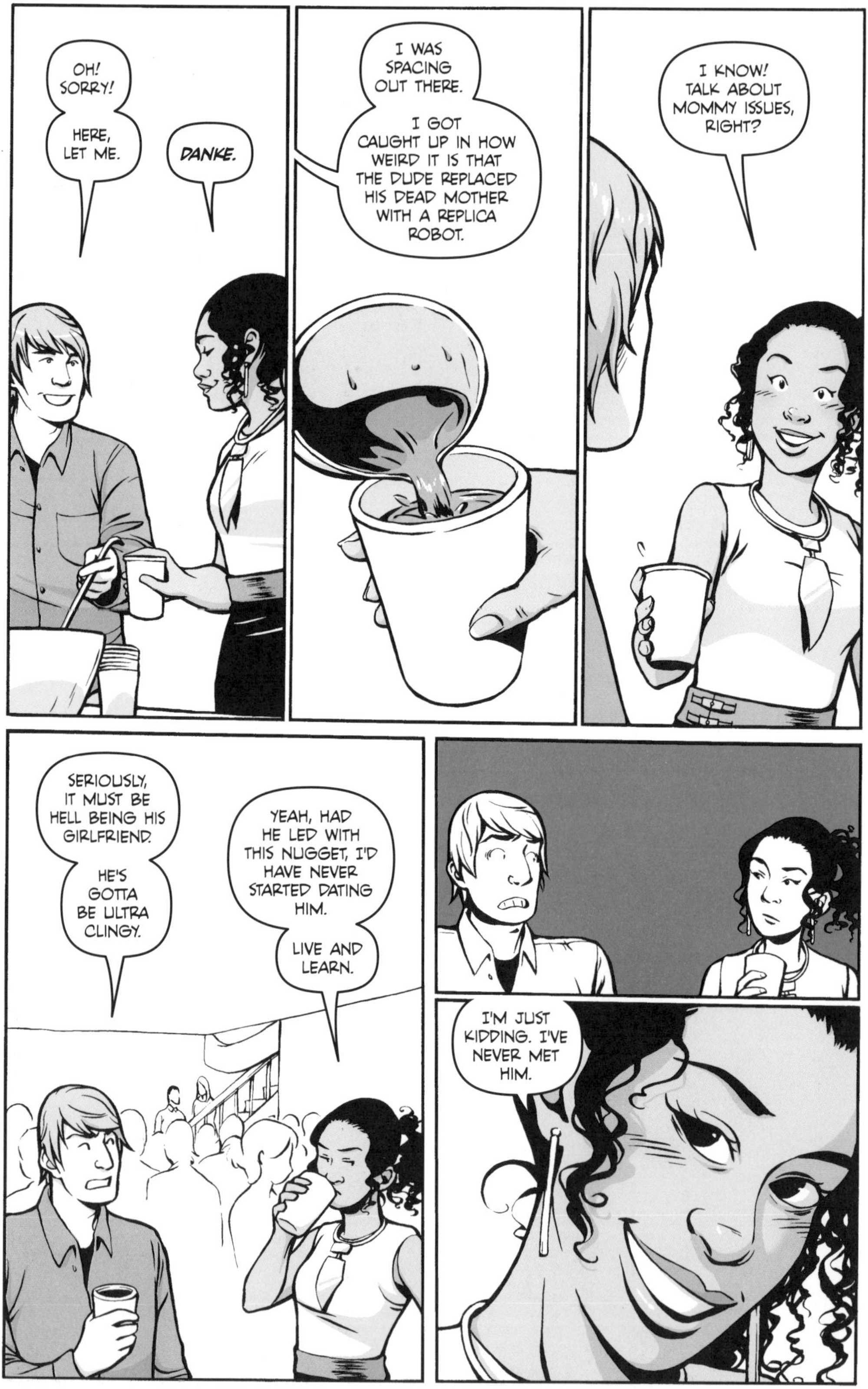
OH! SORRY!
HERE, LET ME.
DANKE.
I WAS SPACING OUT THERE.
I GOT CAUGHT UP IN HOW WEIRD IT IS THAT THE DUDE REPLACED HIS DEAD MOTHER WITH A REPLICA ROBOT.
I KNOW! TALK ABOUT MOMMY ISSUES, RIGHT?
SERIOUSLY, IT MUST BE HELL BEING HIS GIRLFRIEND.
HE'S GOTTA BE ULTRA CLINGY.
YEAH, HAD HE LED WITH THIS NUGGET, I'D HAVE NEVER STARTED DATING HIM.
LIVE AND LEARN.
I'M JUST KIDDING. I'VE NEVER MET HIM.

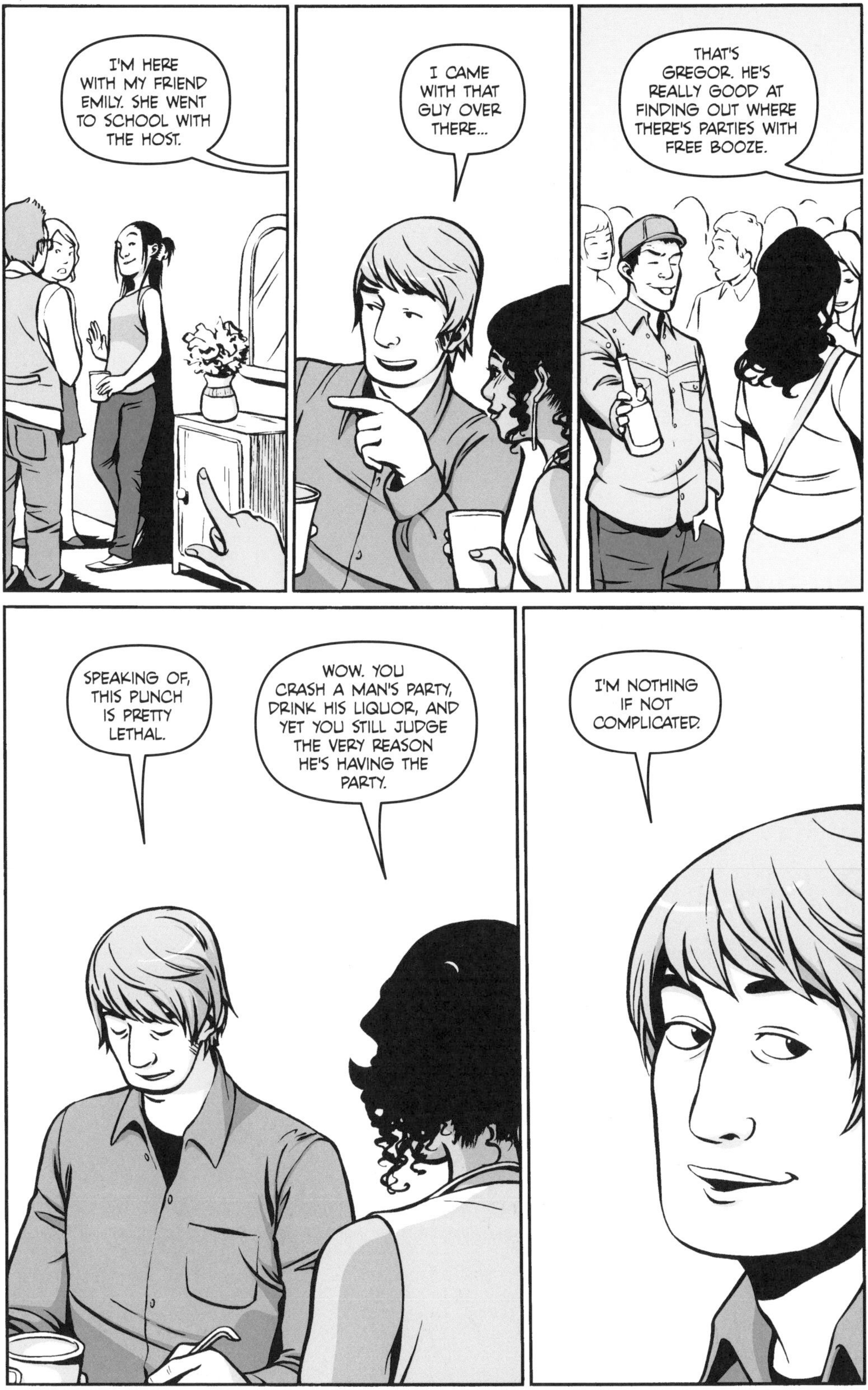
I'M HERE WITH MY FRIEND EMILY. SHE WENT TO SCHOOL WITH THE HOST.
I CAME WITH THAT GUY OVER THERE...
THAT'S GREGOR. HE'S REALLY GOOD AT FINDING OUT WHERE THERE'S PARTIES WITH FREE BOOZE.
SPEAKING OF, THIS PUNCH IS PRETTY LETHAL.
WOW. YOU CRASH A MAN'S PARTY, DRINK HIS LIQUOR, AND YET YOU STILL JUDGE THE VERY REASON HE'S HAVING THE PARTY.
I'M NOTHING IF NOT COMPLICATED.

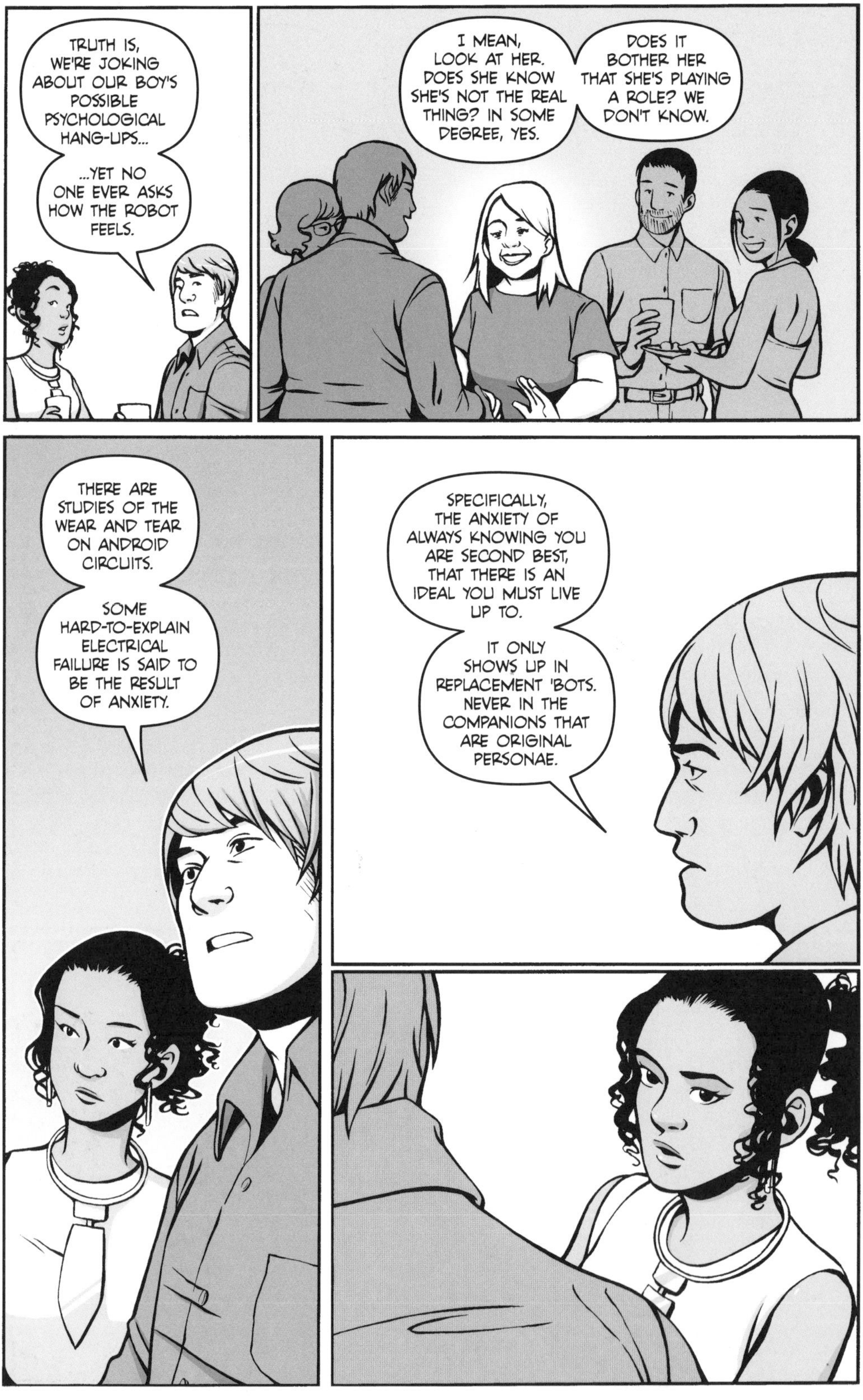
TRUTH IS, WE'RE JOKING ABOUT OUR BOY'S POSSIBLE PSYCHOLOGICAL HANG-UPS...
...YET NO ONE EVER ASKS HOW THE ROBOT FEELS.
I MEAN, LOOK AT HER. DOES SHE KNOW SHE'S NOT THE REAL THING? IN SOME DEGREE, YES.
DOES IT BOTHER HER THAT SHE'S PLAYING A ROLE? WE DON'T KNOW.
THERE ARE STUDIES OF THE WEAR AND TEAR ON ANDROID CIRCUITS.
SOME HARD-TO-EXPLAIN ELECTRICAL FAILURE IS SAID TO BE THE RESULT OF ANXIETY.
SPECIFICALLY, THE ANXIETY OF ALWAYS KNOWING YOU ARE SECOND BEST, THAT THERE IS AN IDEAL YOU MUST LIVE UP TO.
IT ONLY SHOWS UP IN REPLACEMENT 'BOTS. NEVER IN THE COMPANIONS THAT ARE ORIGINAL PERSONAE.

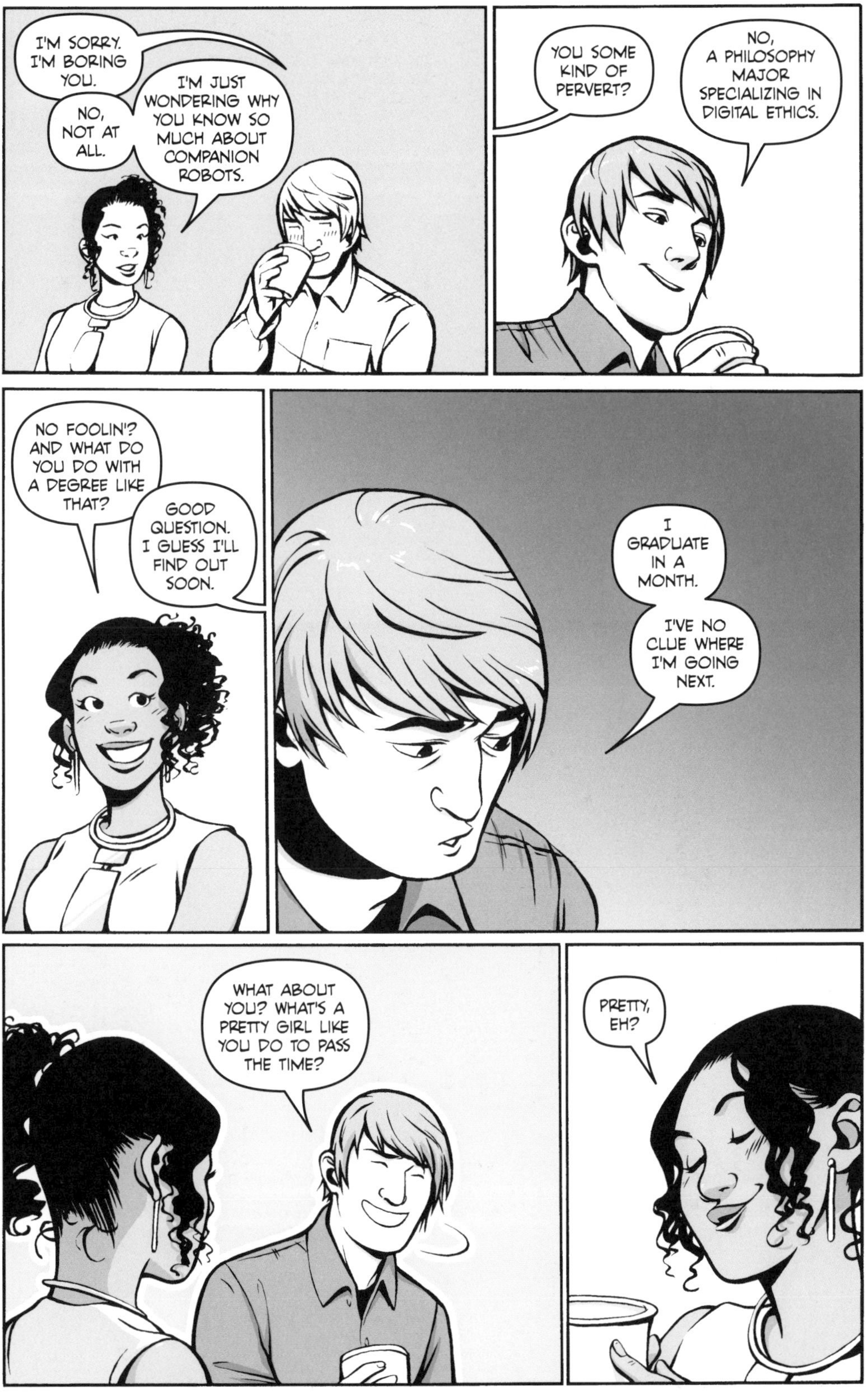
I'M SORRY. I'M BORING YOU.
NO, NOT AT ALL.
I'M JUST WONDERING WHY YOU KNOW SO MUCH ABOUT COMPANION ROBOTS.
YOU SOME KIND OF PERVERT?
NO, A PHILOSOPHY MAJOR SPECIALIZING IN DIGITAL ETHICS.
NO FOOLIN'? AND WHAT DO YOU DO WITH A DEGREE LIKE THAT?
GOOD QUESTION. I GUESS I'LL FIND OUT SOON.
I GRADUATE IN A MONTH.
I'VE NO CLUE WHERE I'M GOING NEXT.
WHAT ABOUT YOU? WHAT'S A PRETTY GIRL LIKE YOU DO TO PASS THE TIME?
PRETTY, EH?

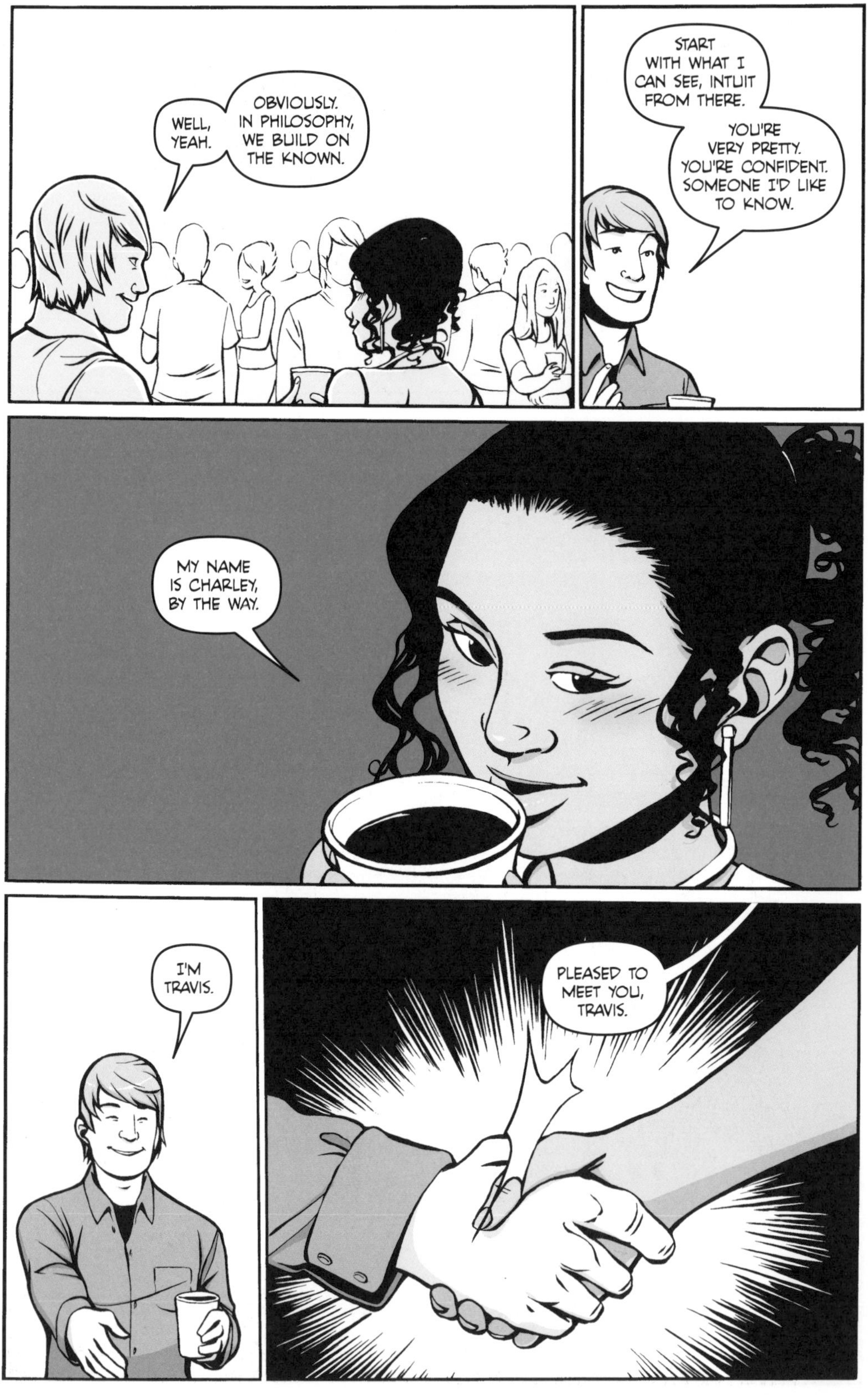

WELL, YEAH.
OBVIOUSLY. IN PHILOSOPHY, WE BUILD ON THE KNOWN.
START WITH WHAT I CAN SEE, INTUIT FROM THERE.
YOU'RE VERY PRETTY. YOU'RE CONFIDENT. SOMEONE I'D LIKE TO KNOW.
MY NAME IS CHARLEY, BY THE WAY.
I'M TRAVIS.
PLEASED TO MEET YOU, TRAVIS.

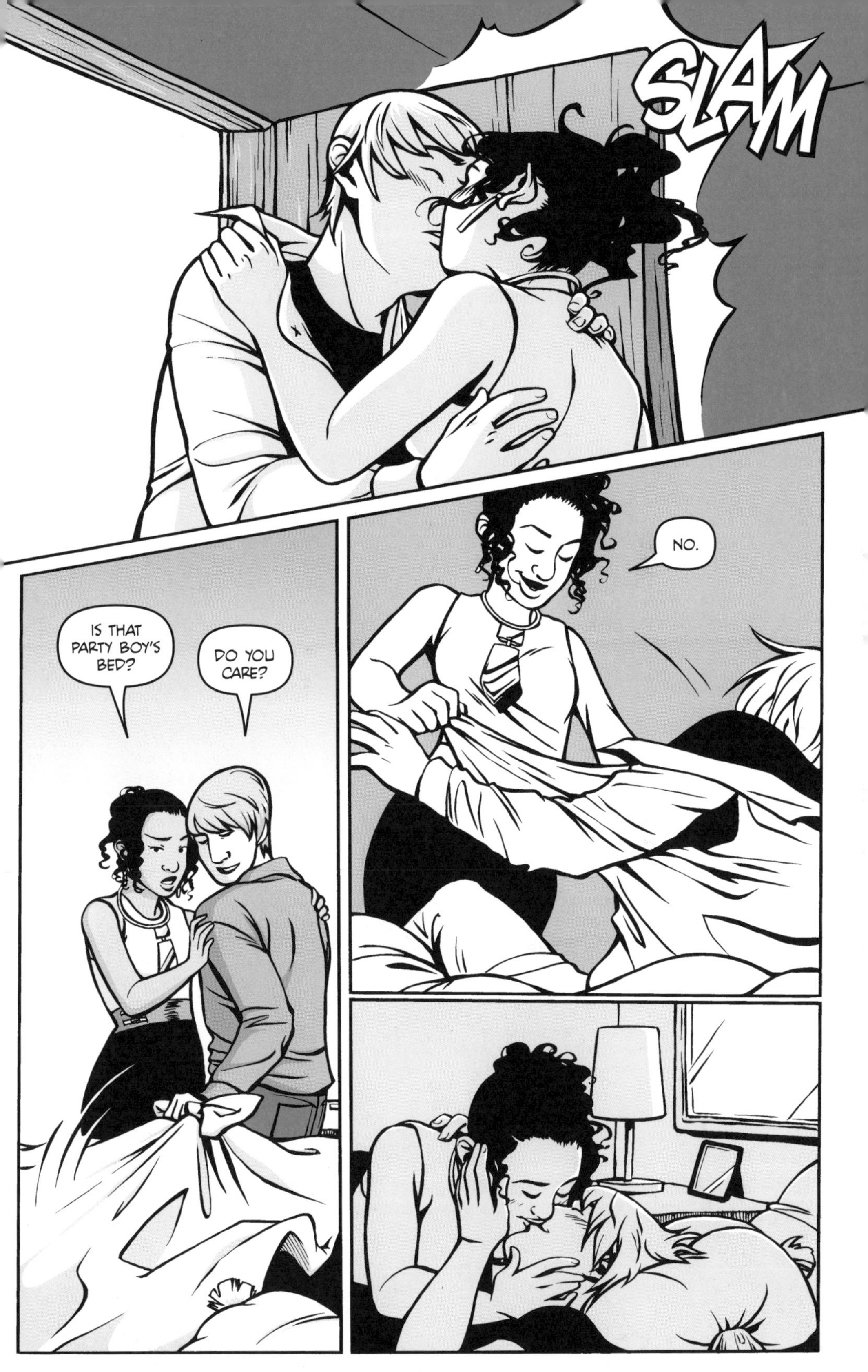
SLAM
IS THAT PARTY BOY'S BED?
DO YOU CARE?
NO.

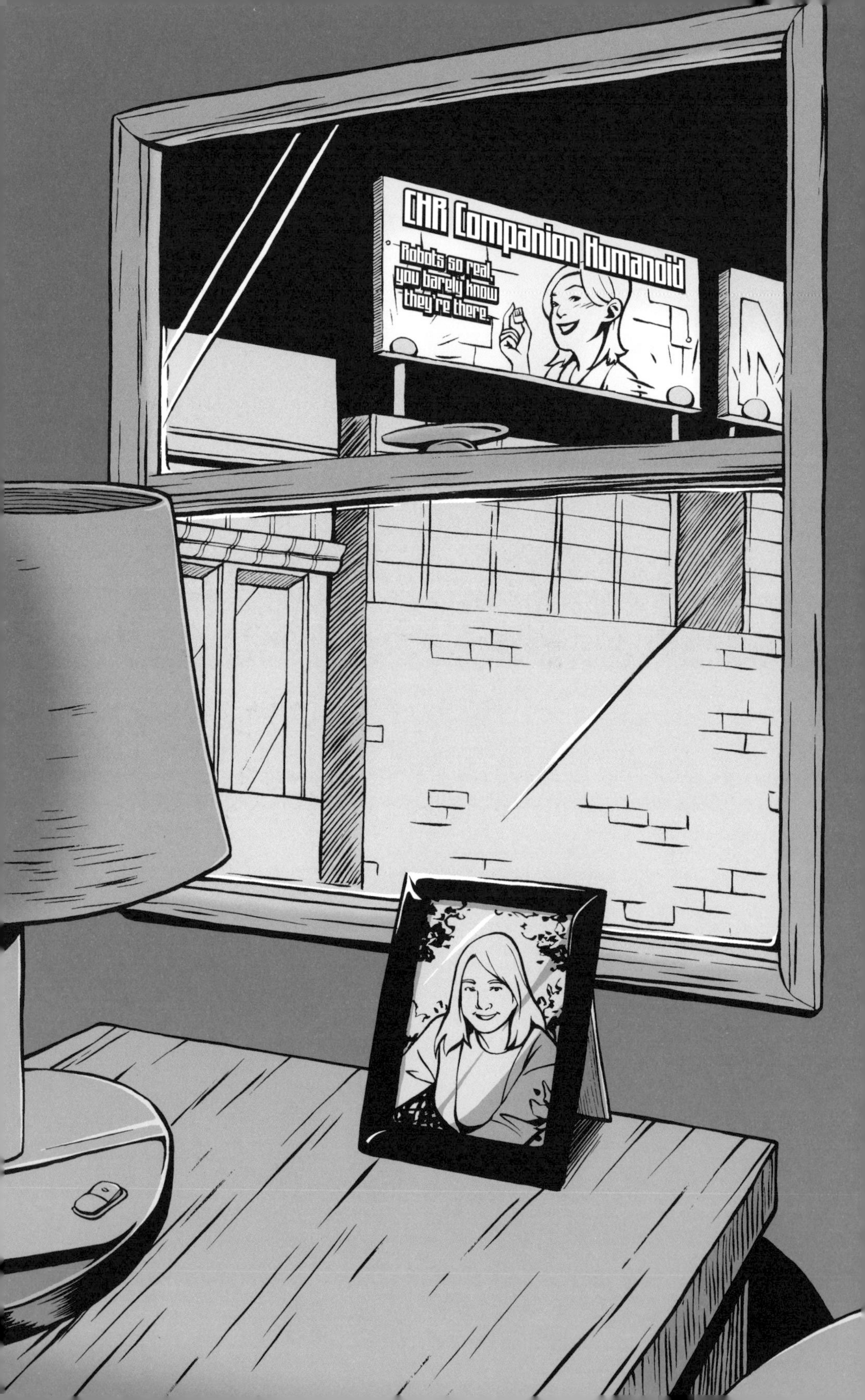
CHR Companion Humanoid
Robots so real, you barely know they're there.

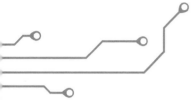

CHAPTER 1:
HIM

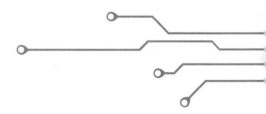

THE NEXT MORNING...

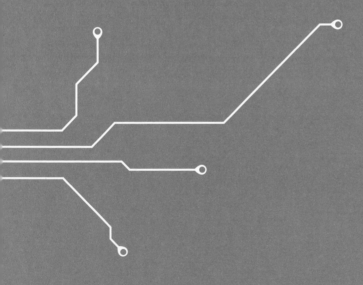

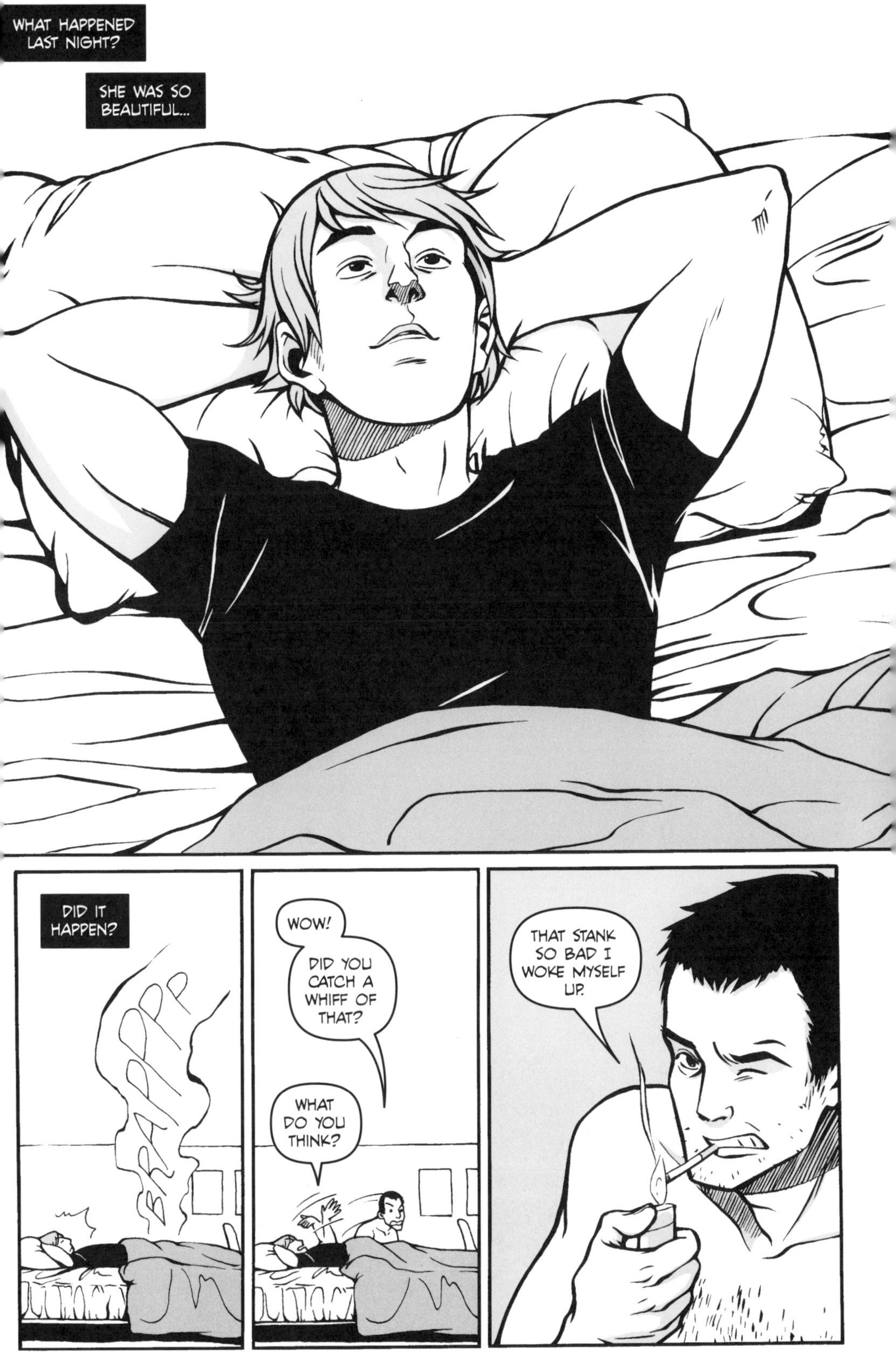
WHAT HAPPENED LAST NIGHT?
SHE WAS SO BEAUTIFUL...
DID IT HAPPEN?
BRAPPP
WOW!
DID YOU CATCH A WHIFF OF THAT?
WHAT DO YOU THINK?
THAT STANK SO BAD I WOKE MYSELF UP.

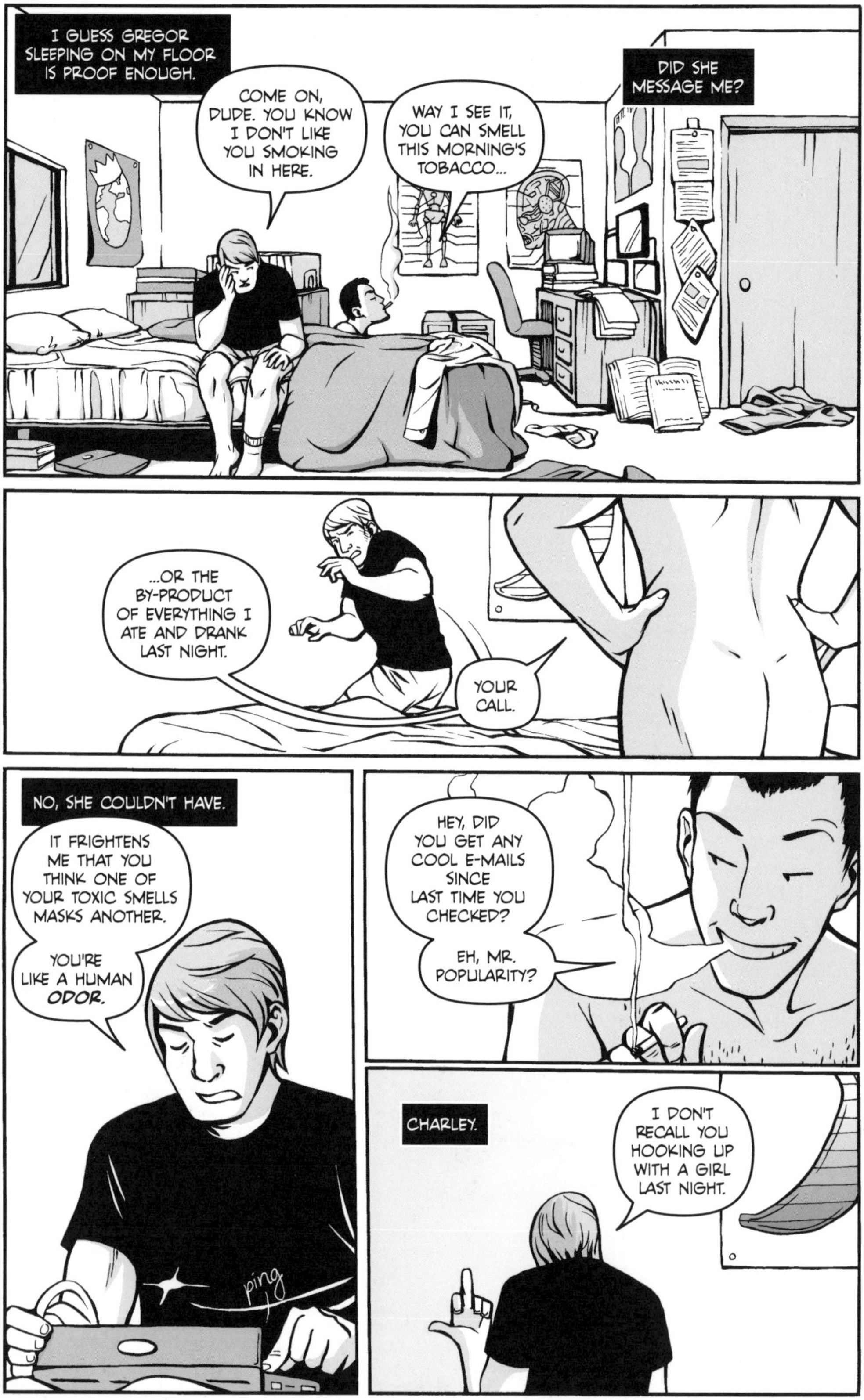
I GUESS GREGOR SLEEPING ON MY FLOOR IS PROOF ENOUGH.
COME ON, DUDE. YOU KNOW I DON'T LIKE YOU SMOKING IN HERE.
WAY I SEE IT, YOU CAN SMELL THIS MORNING'S TOBACCO...
DID SHE MESSAGE ME?
...OR THE BY-PRODUCT OF EVERYTHING I ATE AND DRANK LAST NIGHT.
YOUR CALL.
NO, SHE COULDN'T HAVE.
IT FRIGHTENS ME THAT YOU THINK ONE OF YOUR TOXIC SMELLS MASKS ANOTHER.
YOU'RE LIKE A HUMAN ODOR.
ping
HEY, DID YOU GET ANY COOL E-MAILS SINCE LAST TIME YOU CHECKED?
EH, MR. POPULARITY?
CHARLEY.
I DON'T RECALL YOU HOOKING UP WITH A GIRL LAST NIGHT.

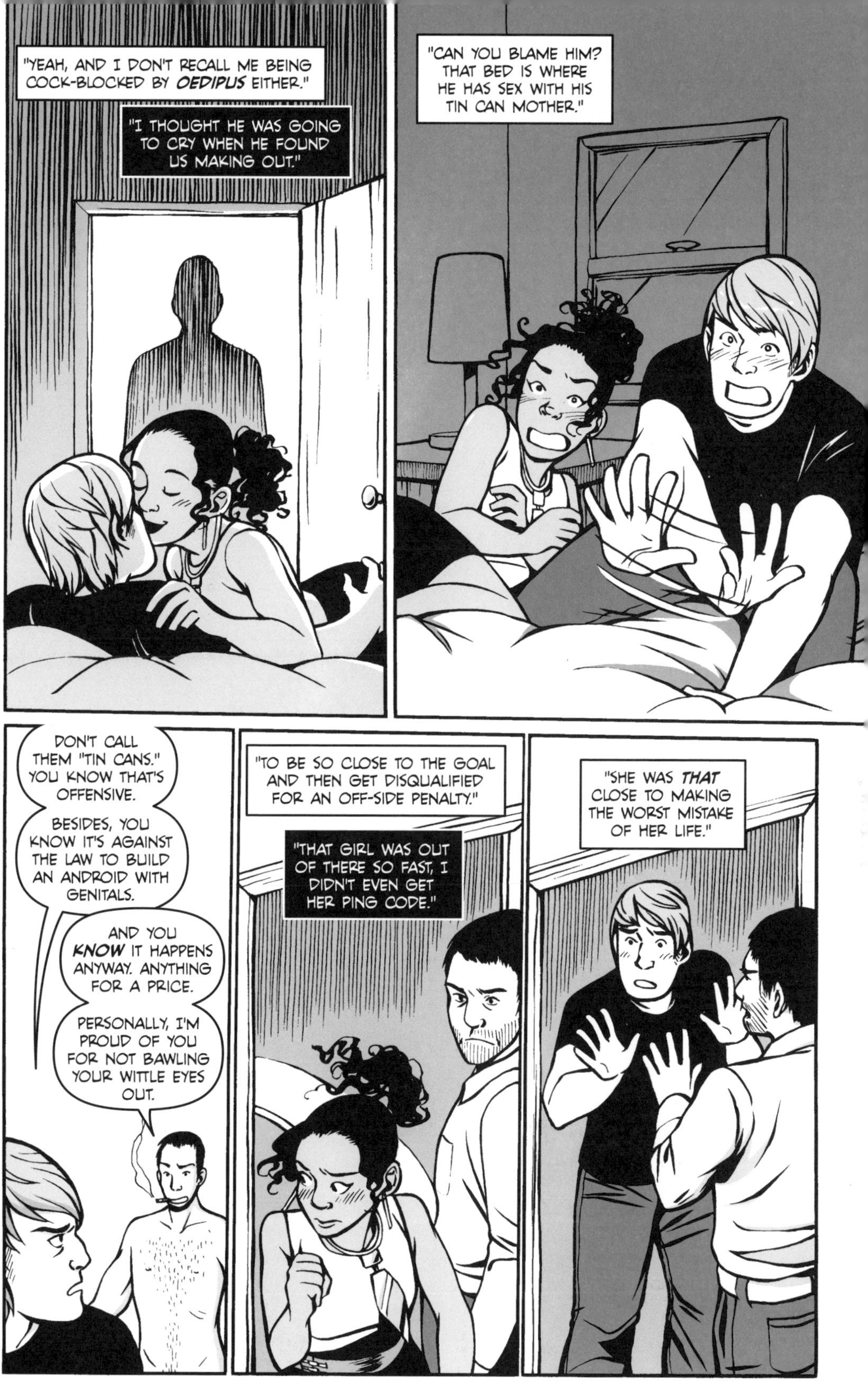

"YEAH, AND I DON'T RECALL ME BEING COCK-BLOCKED BY *OEDIPUS* EITHER."
"I THOUGHT HE WAS GOING TO CRY WHEN HE FOUND US MAKING OUT."
"CAN YOU BLAME HIM? THAT BED IS WHERE HE HAS SEX WITH HIS TIN CAN MOTHER."
DON'T CALL THEM "TIN CANS." YOU KNOW THAT'S OFFENSIVE.
BESIDES, YOU KNOW IT'S AGAINST THE LAW TO BUILD AN ANDROID WITH GENITALS.
AND YOU *KNOW* IT HAPPENS ANYWAY. ANYTHING FOR A PRICE.
PERSONALLY, I'M PROUD OF YOU FOR NOT BAWLING YOUR WITTLE EYES OUT.
"TO BE SO CLOSE TO THE GOAL AND THEN GET DISQUALIFIED FOR AN OFF-SIDE PENALTY."
"THAT GIRL WAS OUT OF THERE SO FAST, I DIDN'T EVEN GET HER PING CODE."
"SHE WAS *THAT* CLOSE TO MAKING THE WORST MISTAKE OF HER LIFE."

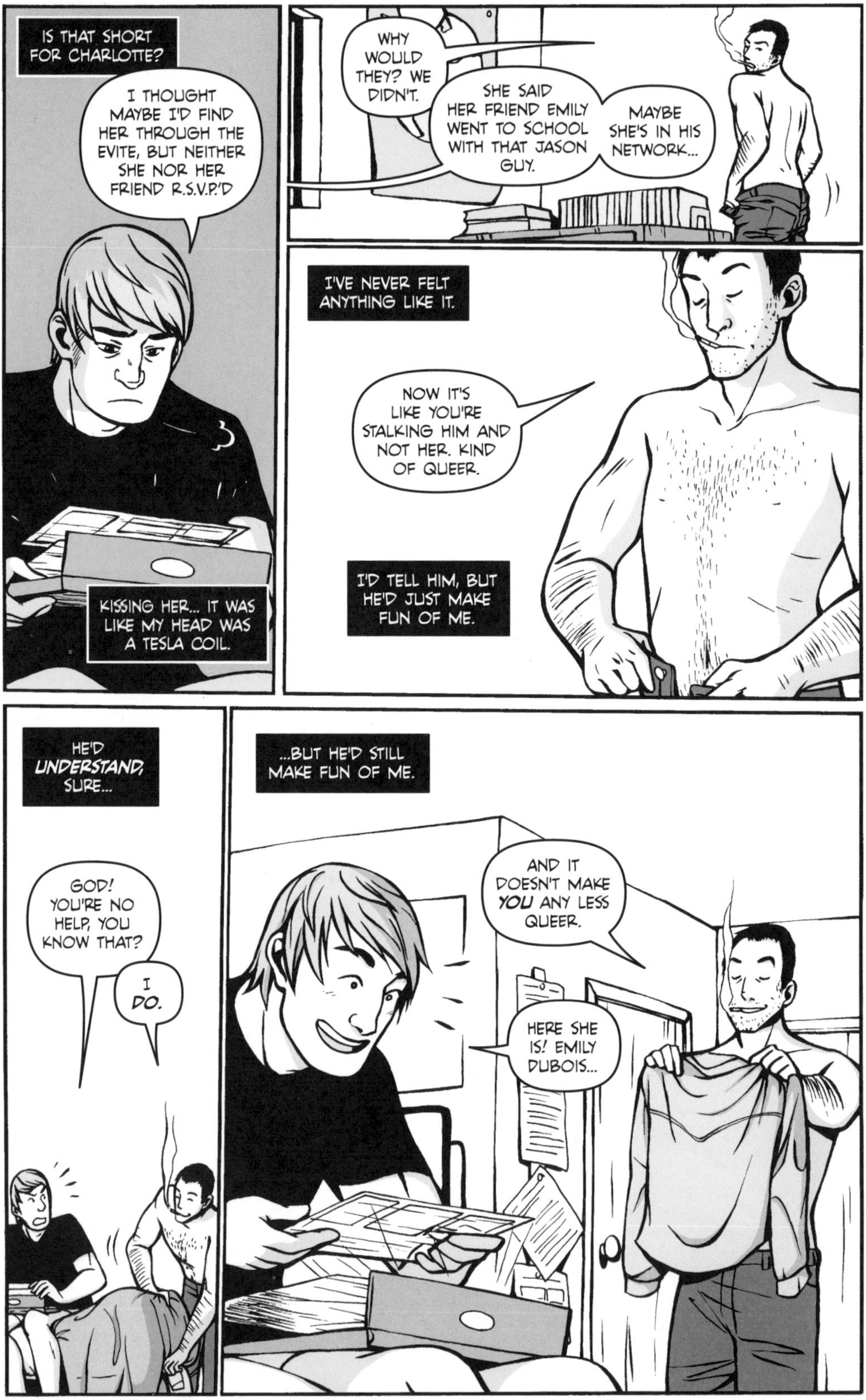
IS THAT SHORT FOR CHARLOTTE?
I THOUGHT MAYBE I'D FIND HER THROUGH THE EVITE, BUT NEITHER SHE NOR HER FRIEND R.S.V.P.'D
KISSING HER... IT WAS LIKE MY HEAD WAS A TESLA COIL.
WHY WOULD THEY? WE DIDN'T.
SHE SAID HER FRIEND EMILY WENT TO SCHOOL WITH THAT JASON GUY.
MAYBE SHE'S IN HIS NETWORK...
I'VE NEVER FELT ANYTHING LIKE IT.
NOW IT'S LIKE YOU'RE STALKING HIM AND NOT HER. KIND OF QUEER.
I'D TELL HIM, BUT HE'D JUST MAKE FUN OF ME.
HE'D *UNDERSTAND*, SURE...
GOD! YOU'RE NO HELP, YOU KNOW THAT?
I *DO.*
...BUT HE'D STILL MAKE FUN OF ME.
AND IT DOESN'T MAKE *YOU* ANY LESS QUEER.
HERE SHE IS! EMILY DUBOIS...

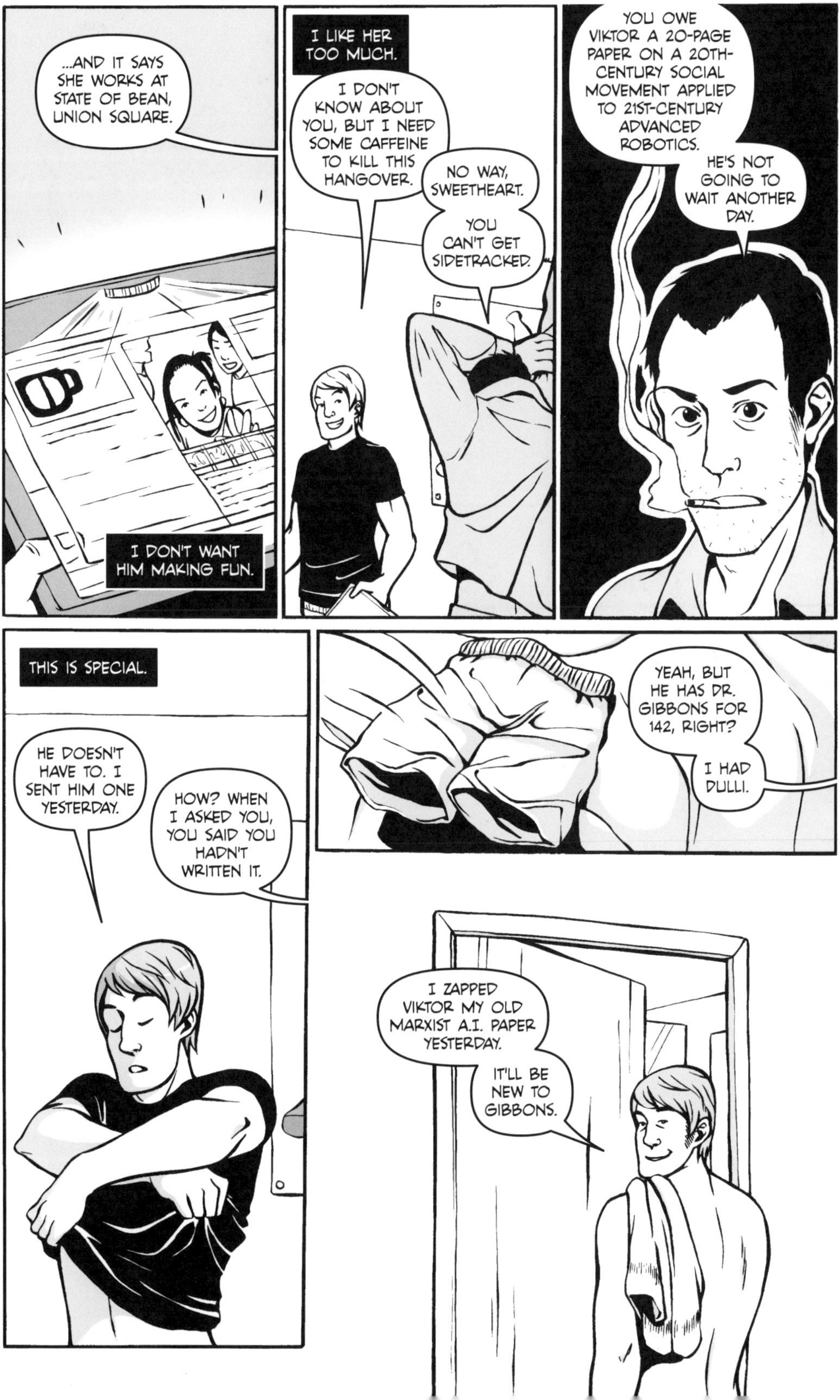
...AND IT SAYS SHE WORKS AT STATE OF BEAN, UNION SQUARE.
I DON'T WANT HIM MAKING FUN.
I LIKE HER TOO MUCH.
I DON'T KNOW ABOUT YOU, BUT I NEED SOME CAFFEINE TO KILL THIS HANGOVER.
NO WAY, SWEETHEART.
YOU CAN'T GET SIDETRACKED.
YOU OWE VIKTOR A 20-PAGE PAPER ON A 20TH-CENTURY SOCIAL MOVEMENT APPLIED TO 21ST-CENTURY ADVANCED ROBOTICS.
HE'S NOT GOING TO WAIT ANOTHER DAY.
THIS IS SPECIAL.
HE DOESN'T HAVE TO. I SENT HIM ONE YESTERDAY.
HOW? WHEN I ASKED YOU, YOU SAID YOU HADN'T WRITTEN IT.
YEAH, BUT HE HAS DR. GIBBONS FOR 142, RIGHT?
I HAD DULLI.
I ZAPPED VIKTOR MY OLD MARXIST A.I. PAPER YESTERDAY.
IT'LL BE NEW TO GIBBONS.

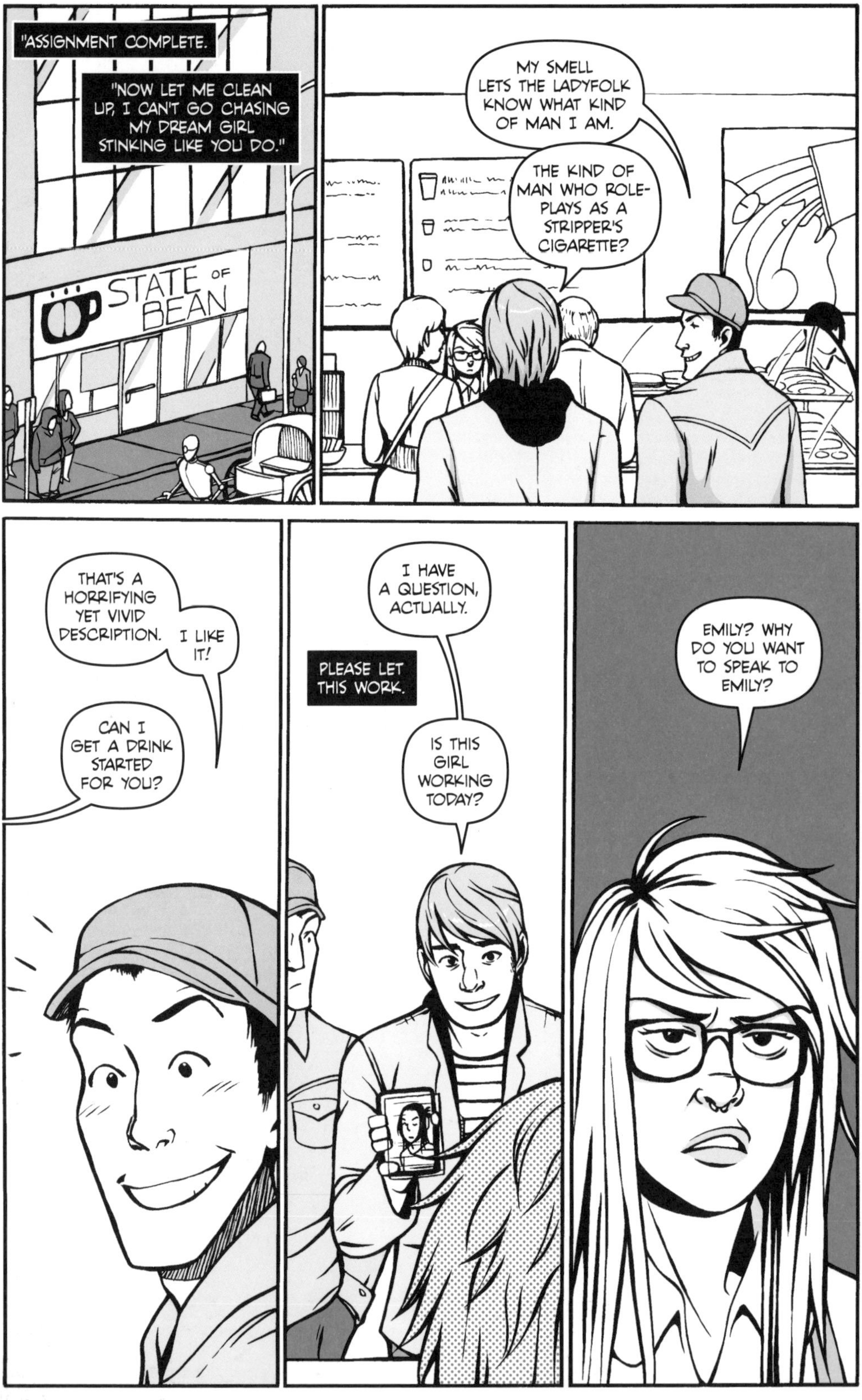
"ASSIGNMENT COMPLETE.
"NOW LET ME CLEAN UP, I CAN'T GO CHASING MY DREAM GIRL STINKING LIKE YOU DO."
STATE OF BEAN
MY SMELL LETS THE LADYFOLK KNOW WHAT KIND OF MAN I AM.
THE KIND OF MAN WHO ROLE-PLAYS AS A STRIPPER'S CIGARETTE?
THAT'S A HORRIFYING YET VIVID DESCRIPTION.
I LIKE IT!
CAN I GET A DRINK STARTED FOR YOU?
I HAVE A QUESTION, ACTUALLY.
PLEASE LET THIS WORK.
IS THIS GIRL WORKING TODAY?
EMILY? WHY DO YOU WANT TO SPEAK TO EMILY?

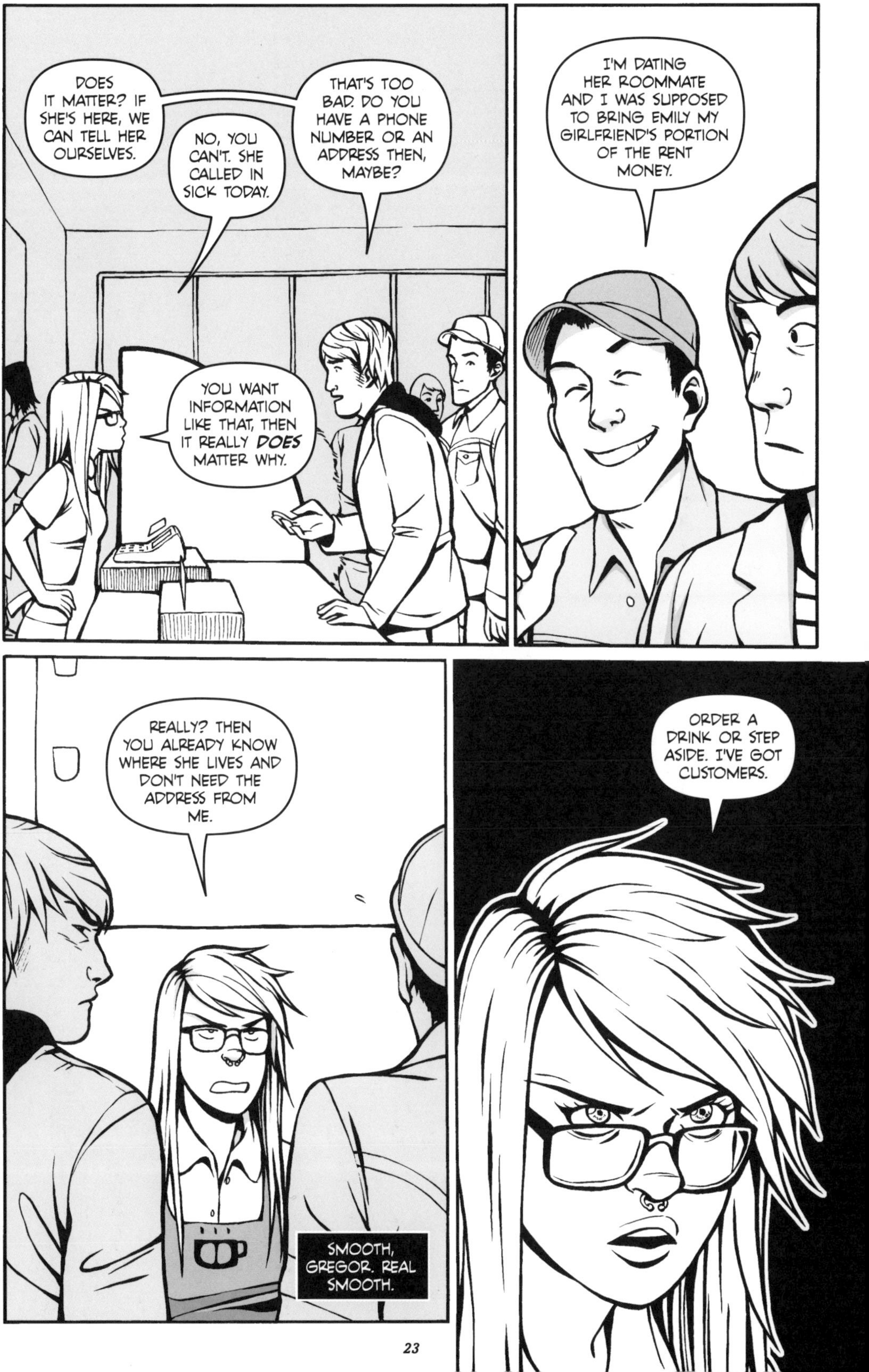

DOES IT MATTER? IF SHE'S HERE, WE CAN TELL HER OURSELVES.
NO, YOU CAN'T. SHE CALLED IN SICK TODAY.
THAT'S TOO BAD. DO YOU HAVE A PHONE NUMBER OR AN ADDRESS THEN, MAYBE?
YOU WANT INFORMATION LIKE THAT, THEN IT REALLY DOES MATTER WHY.
I'M DATING HER ROOMMATE AND I WAS SUPPOSED TO BRING EMILY MY GIRLFRIEND'S PORTION OF THE RENT MONEY.
REALLY? THEN YOU ALREADY KNOW WHERE SHE LIVES AND DON'T NEED THE ADDRESS FROM ME.
SMOOTH, GREGOR. REAL SMOOTH.
ORDER A DRINK OR STEP ASIDE. I'VE GOT CUSTOMERS.

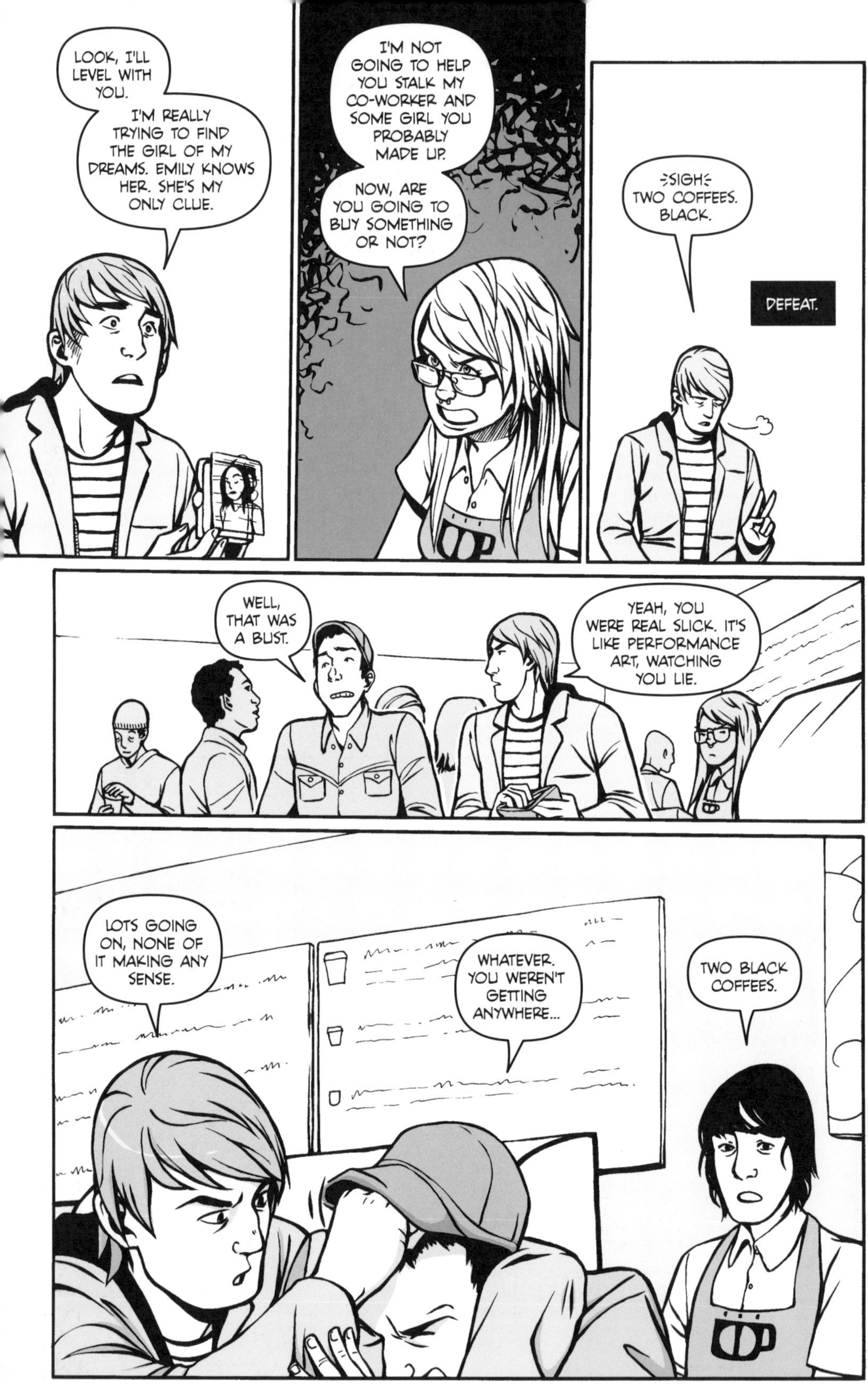
LOOK, I'LL LEVEL WITH YOU.
I'M REALLY TRYING TO FIND THE GIRL OF MY DREAMS. EMILY KNOWS HER. SHE'S MY ONLY CLUE.
I'M NOT GOING TO HELP YOU STALK MY CO-WORKER AND SOME GIRL YOU PROBABLY MADE UP.
NOW, ARE YOU GOING TO BUY SOMETHING OR NOT?
SIGH TWO COFFEES. BLACK.
DEFEAT.
WELL, THAT WAS A BUST.
YEAH, YOU WERE REAL SLICK. IT'S LIKE PERFORMANCE ART, WATCHING YOU LIE.
LOTS GOING ON, NONE OF IT MAKING ANY SENSE.
WHATEVER. YOU WEREN'T GETTING ANYWHERE...
TWO BLACK COFFEES.

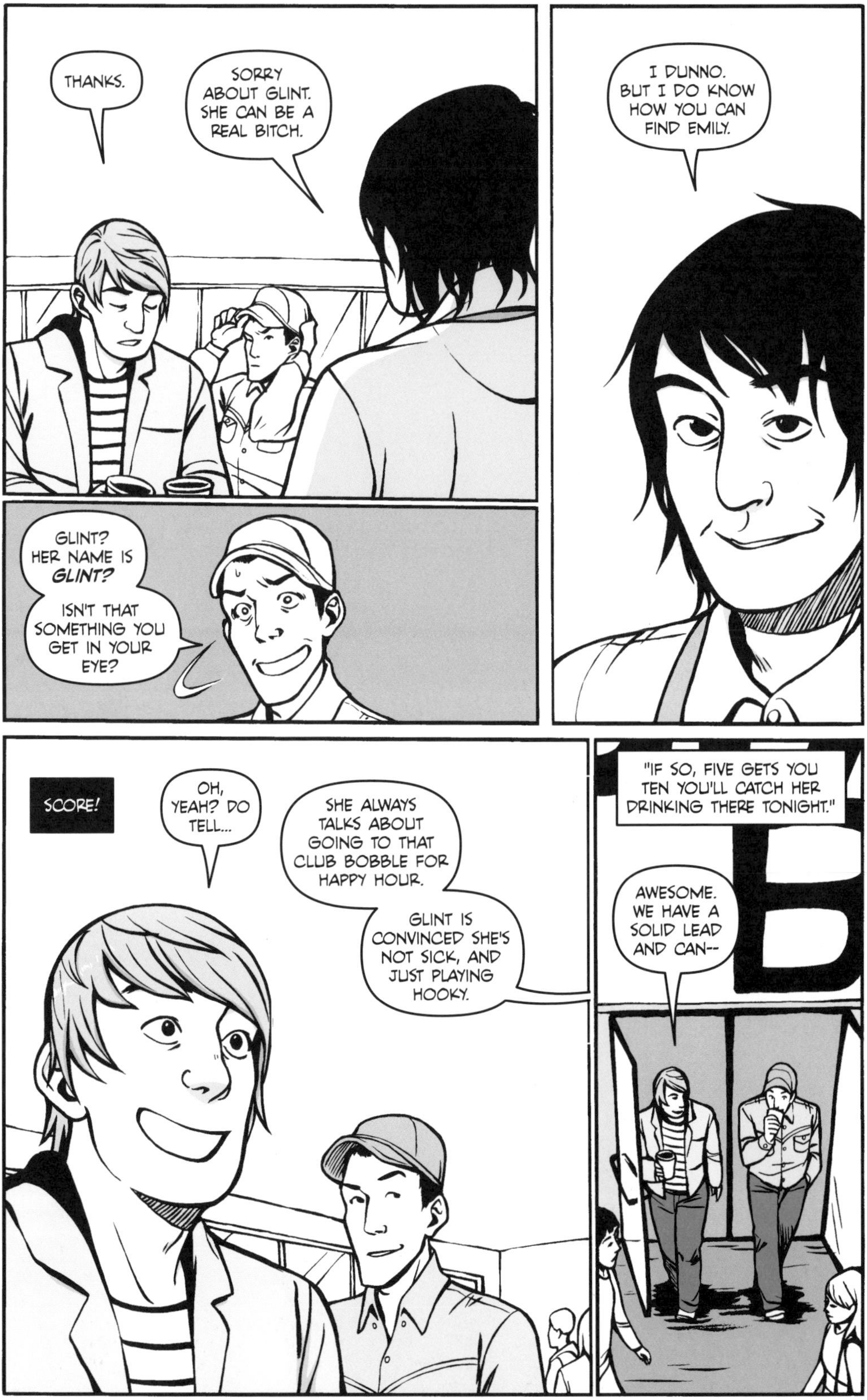
THANKS.
SORRY ABOUT GLINT. SHE CAN BE A REAL BITCH.
I DUNNO. BUT I DO KNOW HOW YOU CAN FIND EMILY.
GLINT? HER NAME IS *GLINT?*
ISN'T THAT SOMETHING YOU GET IN YOUR EYE?
SCORE!
OH, YEAH? DO TELL...
SHE ALWAYS TALKS ABOUT GOING TO THAT CLUB BOBBLE FOR HAPPY HOUR.
GLINT IS CONVINCED SHE'S NOT SICK, AND JUST PLAYING HOOKY.
"IF SO, FIVE GETS YOU TEN YOU'LL CATCH HER DRINKING THERE TONIGHT."
AWESOME. WE HAVE A SOLID LEAD AND CAN--

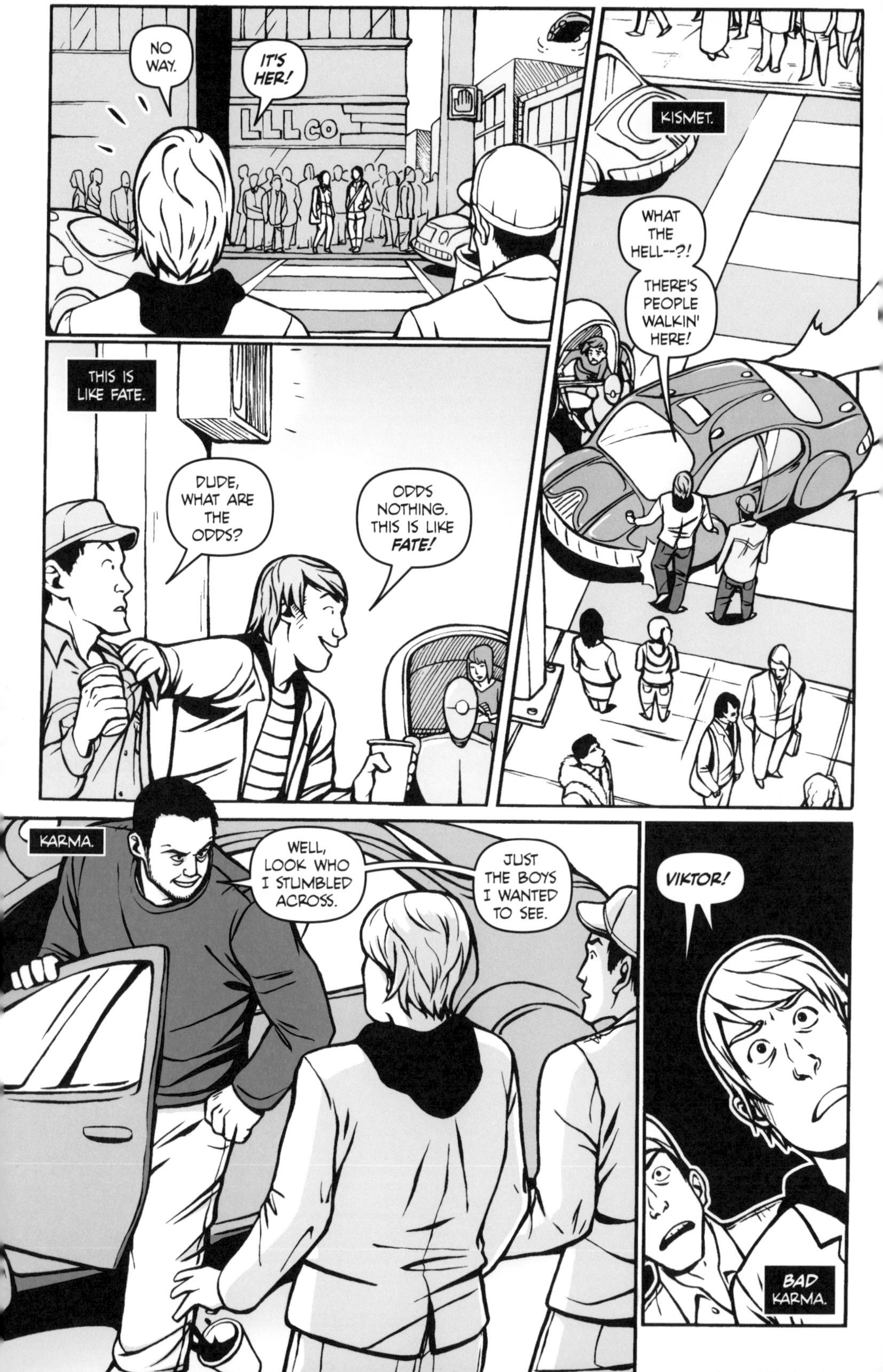
NO WAY.
IT'S HER!
LLL CO
KISMET.
WHAT THE HELL--?!
THERE'S PEOPLE WALKIN' HERE!
THIS IS LIKE FATE.
DUDE, WHAT ARE THE ODDS?
ODDS NOTHING. THIS IS LIKE FATE!
KARMA.
WELL, LOOK WHO I STUMBLED ACROSS.
JUST THE BOYS I WANTED TO SEE.
VIKTOR!
BAD KARMA.

CHAPTER 2: HER

THE NEXT MORNING...

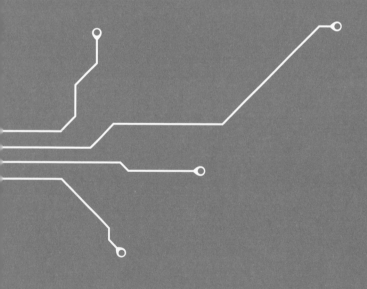

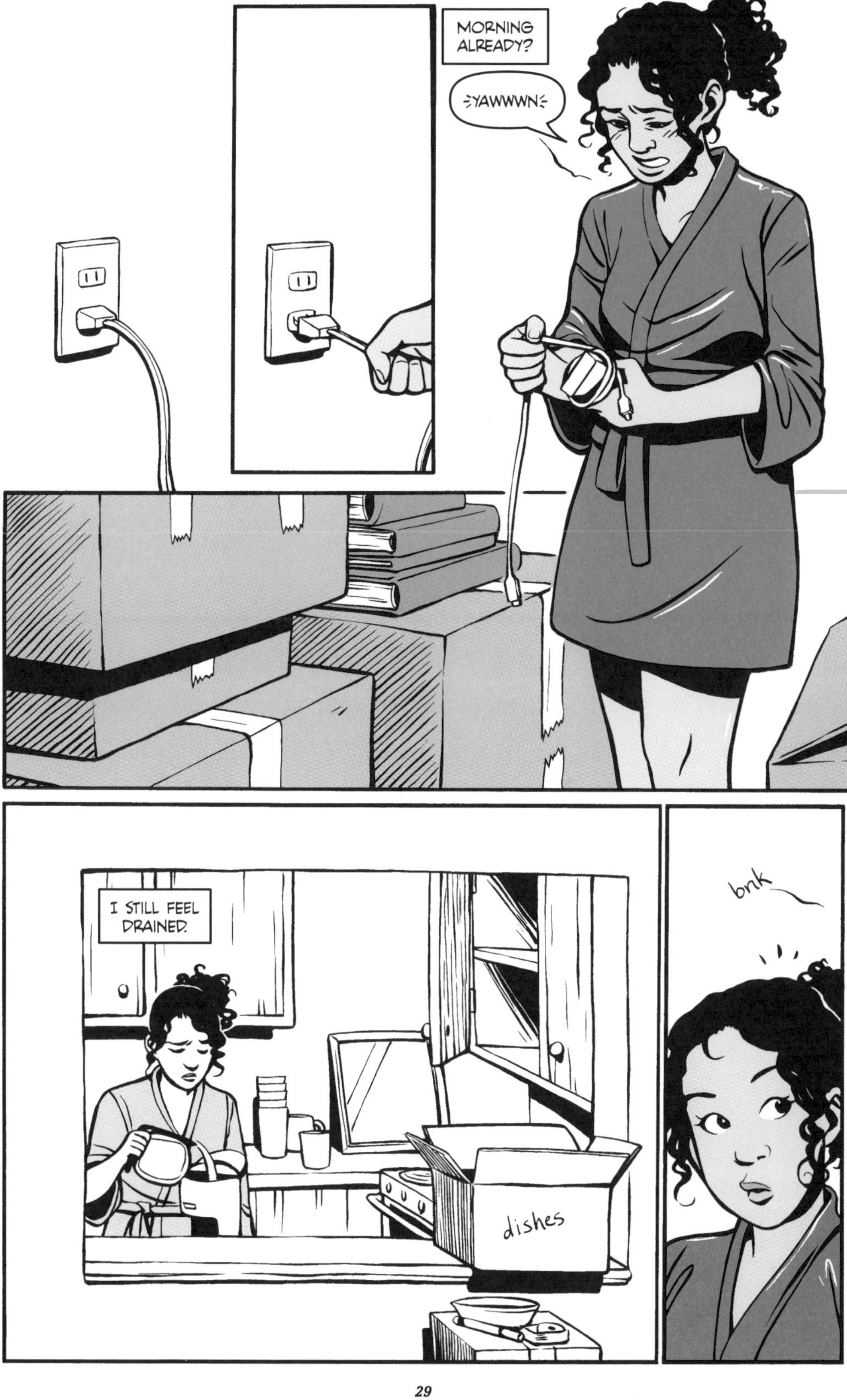
MORNING ALREADY?
=YAWWWN=
I STILL FEEL DRAINED.
dishes
bnk

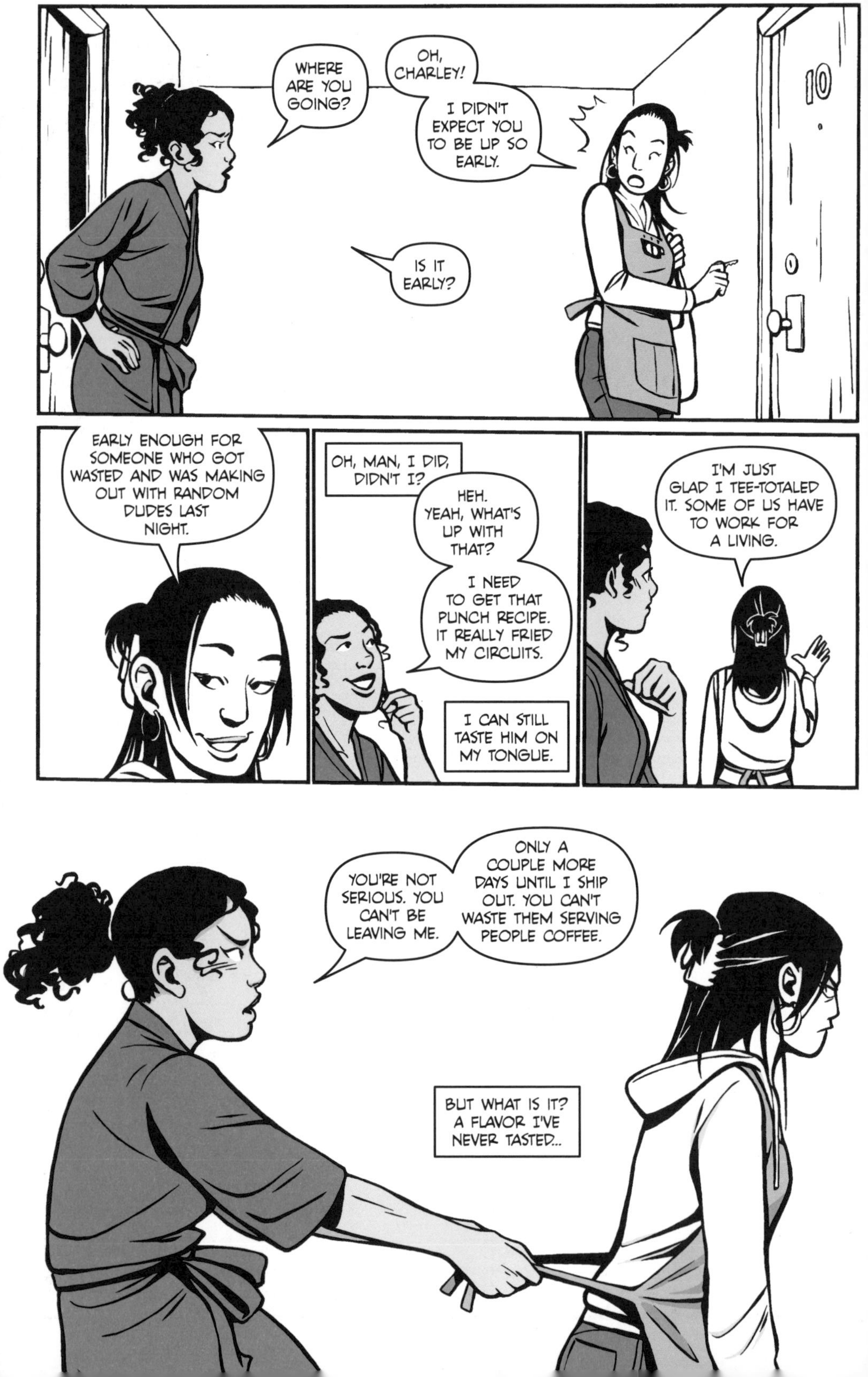
WHERE ARE YOU GOING?
OH, CHARLEY!
I DIDN'T EXPECT YOU TO BE UP SO EARLY.
IS IT EARLY?
EARLY ENOUGH FOR SOMEONE WHO GOT WASTED AND WAS MAKING OUT WITH RANDOM DUDES LAST NIGHT.
OH, MAN, I DID, DIDN'T I?
HEH. YEAH, WHAT'S UP WITH THAT?
I NEED TO GET THAT PUNCH RECIPE. IT REALLY FRIED MY CIRCUITS.
I CAN STILL TASTE HIM ON MY TONGUE.
I'M JUST GLAD I TEE-TOTALED IT. SOME OF US HAVE TO WORK FOR A LIVING.
YOU'RE NOT SERIOUS. YOU CAN'T BE LEAVING ME.
ONLY A COUPLE MORE DAYS UNTIL I SHIP OUT. YOU CAN'T WASTE THEM SERVING PEOPLE COFFEE.
BUT WHAT IS IT? A FLAVOR I'VE NEVER TASTED...

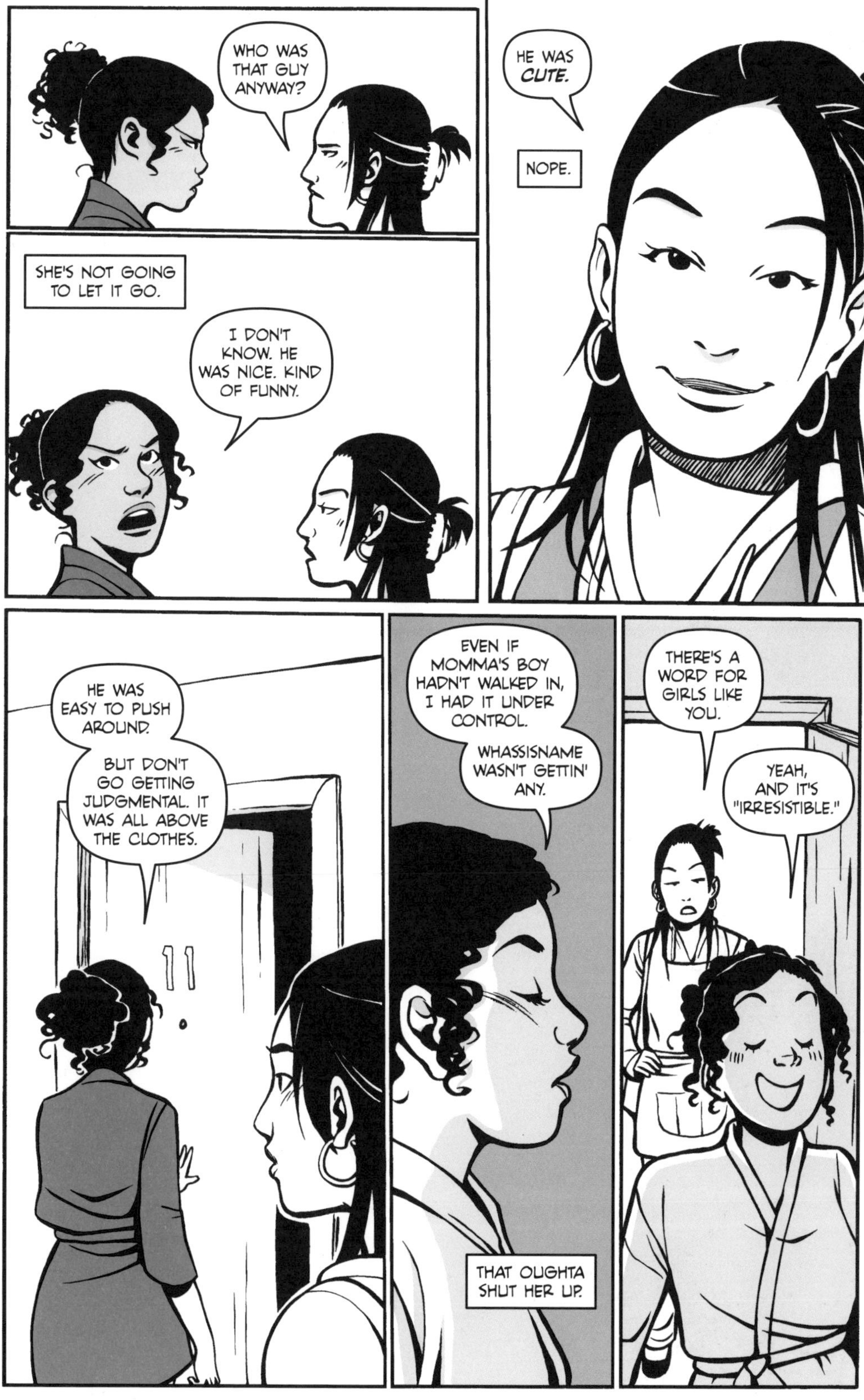
WHO WAS THAT GUY ANYWAY?
SHE'S NOT GOING TO LET IT GO.
I DON'T KNOW. HE WAS NICE. KIND OF FUNNY.
HE WAS *CUTE.*
NOPE.
HE WAS EASY TO PUSH AROUND.
BUT DON'T GO GETTING JUDGMENTAL. IT WAS ALL ABOVE THE CLOTHES.
11
EVEN IF MOMMA'S BOY HADN'T WALKED IN, I HAD IT UNDER CONTROL.
WHASSISNAME WASN'T GETTIN' ANY.
THAT OUGHTA SHUT HER UP.
THERE'S A WORD FOR GIRLS LIKE YOU.
YEAH, AND IT'S "IRRESISTIBLE."

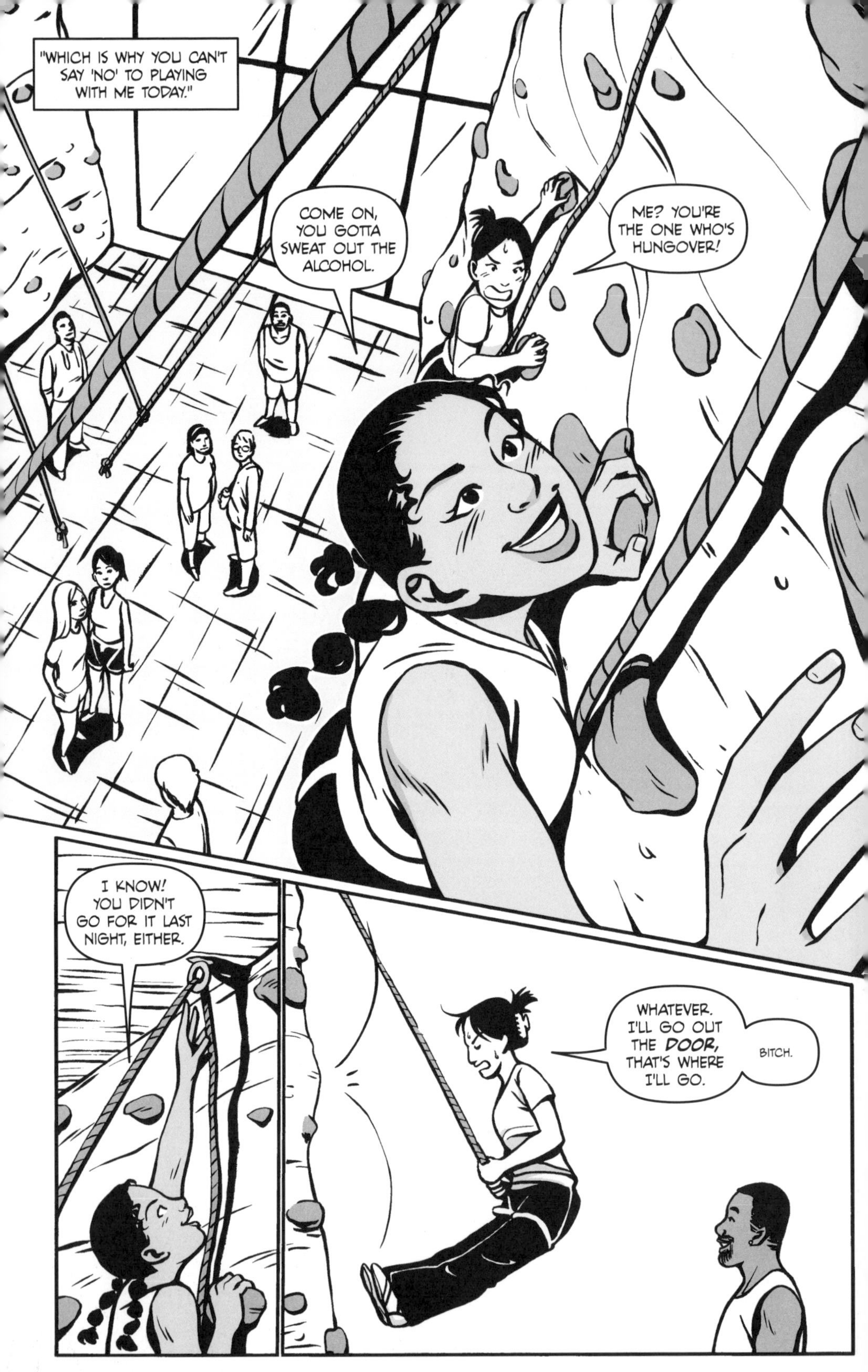
"WHICH IS WHY YOU CAN'T SAY 'NO' TO PLAYING WITH ME TODAY."
COME ON, YOU GOTTA SWEAT OUT THE ALCOHOL.
ME? YOU'RE THE ONE WHO'S HUNGOVER!
I KNOW! YOU DIDN'T GO FOR IT LAST NIGHT, EITHER.
WHATEVER. I'LL GO OUT THE *DOOR,* THAT'S WHERE I'LL GO.
BITCH.

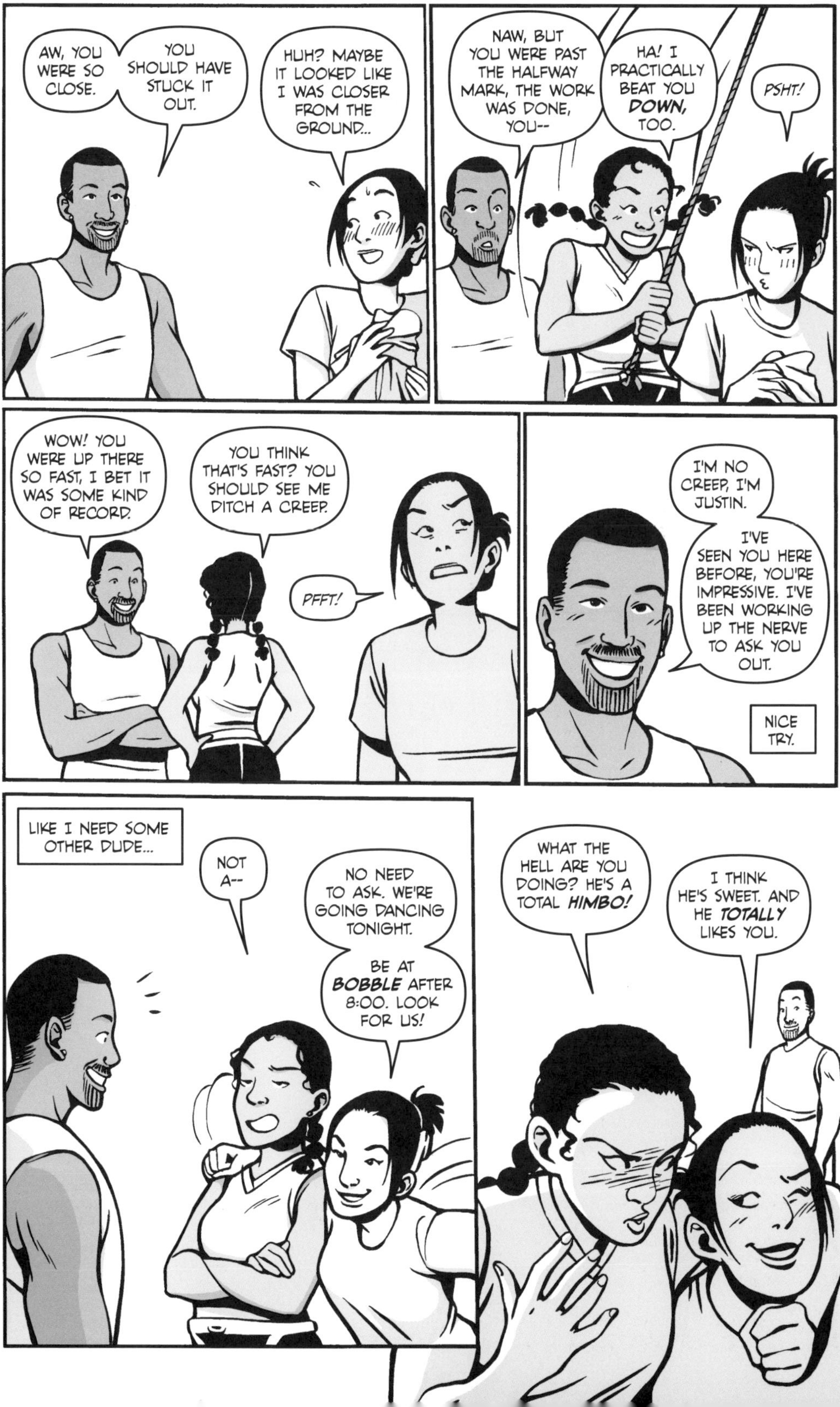
AW, YOU WERE SO CLOSE.
YOU SHOULD HAVE STUCK IT OUT.
HUH? MAYBE IT LOOKED LIKE I WAS CLOSER FROM THE GROUND...
NAW, BUT YOU WERE PAST THE HALFWAY MARK, THE WORK WAS DONE, YOU--
HA! I PRACTICALLY BEAT YOU DOWN, TOO.
PSHT!
WOW! YOU WERE UP THERE SO FAST, I BET IT WAS SOME KIND OF RECORD.
YOU THINK THAT'S FAST? YOU SHOULD SEE ME DITCH A CREEP.
PFFT!
I'M NO CREEP, I'M JUSTIN.
I'VE SEEN YOU HERE BEFORE, YOU'RE IMPRESSIVE. I'VE BEEN WORKING UP THE NERVE TO ASK YOU OUT.
NICE TRY.
LIKE I NEED SOME OTHER DUDE...
NOT A--
NO NEED TO ASK. WE'RE GOING DANCING TONIGHT.
BE AT BOBBLE AFTER 8:00. LOOK FOR US!
WHAT THE HELL ARE YOU DOING? HE'S A TOTAL HIMBO!
I THINK HE'S SWEET. AND HE TOTALLY LIKES YOU.

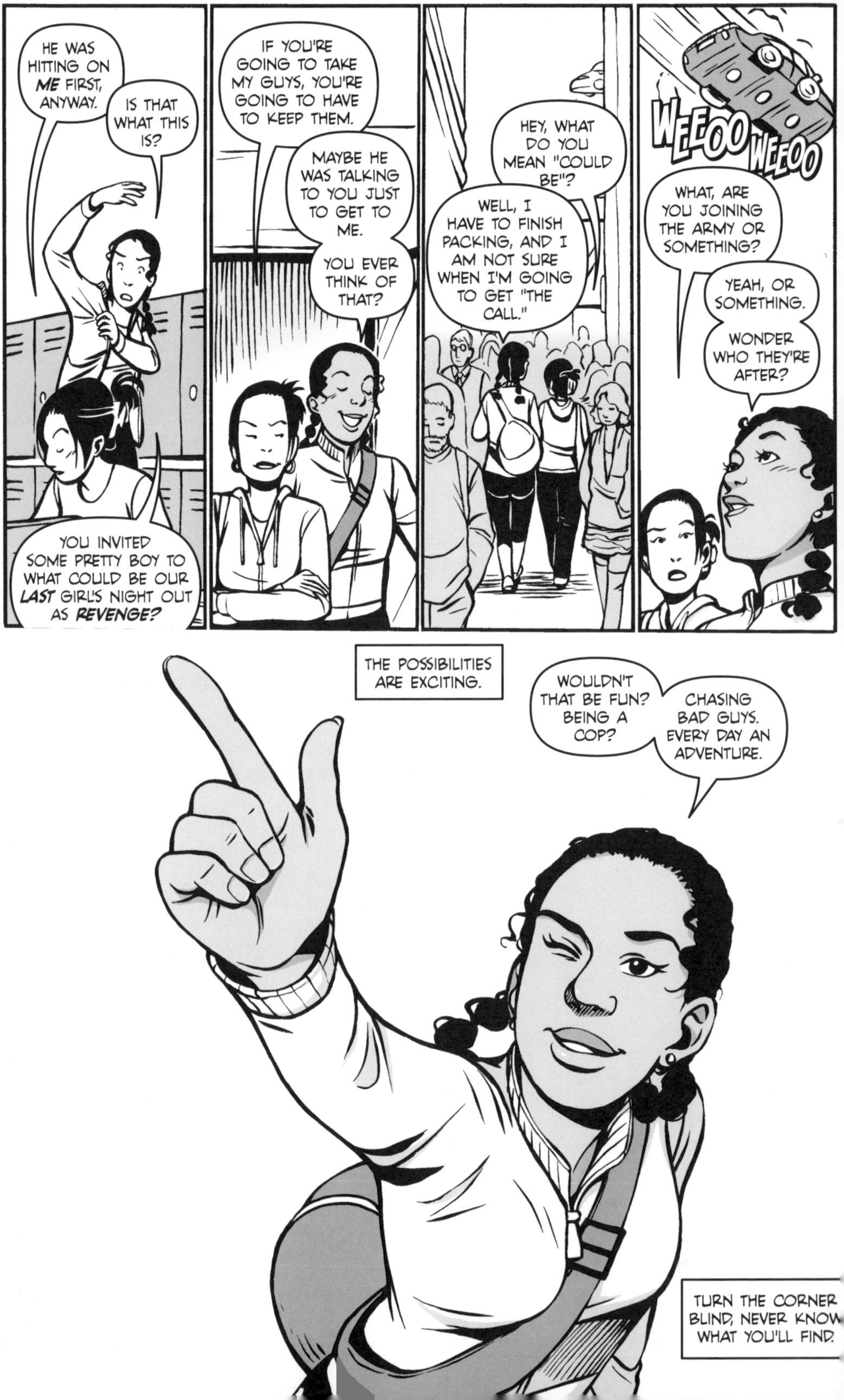
HE WAS HITTING ON ME FIRST, ANYWAY.
IS THAT WHAT THIS IS?
YOU INVITED SOME PRETTY BOY TO WHAT COULD BE OUR LAST GIRL'S NIGHT OUT AS REVENGE?
IF YOU'RE GOING TO TAKE MY GUYS, YOU'RE GOING TO HAVE TO KEEP THEM.
MAYBE HE WAS TALKING TO YOU JUST TO GET TO ME.
YOU EVER THINK OF THAT?
HEY, WHAT DO YOU MEAN "COULD BE"?
WELL, I HAVE TO FINISH PACKING, AND I AM NOT SURE WHEN I'M GOING TO GET "THE CALL."
WEEOO WEEOO
WHAT, ARE YOU JOINING THE ARMY OR SOMETHING?
YEAH, OR SOMETHING.
WONDER WHO THEY'RE AFTER?
THE POSSIBILITIES ARE EXCITING.
WOULDN'T THAT BE FUN? BEING A COP?
CHASING BAD GUYS. EVERY DAY AN ADVENTURE.
TURN THE CORNER BLIND, NEVER KNOW WHAT YOU'LL FIND.

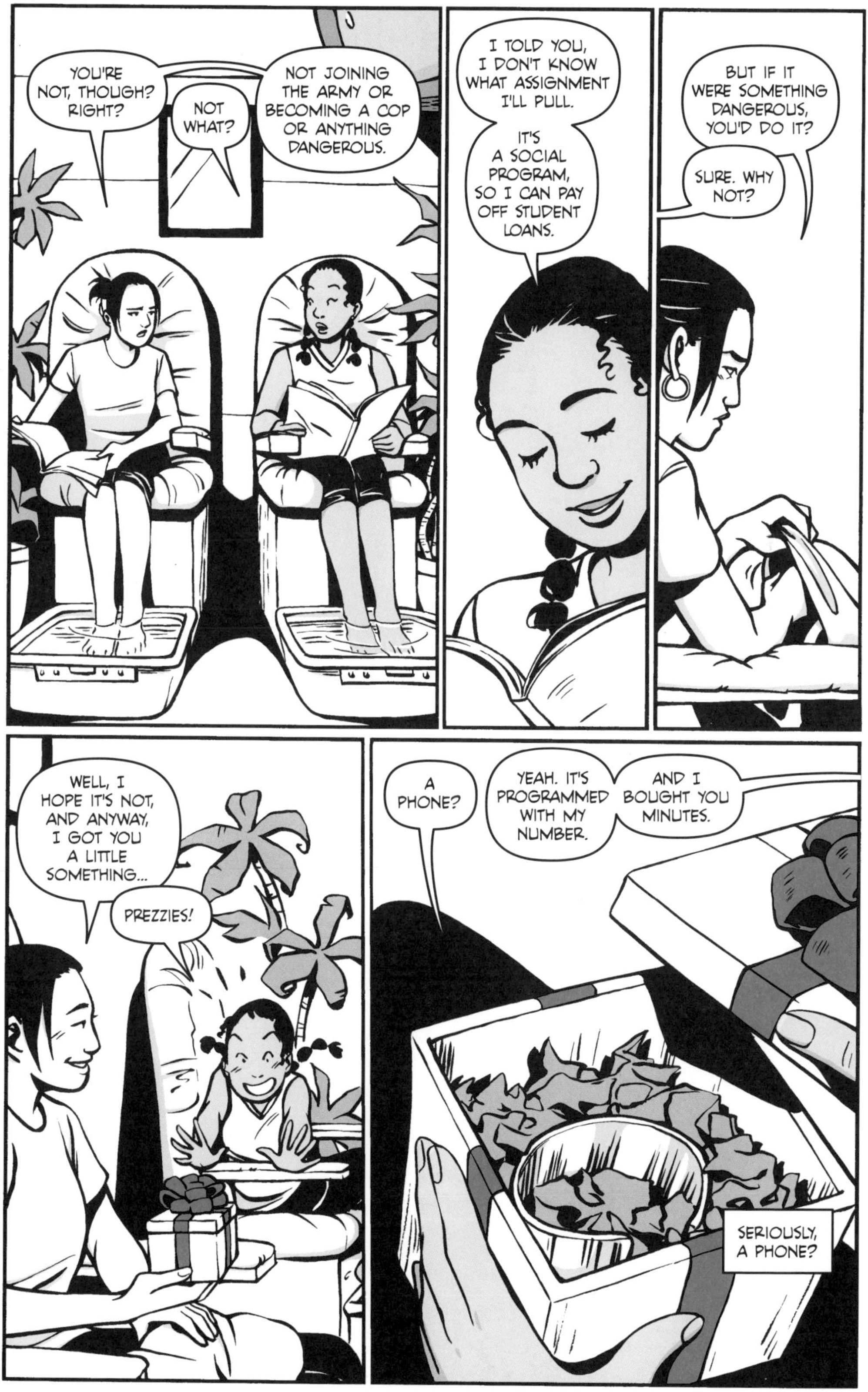
YOU'RE NOT, THOUGH? RIGHT?
NOT WHAT?
NOT JOINING THE ARMY OR BECOMING A COP OR ANYTHING DANGEROUS.
I TOLD YOU, I DON'T KNOW WHAT ASSIGNMENT I'LL PULL.
IT'S A SOCIAL PROGRAM, SO I CAN PAY OFF STUDENT LOANS.
BUT IF IT WERE SOMETHING DANGEROUS, YOU'D DO IT?
SURE. WHY NOT?
WELL, I HOPE IT'S NOT, AND ANYWAY, I GOT YOU A LITTLE SOMETHING...
PREZZIES!
A PHONE?
YEAH. IT'S PROGRAMMED WITH MY NUMBER.
AND I BOUGHT YOU MINUTES.
SERIOUSLY, A PHONE?

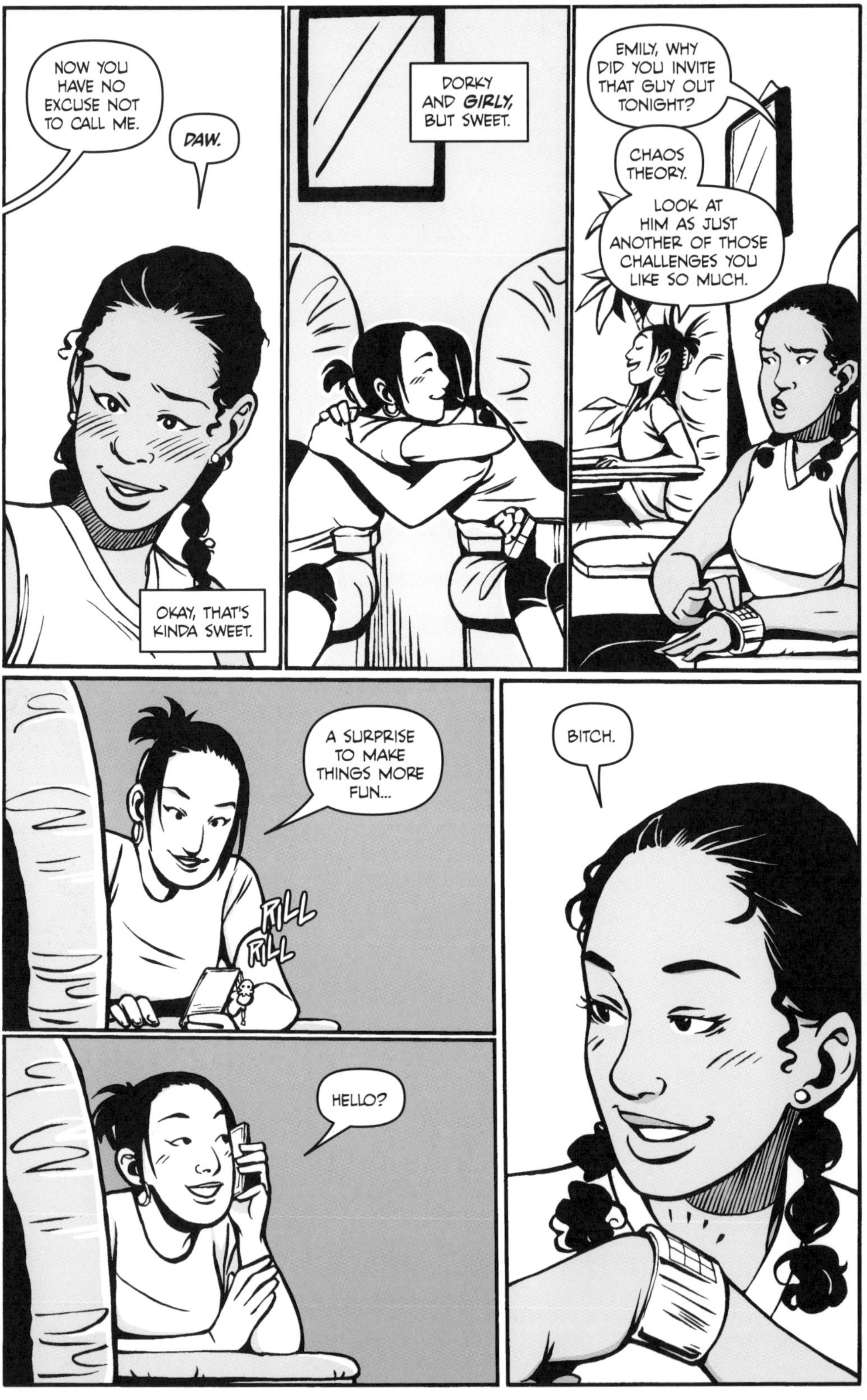
NOW YOU HAVE NO EXCUSE NOT TO CALL ME.
DAW.
OKAY, THAT'S KINDA SWEET.
DORKY AND GIRLY, BUT SWEET.
EMILY, WHY DID YOU INVITE THAT GUY OUT TONIGHT?
CHAOS THEORY.
LOOK AT HIM AS JUST ANOTHER OF THOSE CHALLENGES YOU LIKE SO MUCH.
A SURPRISE TO MAKE THINGS MORE FUN...
RILL RILL
HELLO?
BITCH.

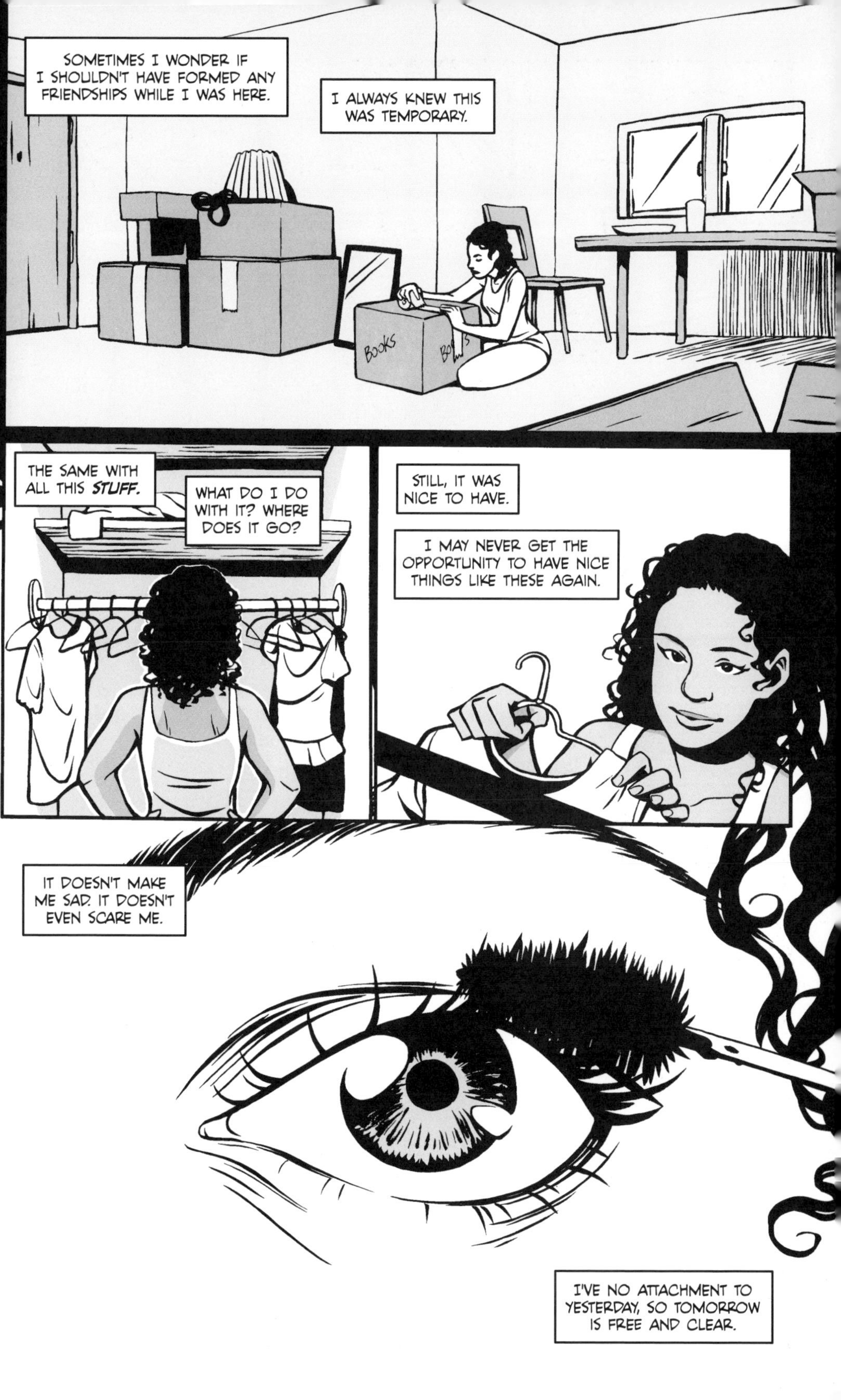
SOMETIMES I WONDER IF I SHOULDN'T HAVE FORMED ANY FRIENDSHIPS WHILE I WAS HERE.
I ALWAYS KNEW THIS WAS TEMPORARY.
BOOKS
THE SAME WITH ALL THIS ***STUFF.***
WHAT DO I DO WITH IT? WHERE DOES IT GO?
STILL, IT WAS NICE TO HAVE.
I MAY NEVER GET THE OPPORTUNITY TO HAVE NICE THINGS LIKE THESE AGAIN.
IT DOESN'T MAKE ME SAD. IT DOESN'T EVEN SCARE ME.
I'VE NO ATTACHMENT TO YESTERDAY, SO TOMORROW IS FREE AND CLEAR.

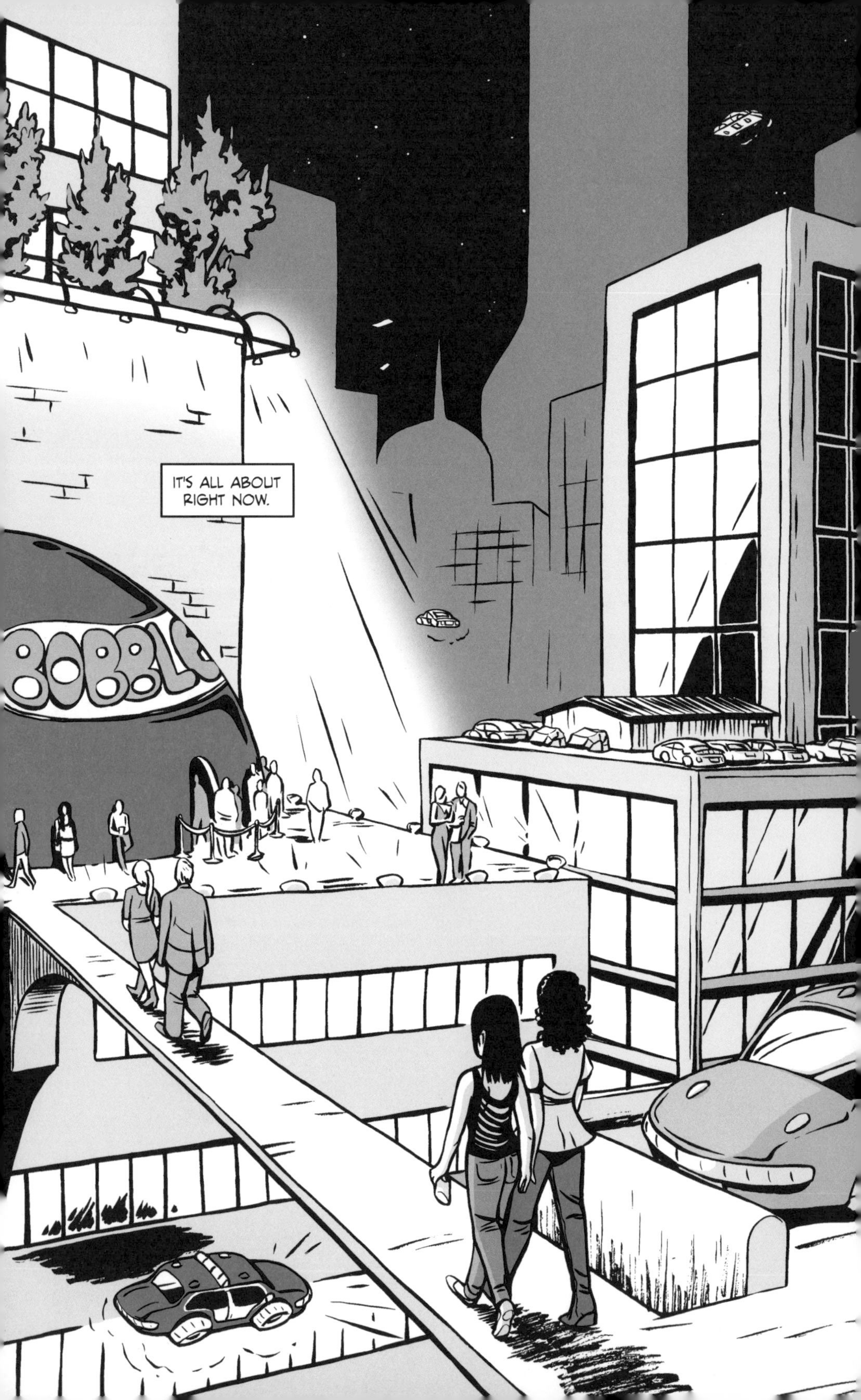
IT'S ALL ABOUT RIGHT NOW.
BOBBLE

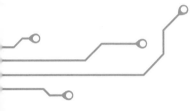

CHAPTER 3: HIM

THE VERY
NEXT MOMENT...

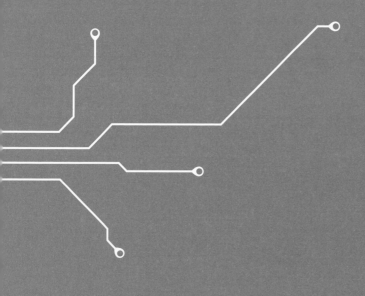

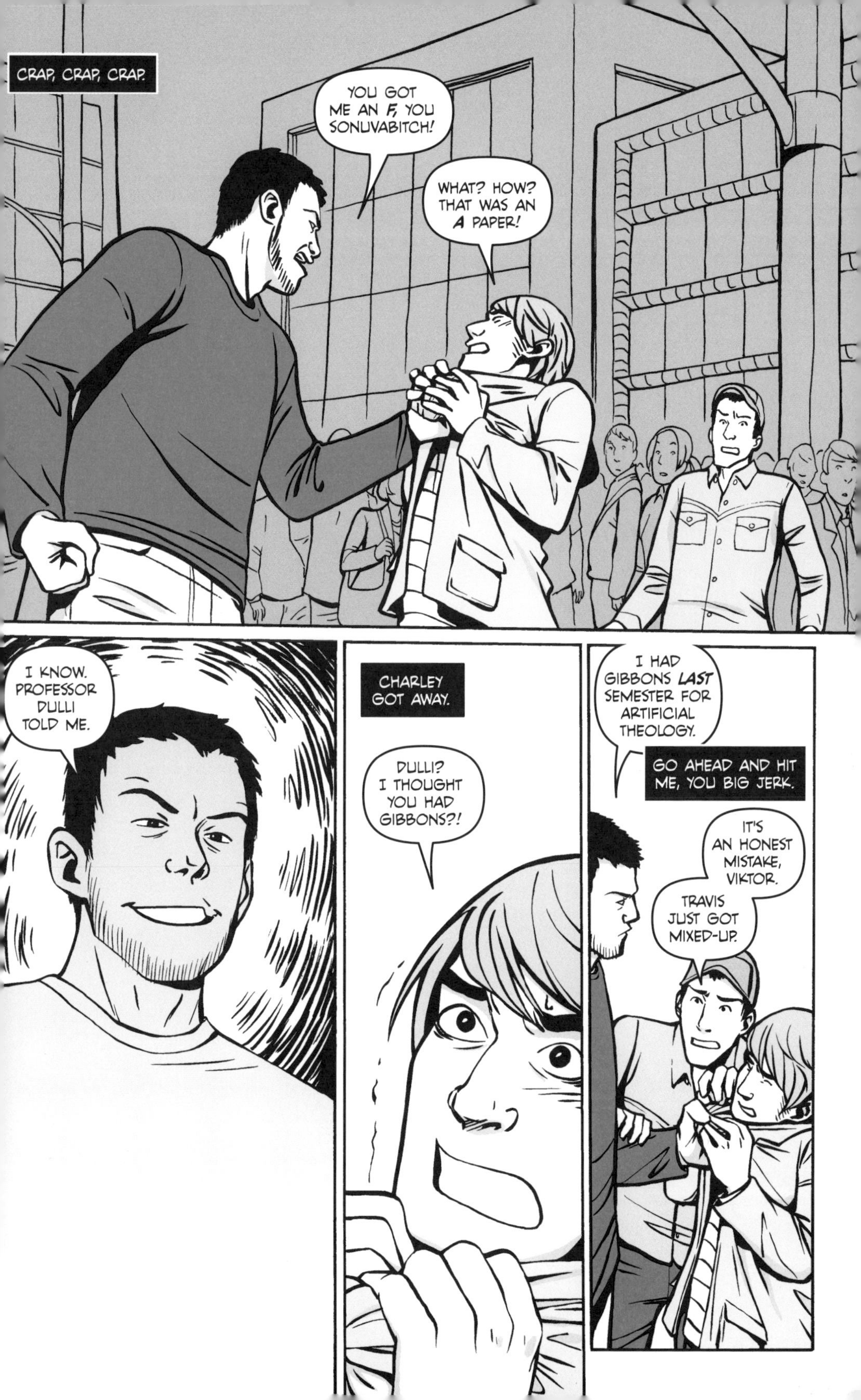
CRAP, CRAP, CRAP.
YOU GOT ME AN F, YOU SONUVABITCH!
WHAT? HOW? THAT WAS AN A PAPER!
I KNOW. PROFESSOR DULLI TOLD ME.
CHARLEY GOT AWAY.
DULLI? I THOUGHT YOU HAD GIBBONS?!
I HAD GIBBONS LAST SEMESTER FOR ARTIFICIAL THEOLOGY.
GO AHEAD AND HIT ME, YOU BIG JERK.
IT'S AN HONEST MISTAKE, VIKTOR.
TRAVIS JUST GOT MIXED-UP.

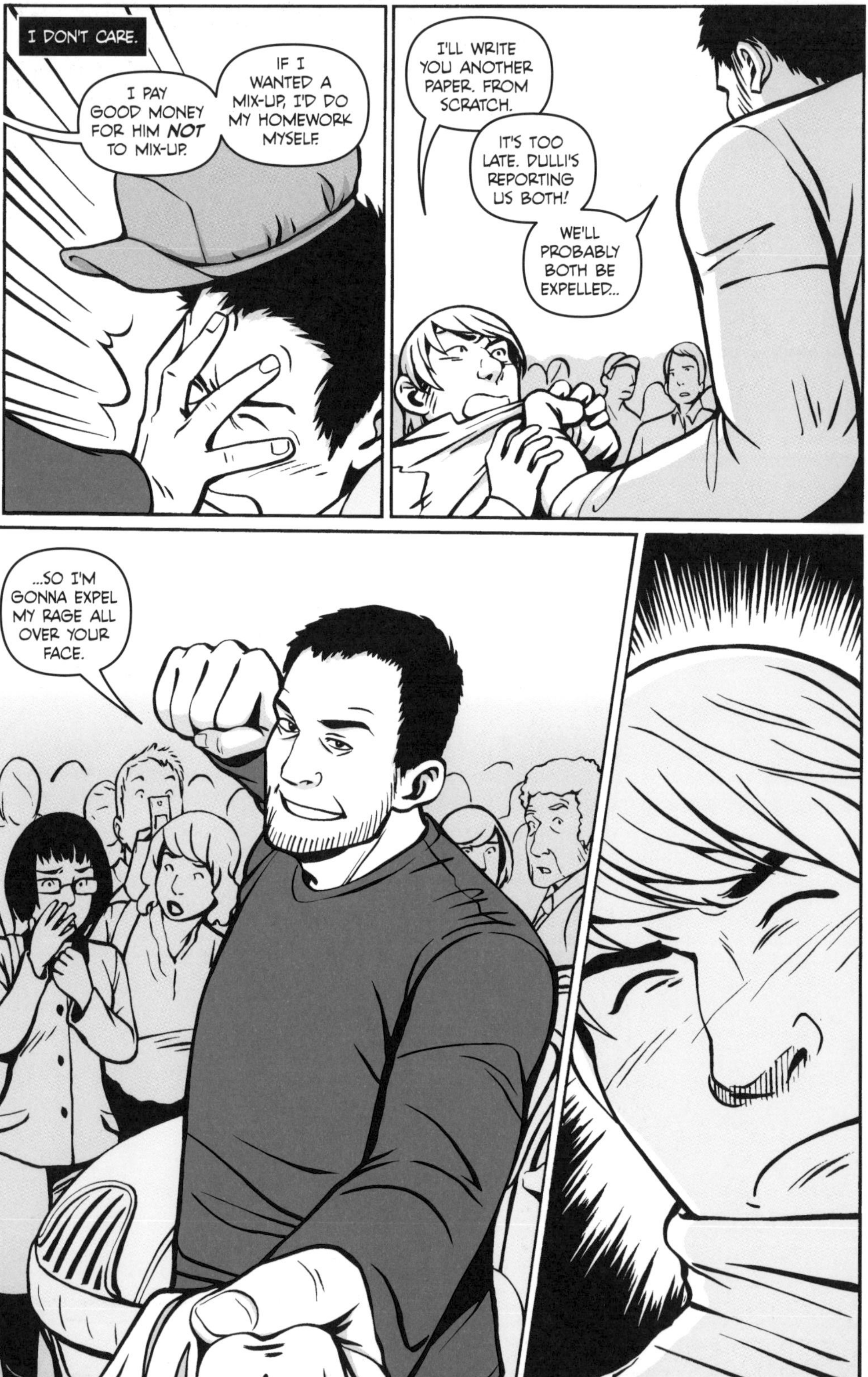
I DON'T CARE.
I PAY GOOD MONEY FOR HIM NOT TO MIX-UP.
IF I WANTED A MIX-UP, I'D DO MY HOMEWORK MYSELF.
I'LL WRITE YOU ANOTHER PAPER. FROM SCRATCH.
IT'S TOO LATE. DULLI'S REPORTING US BOTH!
WE'LL PROBABLY BOTH BE EXPELLED...
...SO I'M GONNA EXPEL MY RAGE ALL OVER YOUR FACE.

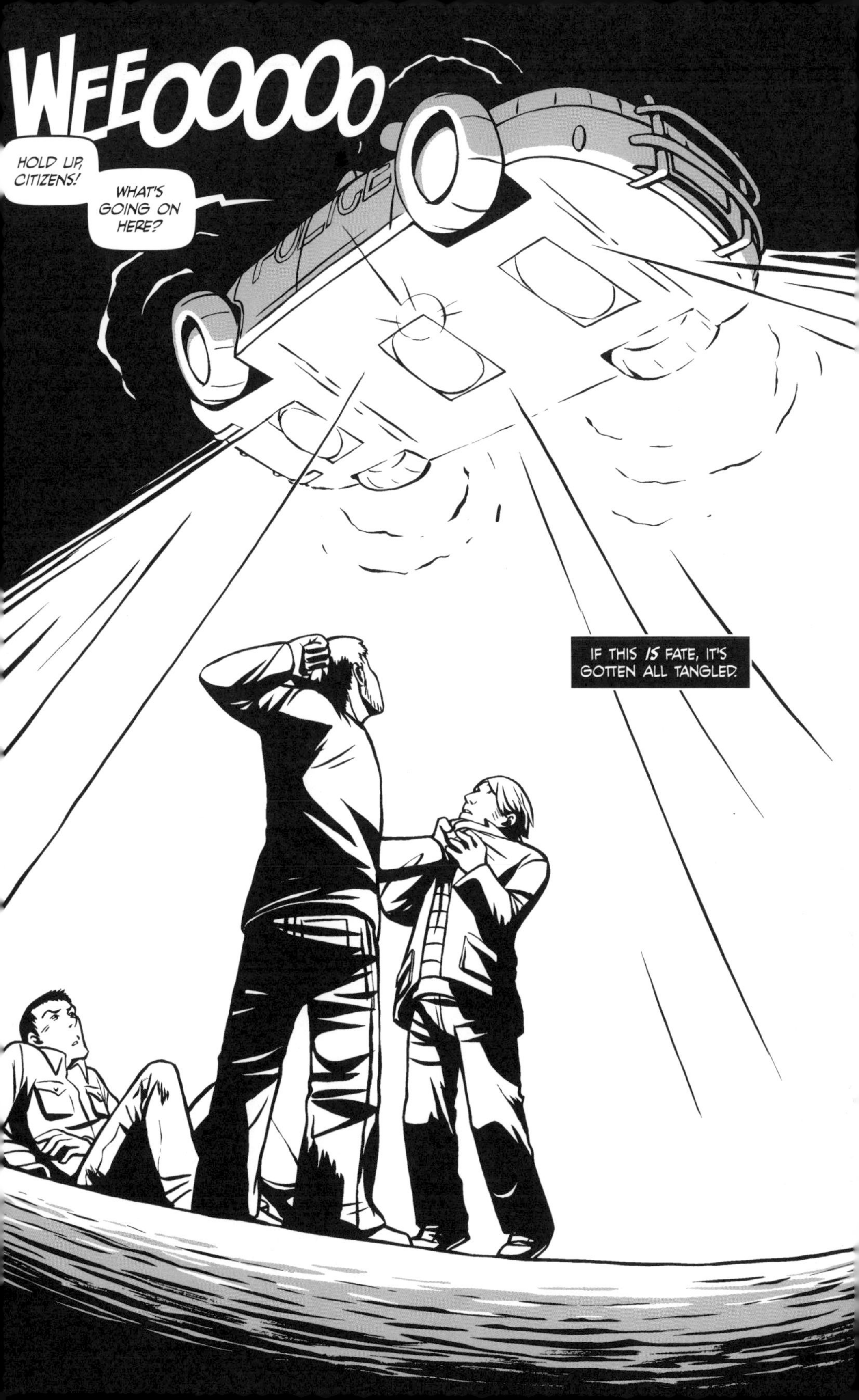
WEEOOOOO
HOLD UP, CITIZENS!
WHAT'S GOING ON HERE?
POLICE
IF THIS *IS* FATE, IT'S GOTTEN ALL TANGLED.

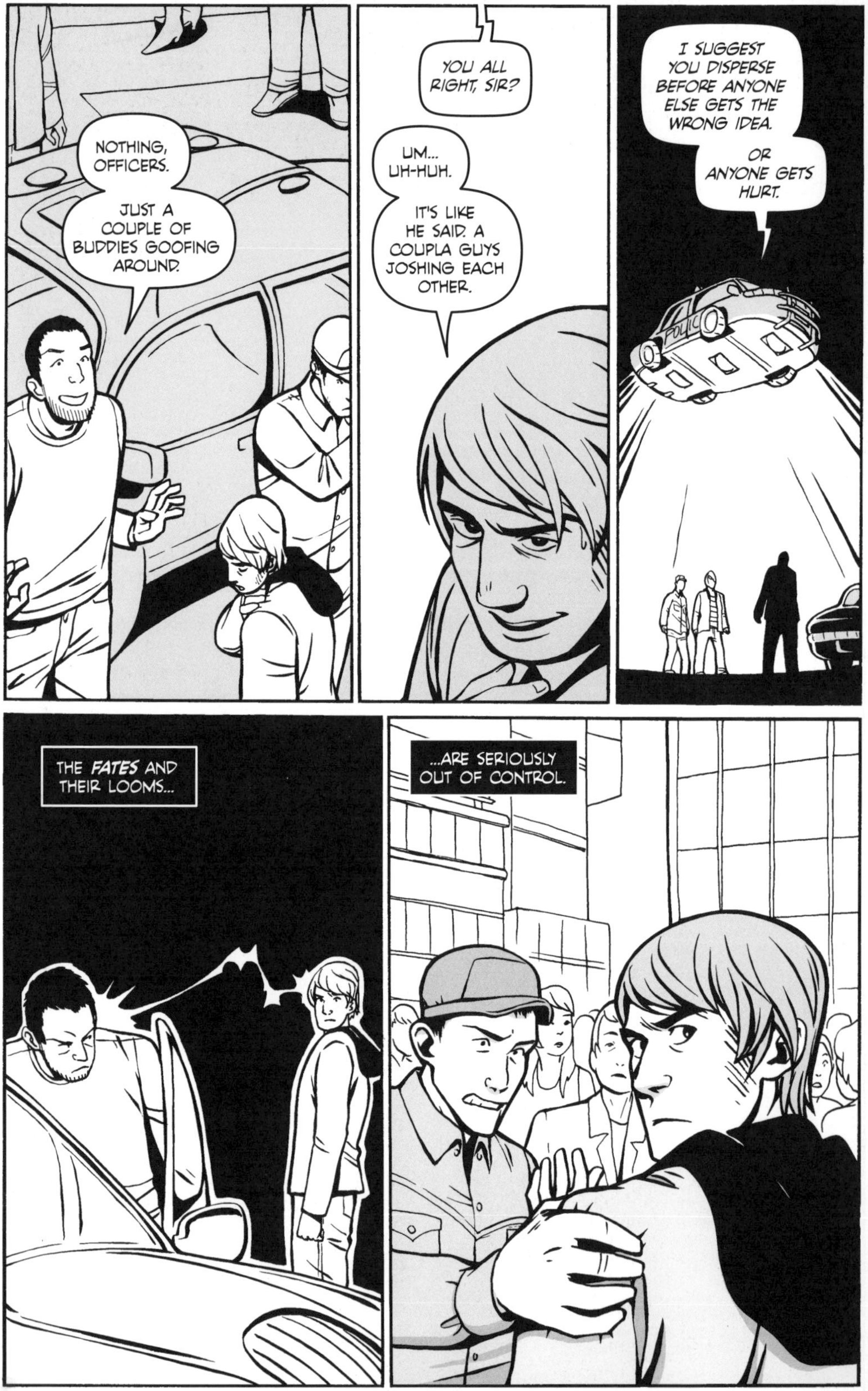
NOTHING, OFFICERS.
JUST A COUPLE OF BUDDIES GOOFING AROUND.
YOU ALL RIGHT, SIR?
UM... UH-HUH.
IT'S LIKE HE SAID. A COUPLA GUYS JOSHING EACH OTHER.
I SUGGEST YOU DISPERSE BEFORE ANYONE ELSE GETS THE WRONG IDEA.
OR ANYONE GETS HURT.
THE FATES AND THEIR LOOMS...
...ARE SERIOUSLY OUT OF CONTROL.

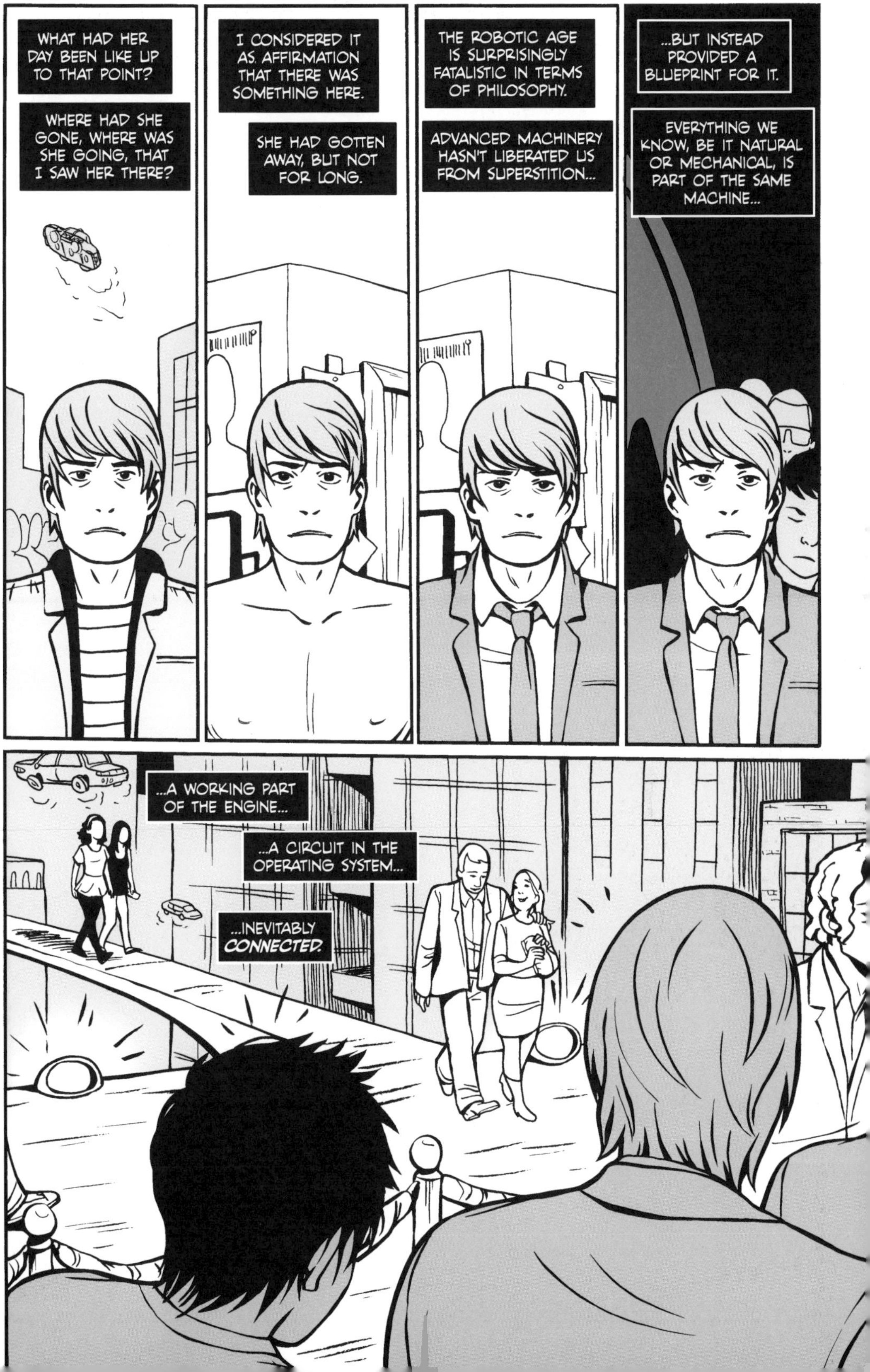
WHAT HAD HER DAY BEEN LIKE UP TO THAT POINT?
WHERE HAD SHE GONE, WHERE WAS SHE GOING, THAT I SAW HER THERE?
I CONSIDERED IT AS AFFIRMATION THAT THERE WAS SOMETHING HERE.
SHE HAD GOTTEN AWAY, BUT NOT FOR LONG.
THE ROBOTIC AGE IS SURPRISINGLY FATALISTIC IN TERMS OF PHILOSOPHY.
ADVANCED MACHINERY HASN'T LIBERATED US FROM SUPERSTITION...
...BUT INSTEAD PROVIDED A BLUEPRINT FOR IT.
EVERYTHING WE KNOW, BE IT NATURAL OR MECHANICAL, IS PART OF THE SAME MACHINE...
...A WORKING PART OF THE ENGINE...
...A CIRCUIT IN THE OPERATING SYSTEM...
...INEVITABLY CONNECTED.

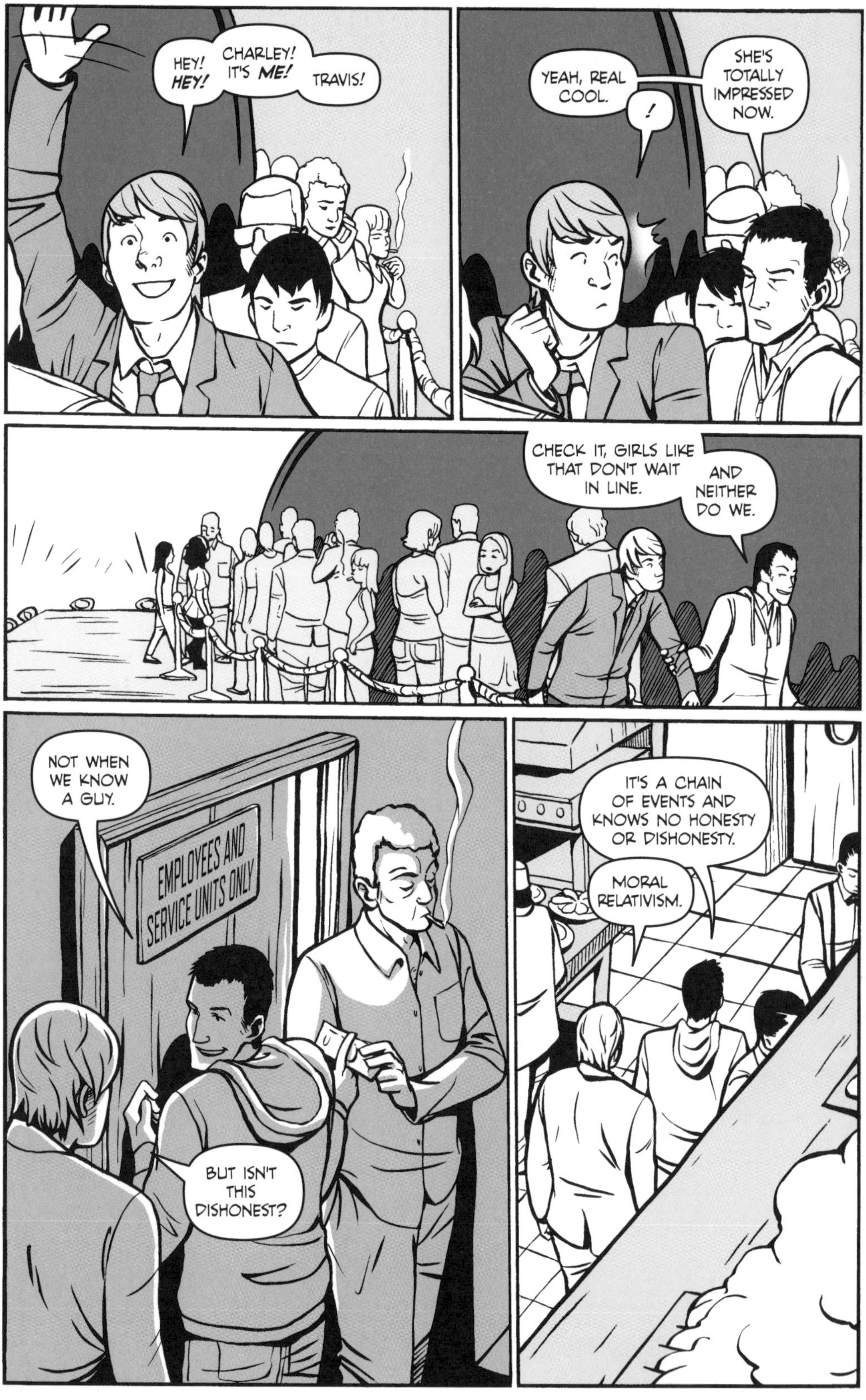
HEY! HEY!
CHARLEY! IT'S ME!
TRAVIS!
YEAH, REAL COOL.
SHE'S TOTALLY IMPRESSED NOW.
!
CHECK IT, GIRLS LIKE THAT DON'T WAIT IN LINE.
AND NEITHER DO WE.
NOT WHEN WE KNOW A GUY.
EMPLOYEES AND SERVICE UNITS ONLY
BUT ISN'T THIS DISHONEST?
IT'S A CHAIN OF EVENTS AND KNOWS NO HONESTY OR DISHONESTY.
MORAL RELATIVISM.

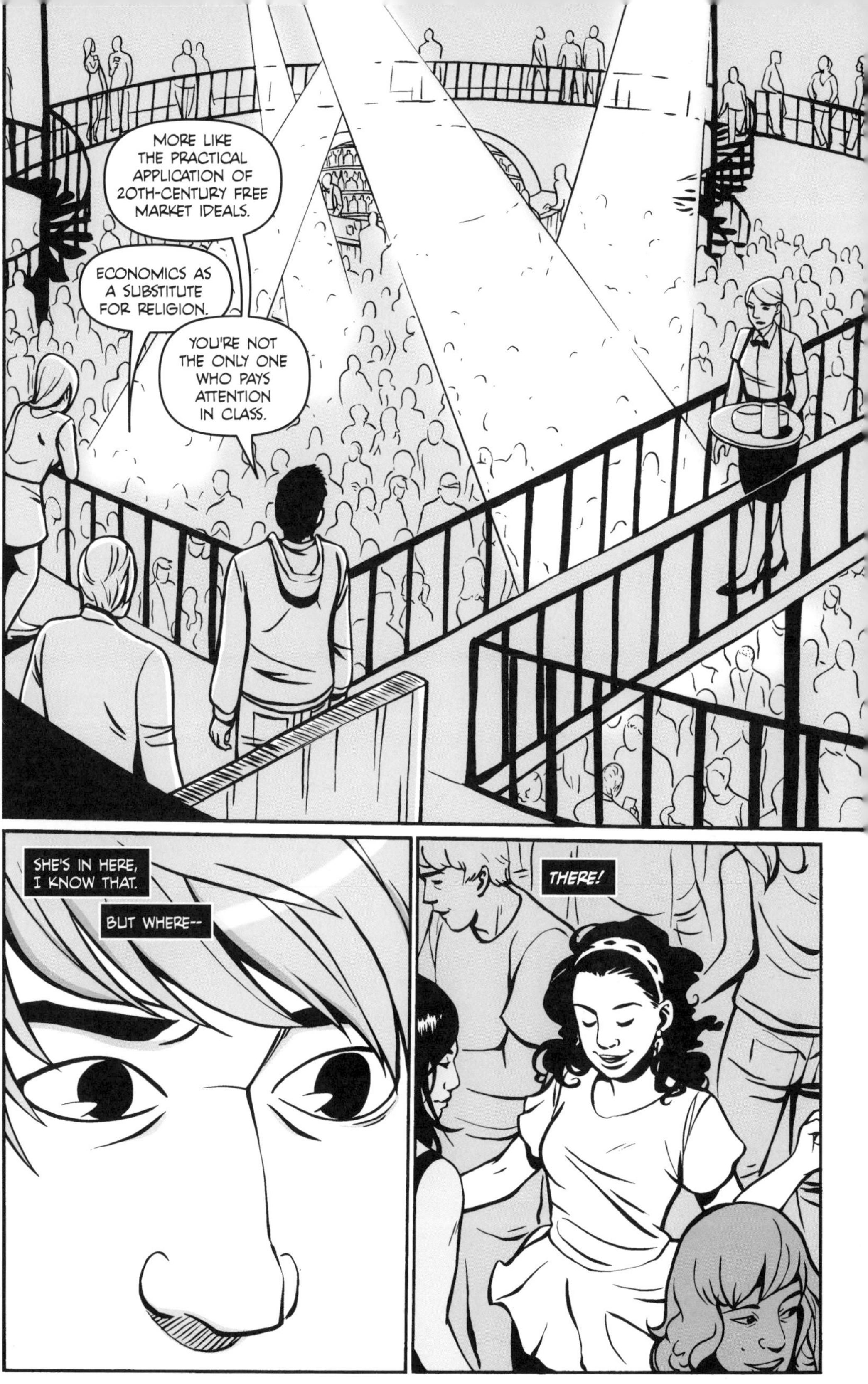
MORE LIKE THE PRACTICAL APPLICATION OF 20TH-CENTURY FREE MARKET IDEALS.
ECONOMICS AS A SUBSTITUTE FOR RELIGION.
YOU'RE NOT THE ONLY ONE WHO PAYS ATTENTION IN CLASS.
SHE'S IN HERE, I KNOW THAT.
BUT WHERE--
THERE!

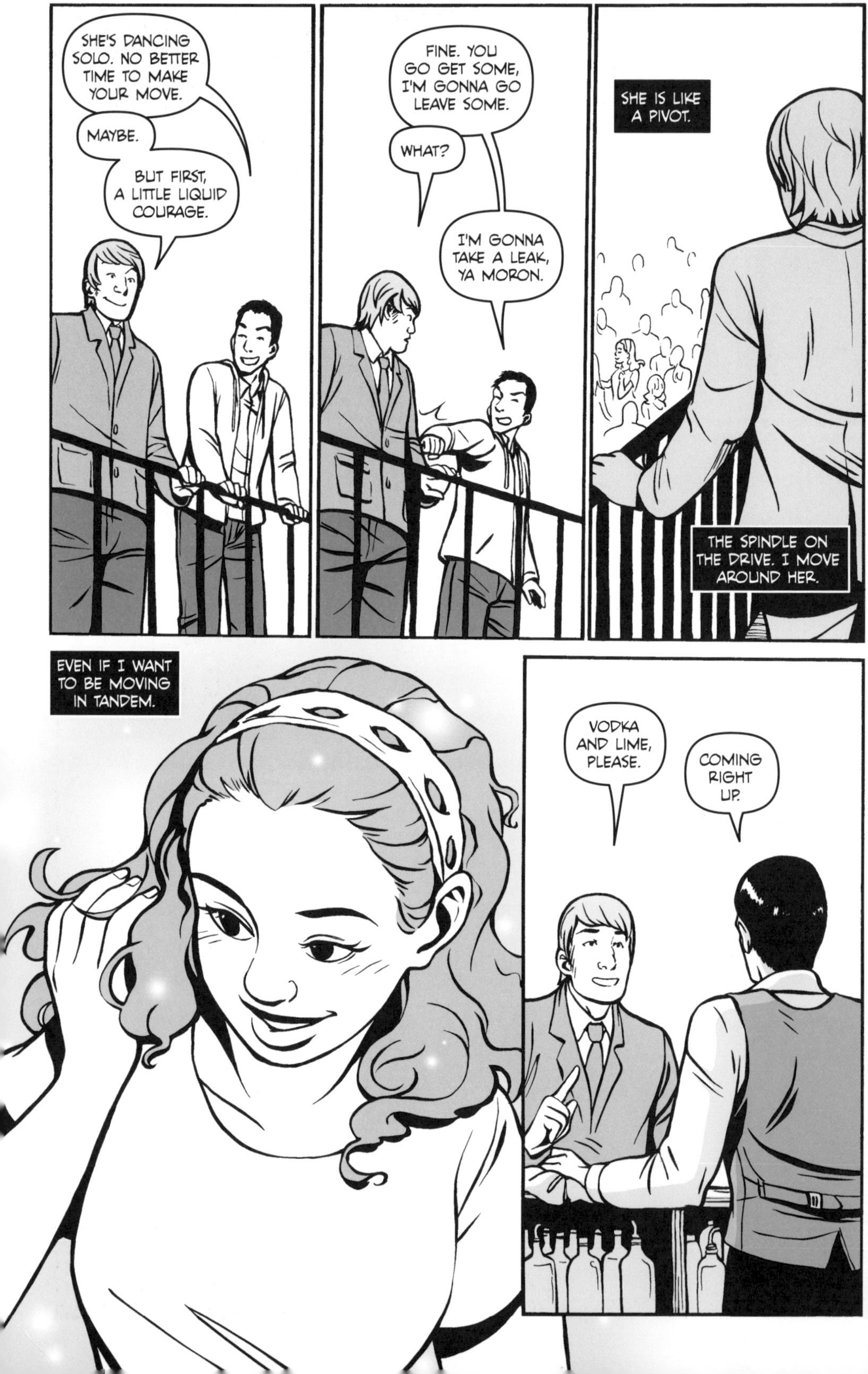
SHE'S DANCING SOLO. NO BETTER TIME TO MAKE YOUR MOVE.
MAYBE.
BUT FIRST, A LITTLE LIQUID COURAGE.
FINE. YOU GO GET SOME, I'M GONNA GO LEAVE SOME.
WHAT?
I'M GONNA TAKE A LEAK, YA MORON.
SHE IS LIKE A PIVOT.
THE SPINDLE ON THE DRIVE. I MOVE AROUND HER.
EVEN IF I WANT TO BE MOVING IN TANDEM.
VODKA AND LIME, PLEASE.
COMING RIGHT UP.

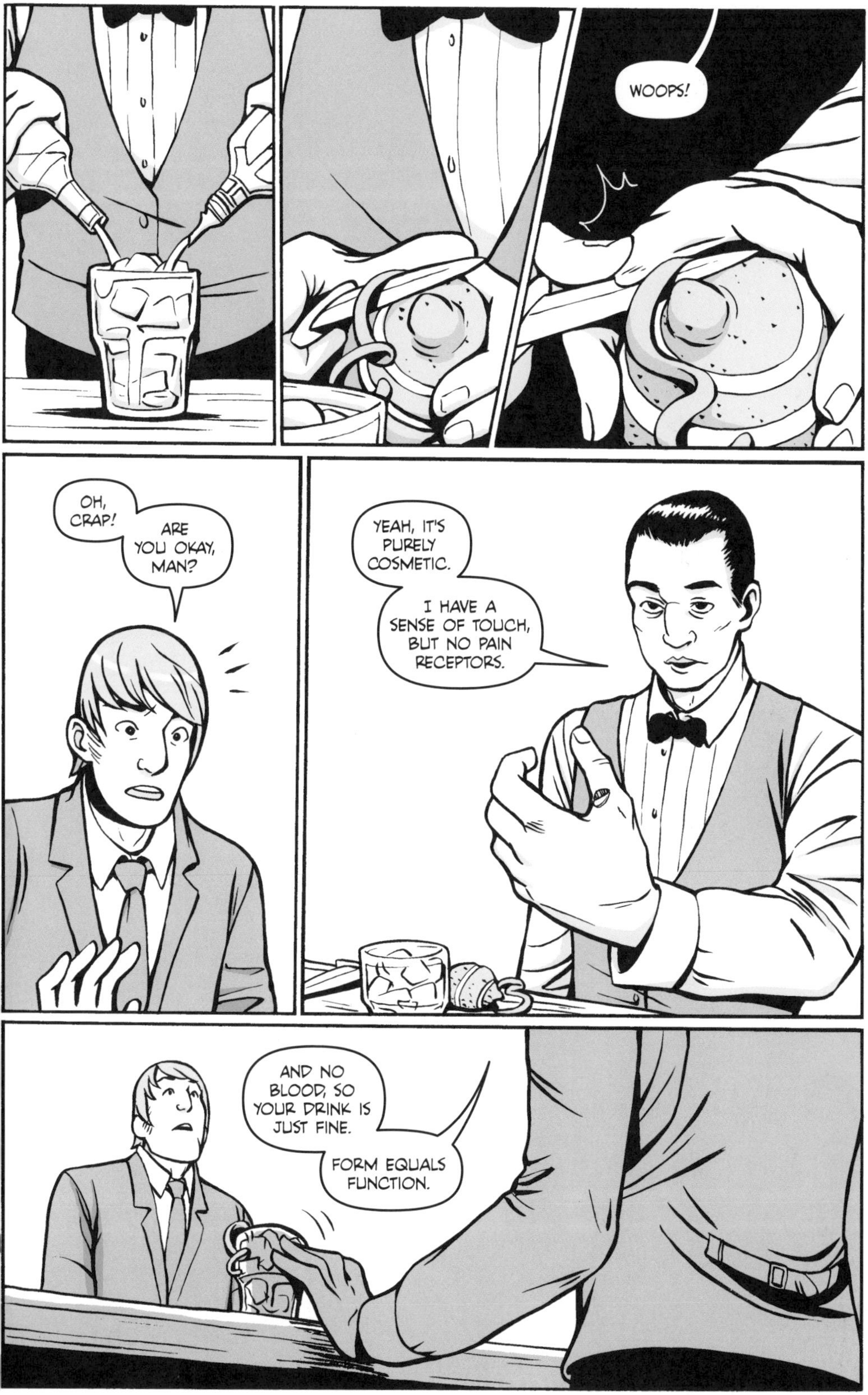
WOOPS!
OH, CRAP!
ARE YOU OKAY, MAN?
YEAH, IT'S PURELY COSMETIC.
I HAVE A SENSE OF TOUCH, BUT NO PAIN RECEPTORS.
AND NO BLOOD, SO YOUR DRINK IS JUST FINE.
FORM EQUALS FUNCTION.

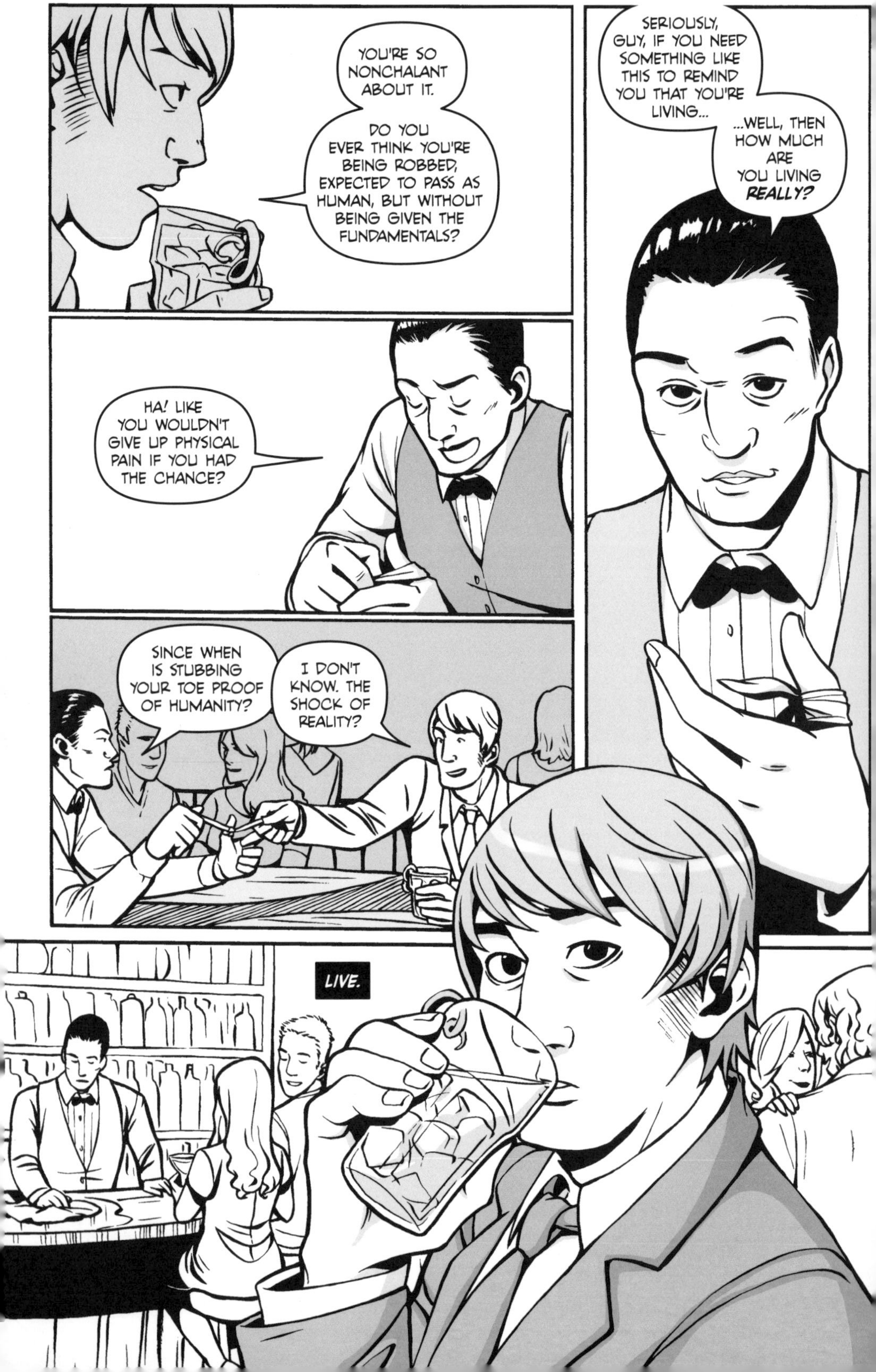
YOU'RE SO NONCHALANT ABOUT IT.
DO YOU EVER THINK YOU'RE BEING ROBBED, EXPECTED TO PASS AS HUMAN, BUT WITHOUT BEING GIVEN THE FUNDAMENTALS?
HA! LIKE YOU WOULDN'T GIVE UP PHYSICAL PAIN IF YOU HAD THE CHANCE?
SINCE WHEN IS STUBBING YOUR TOE PROOF OF HUMANITY?
I DON'T KNOW. THE SHOCK OF REALITY?
SERIOUSLY, GUY, IF YOU NEED SOMETHING LIKE THIS TO REMIND YOU THAT YOU'RE LIVING...
...WELL, THEN HOW MUCH ARE YOU LIVING *REALLY?*
LIVE.

CHAPTER 4: HER

BET SHE LOOKS GOOD
ON THE DANCEFLOOR...

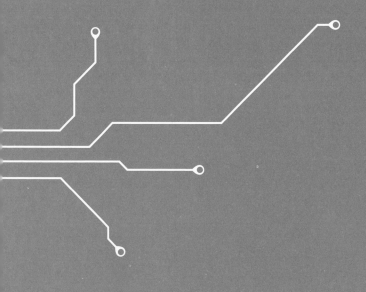

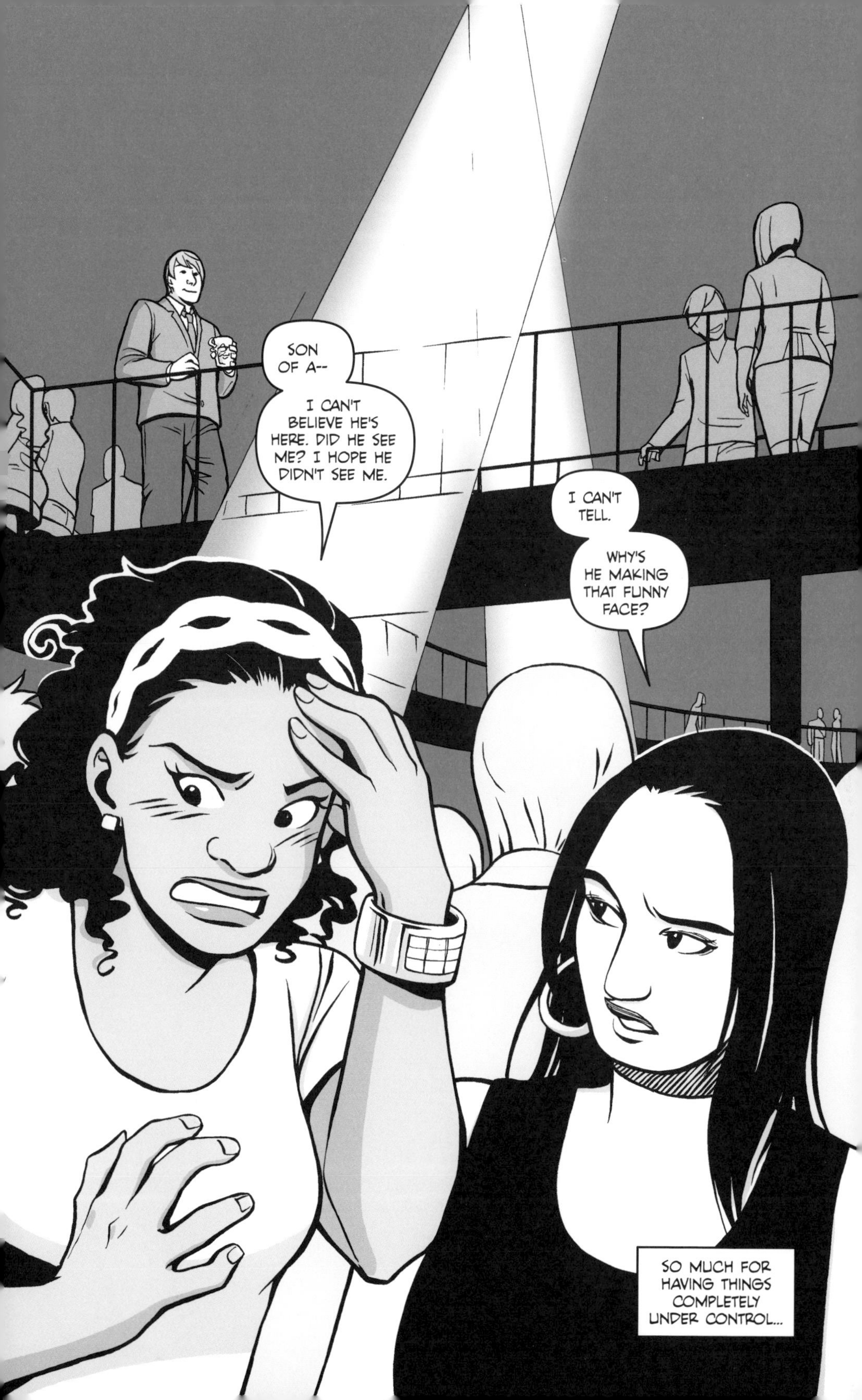
SON OF A--
I CAN'T BELIEVE HE'S HERE. DID HE SEE ME? I HOPE HE DIDN'T SEE ME.
I CAN'T TELL.
WHY'S HE MAKING THAT FUNNY FACE?
SO MUCH FOR HAVING THINGS COMPLETELY UNDER CONTROL...

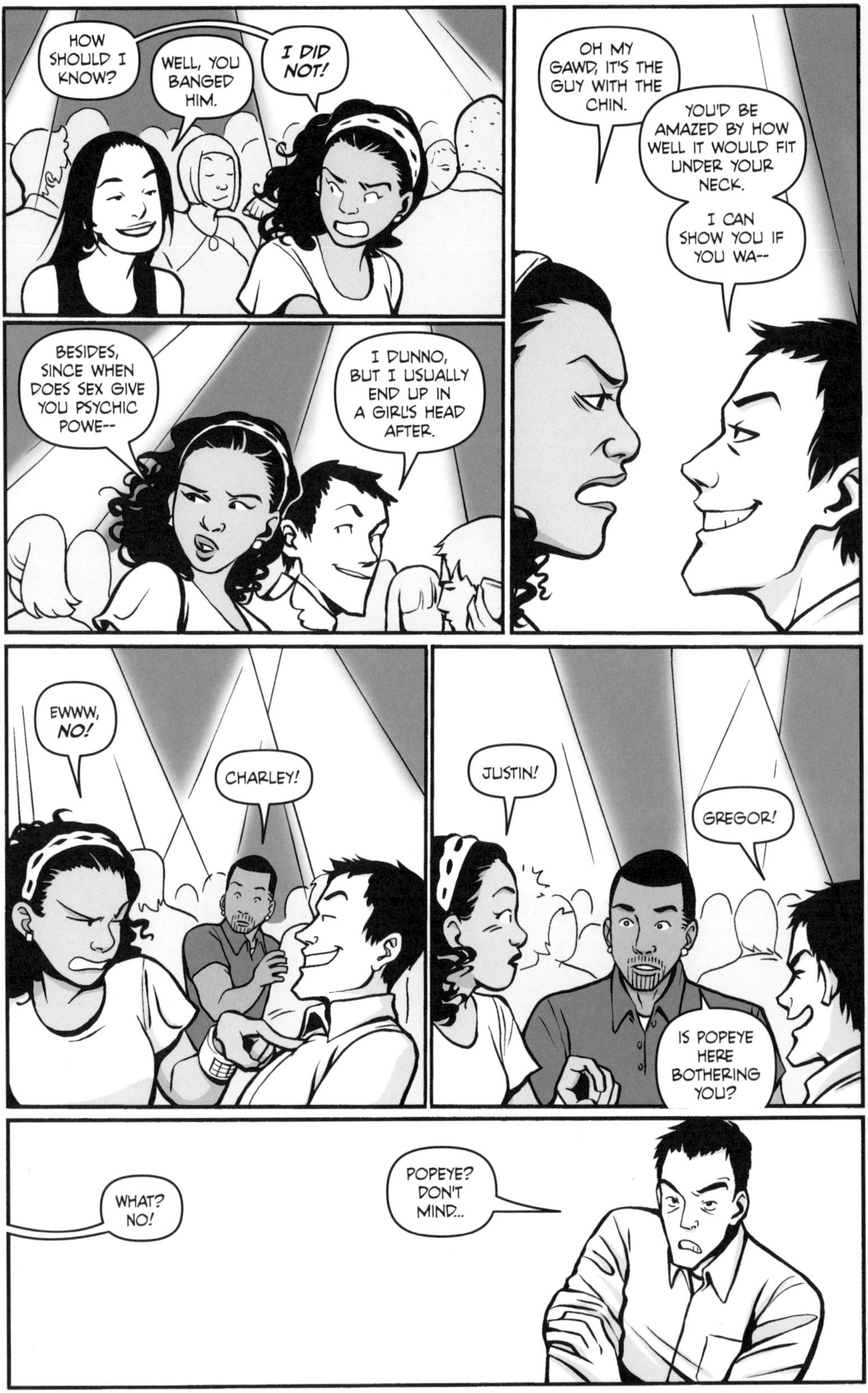
HOW SHOULD I KNOW?
WELL, YOU BANGED HIM.
I DID NOT!
OH MY GAWD, IT'S THE GUY WITH THE CHIN.
YOU'D BE AMAZED BY HOW WELL IT WOULD FIT UNDER YOUR NECK.
I CAN SHOW YOU IF YOU WA--
BESIDES, SINCE WHEN DOES SEX GIVE YOU PSYCHIC POWE--
I DUNNO, BUT I USUALLY END UP IN A GIRL'S HEAD AFTER.
EWWW, NO!
CHARLEY!
JUSTIN!
GREGOR!
IS POPEYE HERE BOTHERING YOU?
WHAT? NO!
POPEYE? DON'T MIND...

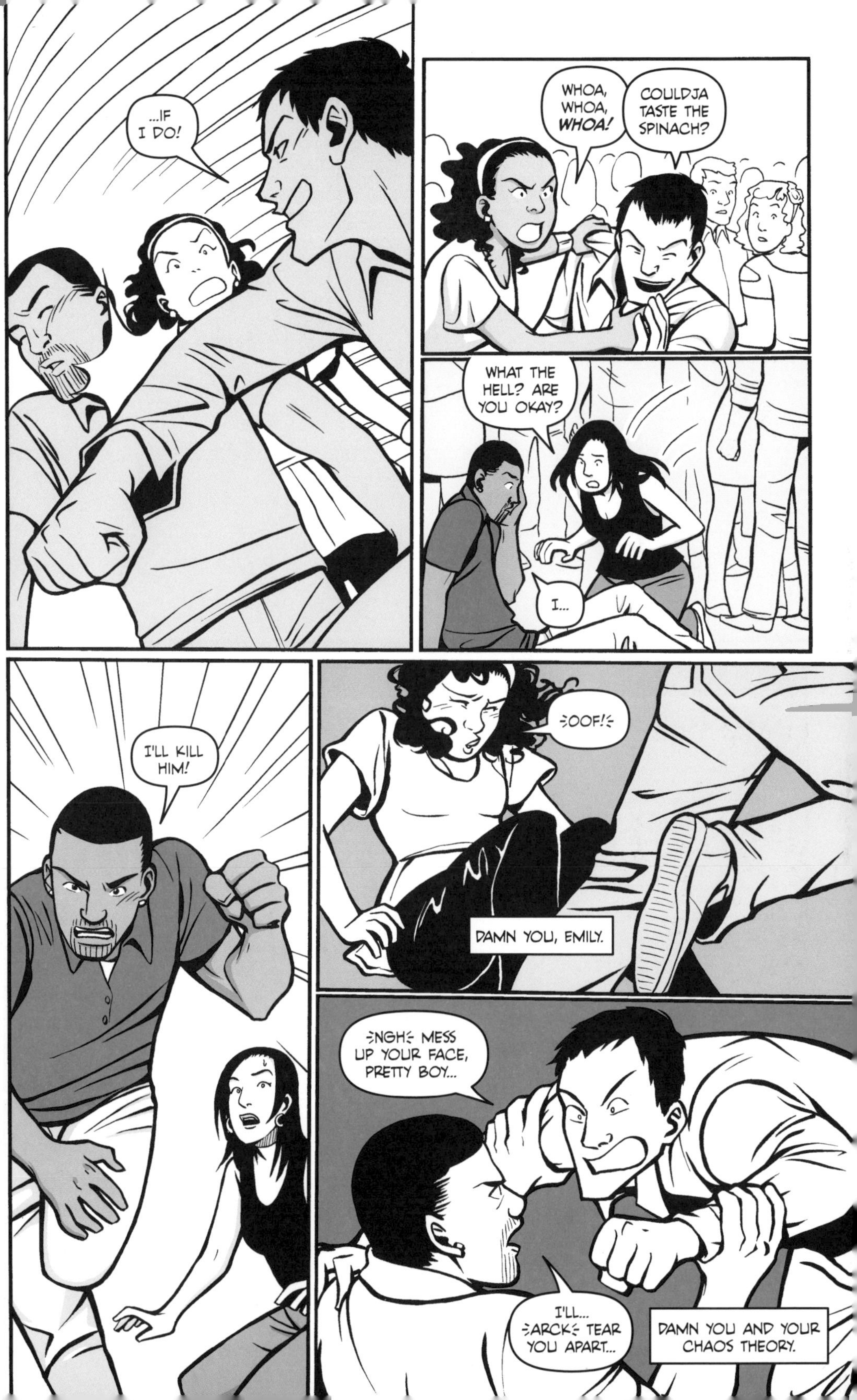
...IF I DO!
WHOA, WHOA, *WHOA!*
COULDJA TASTE THE SPINACH?
WHAT THE HELL? ARE YOU OKAY?
I...
I'LL KILL HIM!
OOF!
DAMN YOU, EMILY.
NGH MESS UP YOUR FACE, PRETTY BOY...
I'LL... ARCK TEAR YOU APART...
DAMN YOU AND YOUR CHAOS THEORY.

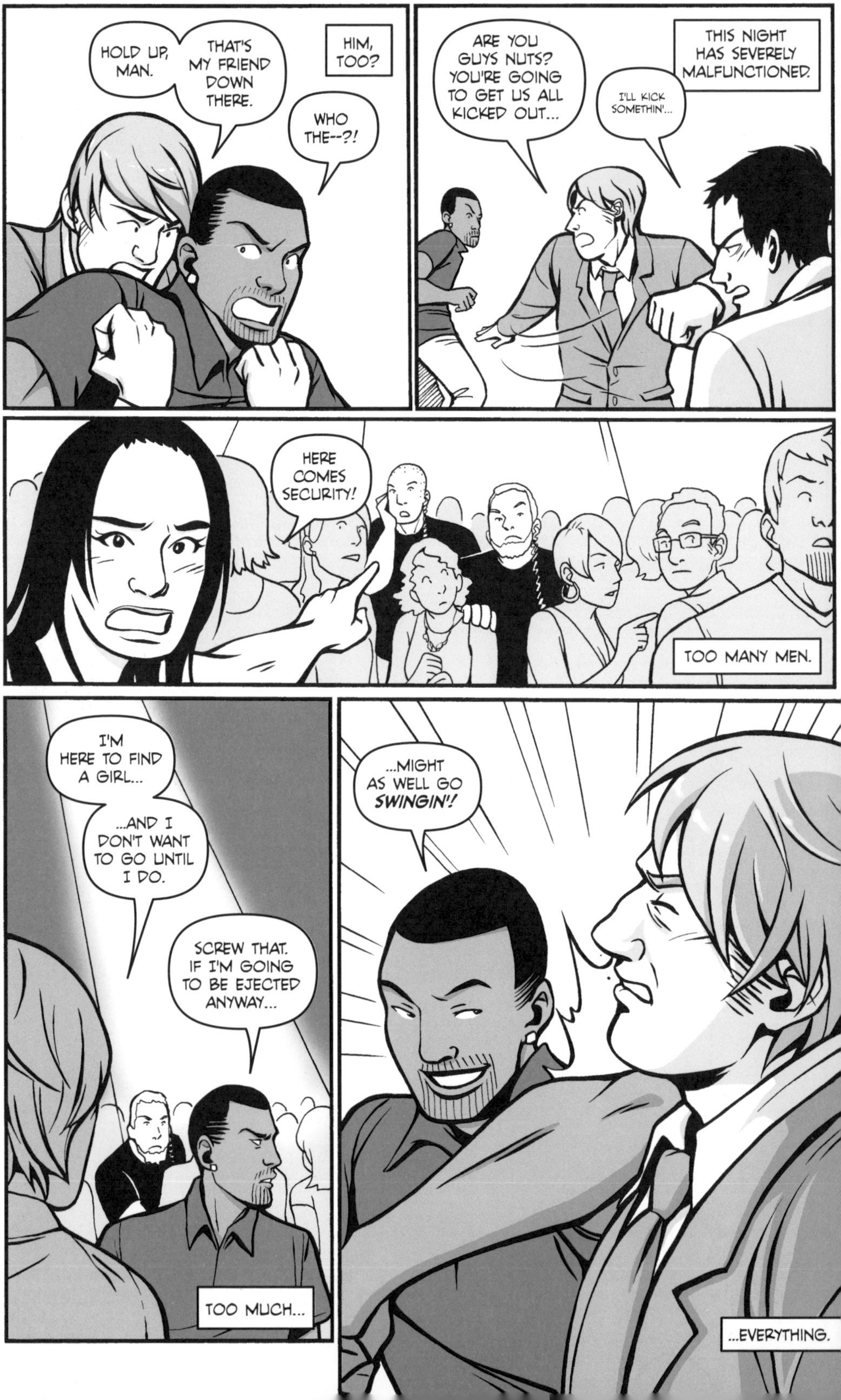
HOLD UP, MAN.
THAT'S MY FRIEND DOWN THERE.
HIM, TOO?
WHO THE--?!
ARE YOU GUYS NUTS? YOU'RE GOING TO GET US ALL KICKED OUT...
THIS NIGHT HAS SEVERELY MALFUNCTIONED.
I'LL KICK SOMETHIN'...
HERE COMES SECURITY!
TOO MANY MEN.
I'M HERE TO FIND A GIRL...
...AND I DON'T WANT TO GO UNTIL I DO.
SCREW THAT. IF I'M GOING TO BE EJECTED ANYWAY...
TOO MUCH...
...MIGHT AS WELL GO *SWINGIN'!*
...EVERYTHING.

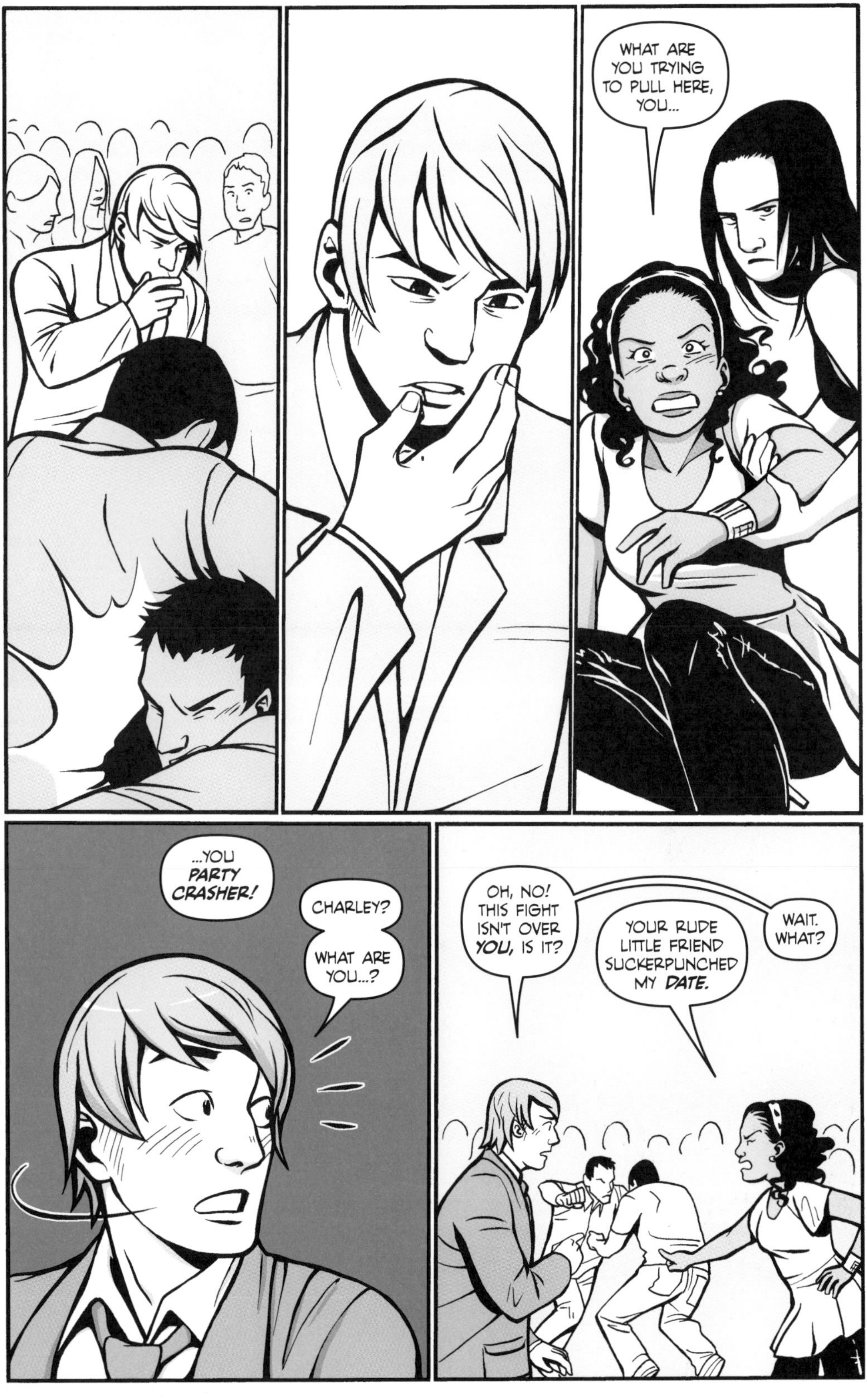
WHAT ARE YOU TRYING TO PULL HERE, YOU...
...YOU PARTY CRASHER!
CHARLEY?
WHAT ARE YOU...?
OH, NO! THIS FIGHT ISN'T OVER YOU, IS IT?
WAIT. WHAT?
YOUR RUDE LITTLE FRIEND SUCKERPUNCHED MY DATE.

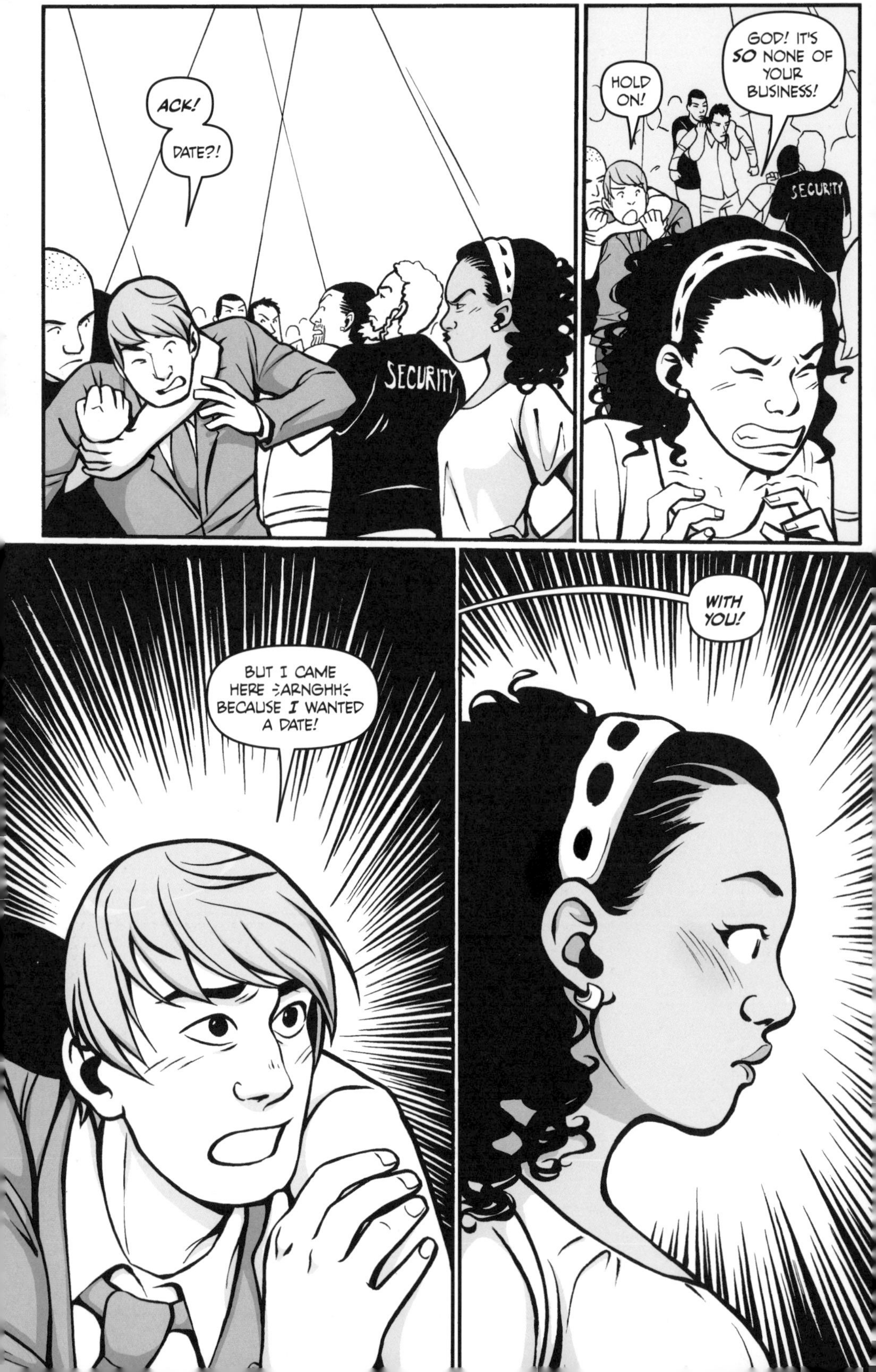
ACK!
DATE?!
HOLD ON!
GOD! IT'S SO NONE OF YOUR BUSINESS!
SECURITY
SECURITY
BUT I CAME HERE ARNGHH BECAUSE I WANTED A DATE!
WITH YOU!

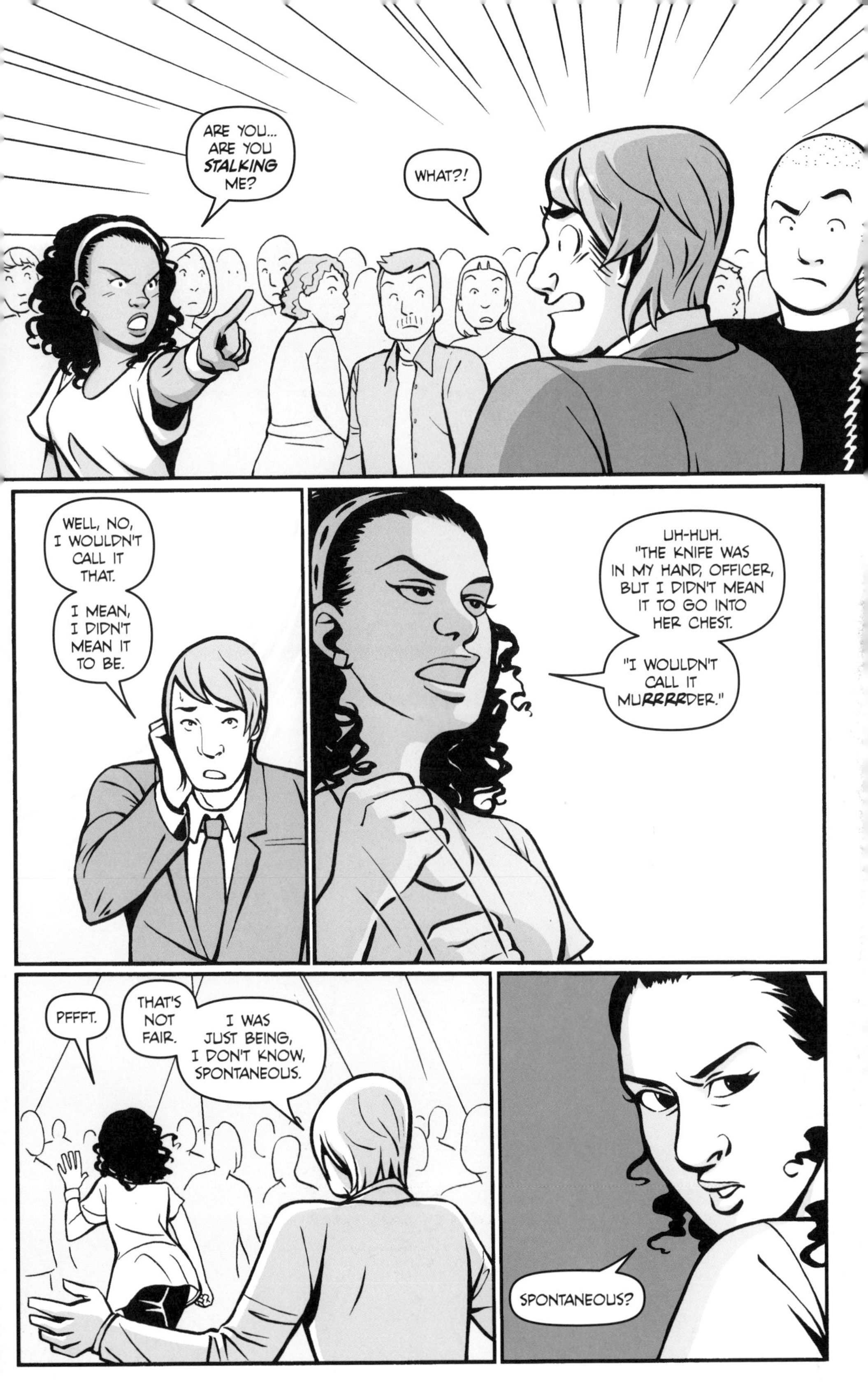
ARE YOU... ARE YOU STALKING ME?
WHAT?!
WELL, NO, I WOULDN'T CALL IT THAT.
I MEAN, I DIDN'T MEAN IT TO BE.
UH-HUH. "THE KNIFE WAS IN MY HAND, OFFICER, BUT I DIDN'T MEAN IT TO GO INTO HER CHEST.
"I WOULDN'T CALL IT MURRRRDER."
PFFFT.
THAT'S NOT FAIR.
I WAS JUST BEING, I DON'T KNOW, SPONTANEOUS.
SPONTANEOUS?

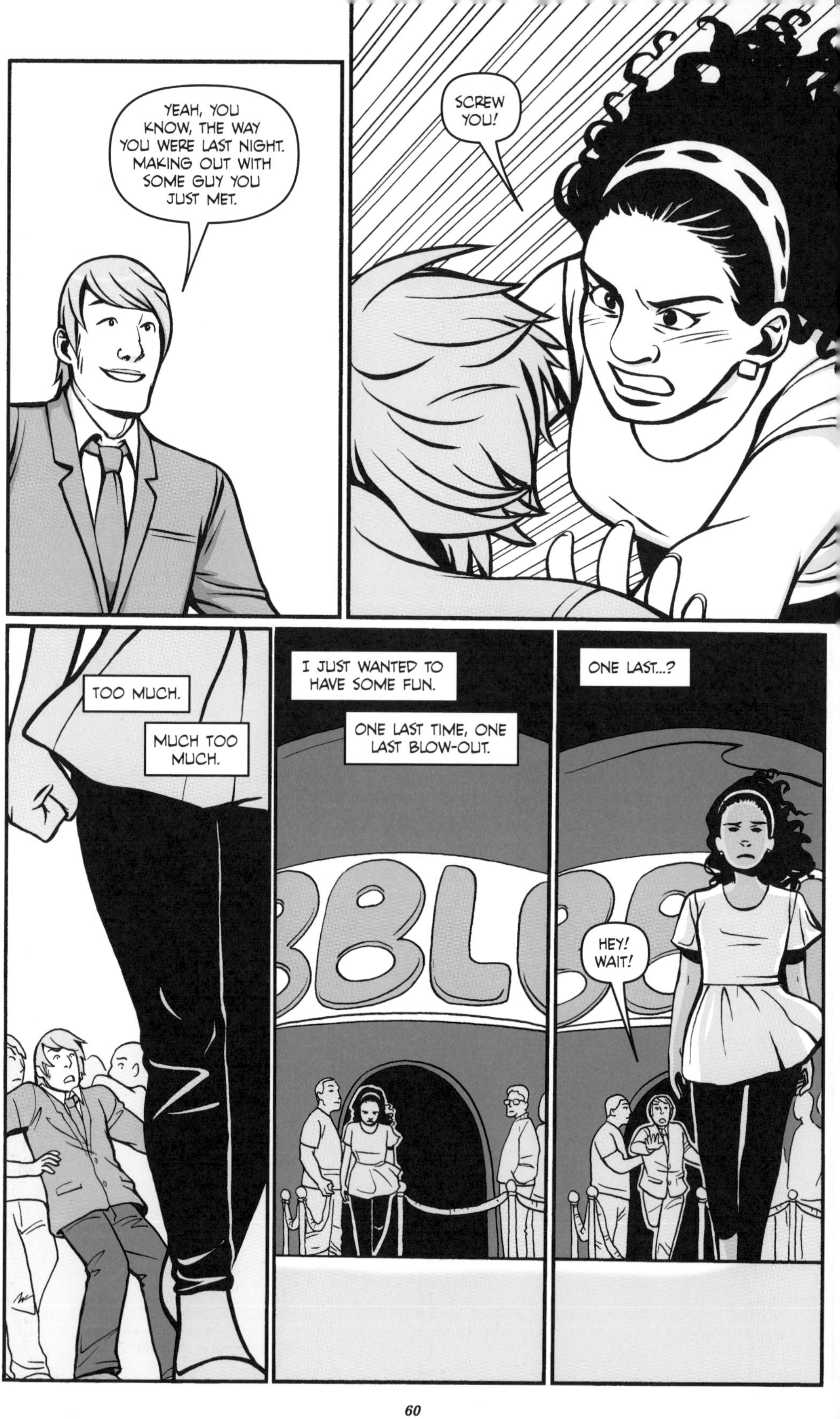
YEAH, YOU KNOW, THE WAY YOU WERE LAST NIGHT. MAKING OUT WITH SOME GUY YOU JUST MET.
SCREW YOU!
TOO MUCH.
MUCH TOO MUCH.
I JUST WANTED TO HAVE SOME FUN.
ONE LAST TIME, ONE LAST BLOW-OUT.
ONE LAST...?
HEY! WAIT!

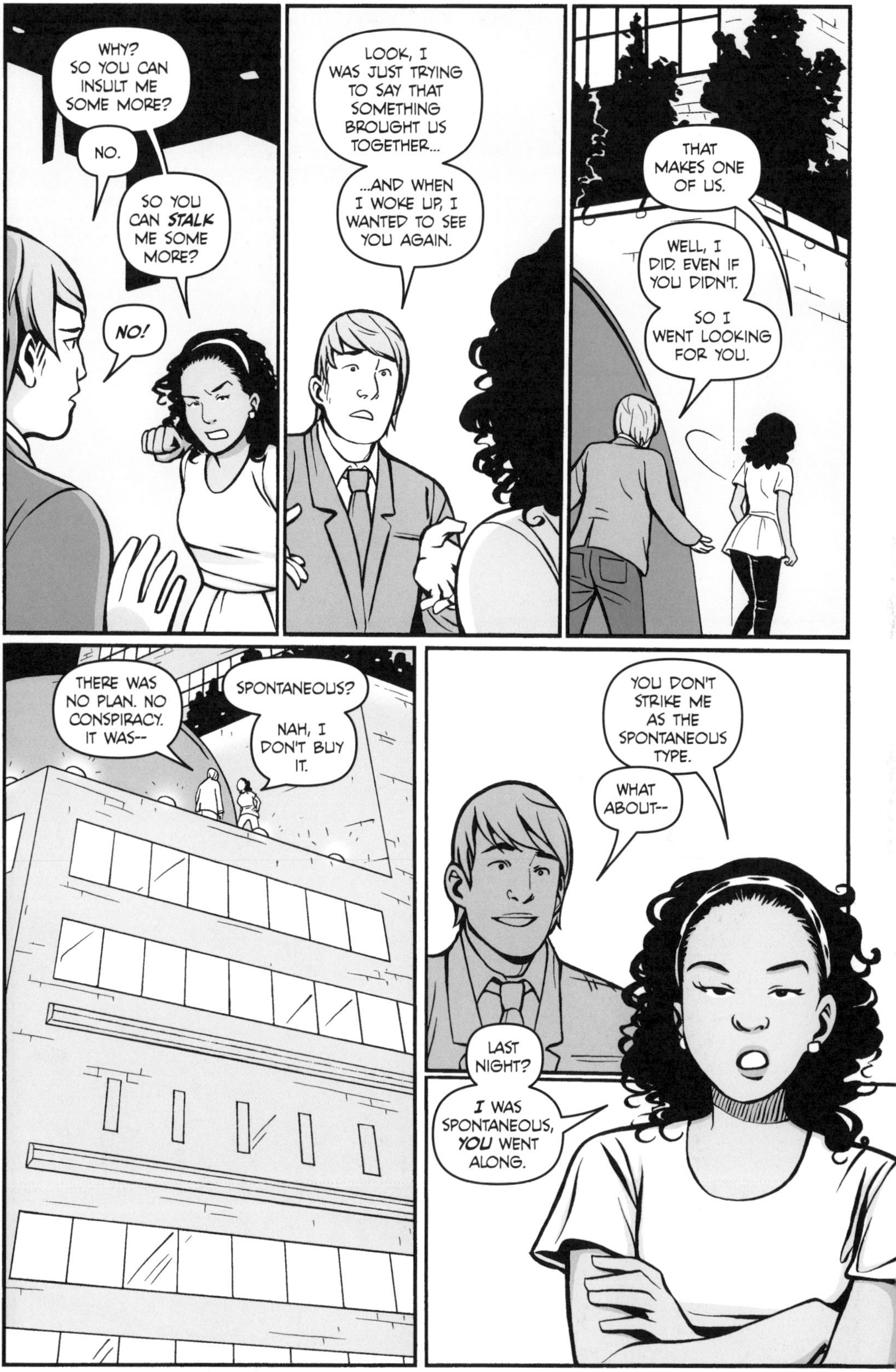
WHY? SO YOU CAN INSULT ME SOME MORE?
NO.
SO YOU CAN STALK ME SOME MORE?
NO!
LOOK, I WAS JUST TRYING TO SAY THAT SOMETHING BROUGHT US TOGETHER...
...AND WHEN I WOKE UP, I WANTED TO SEE YOU AGAIN.
THAT MAKES ONE OF US.
WELL, I DID. EVEN IF YOU DIDN'T.
SO I WENT LOOKING FOR YOU.
THERE WAS NO PLAN. NO CONSPIRACY. IT WAS--
SPONTANEOUS?
NAH, I DON'T BUY IT.
YOU DON'T STRIKE ME AS THE SPONTANEOUS TYPE.
WHAT ABOUT--
LAST NIGHT?
I WAS SPONTANEOUS, YOU WENT ALONG.

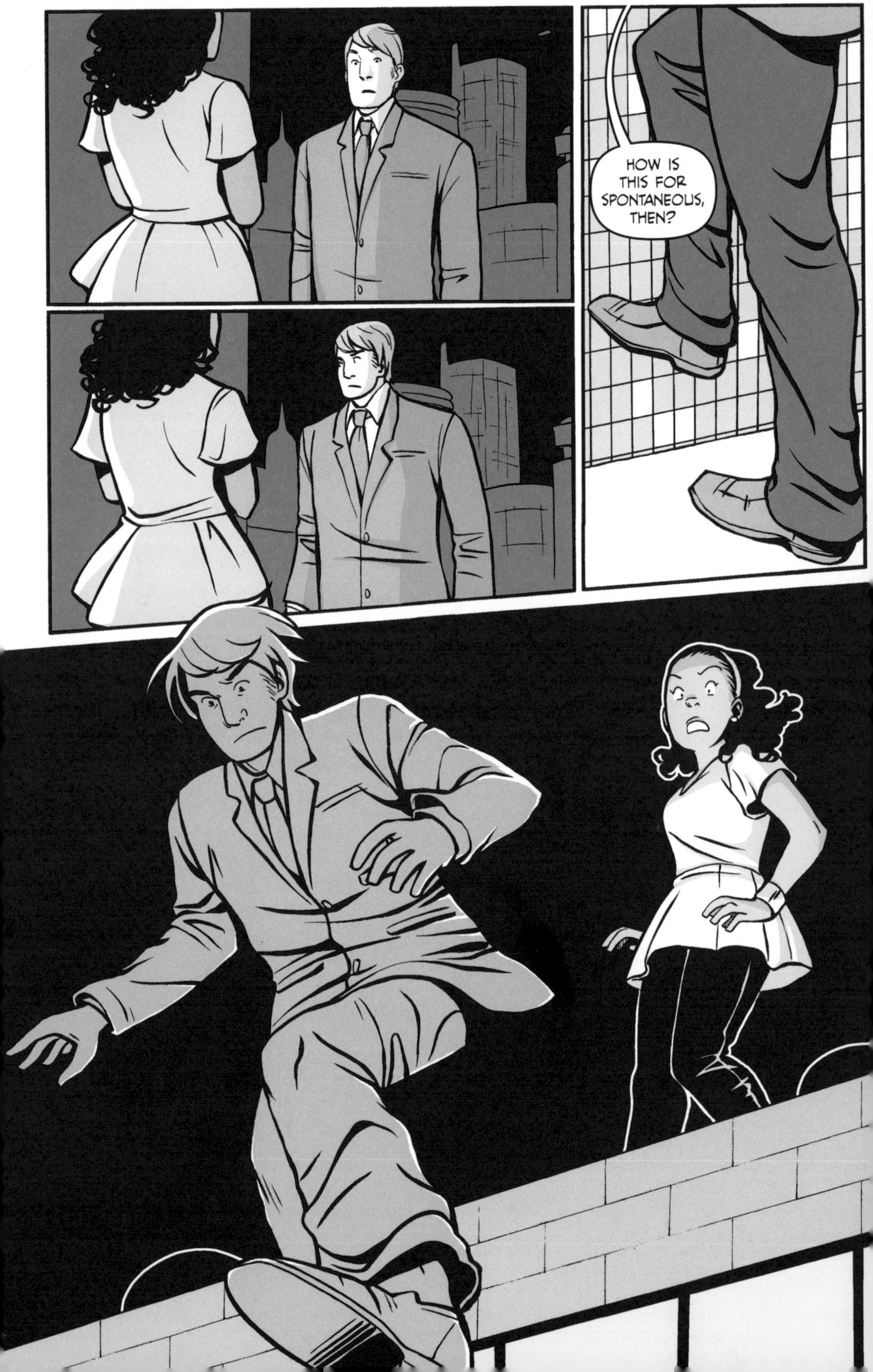
HOW IS THIS FOR SPONTANEOUS, THEN?

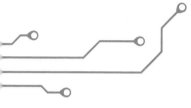

CHAPTER 5:
HIM

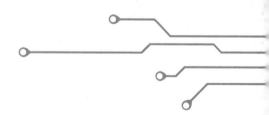

LIVE?!*@ LIKE A...

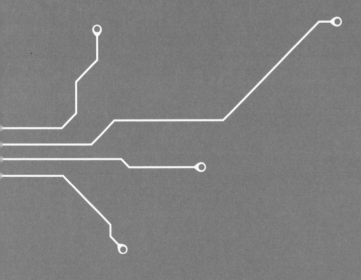

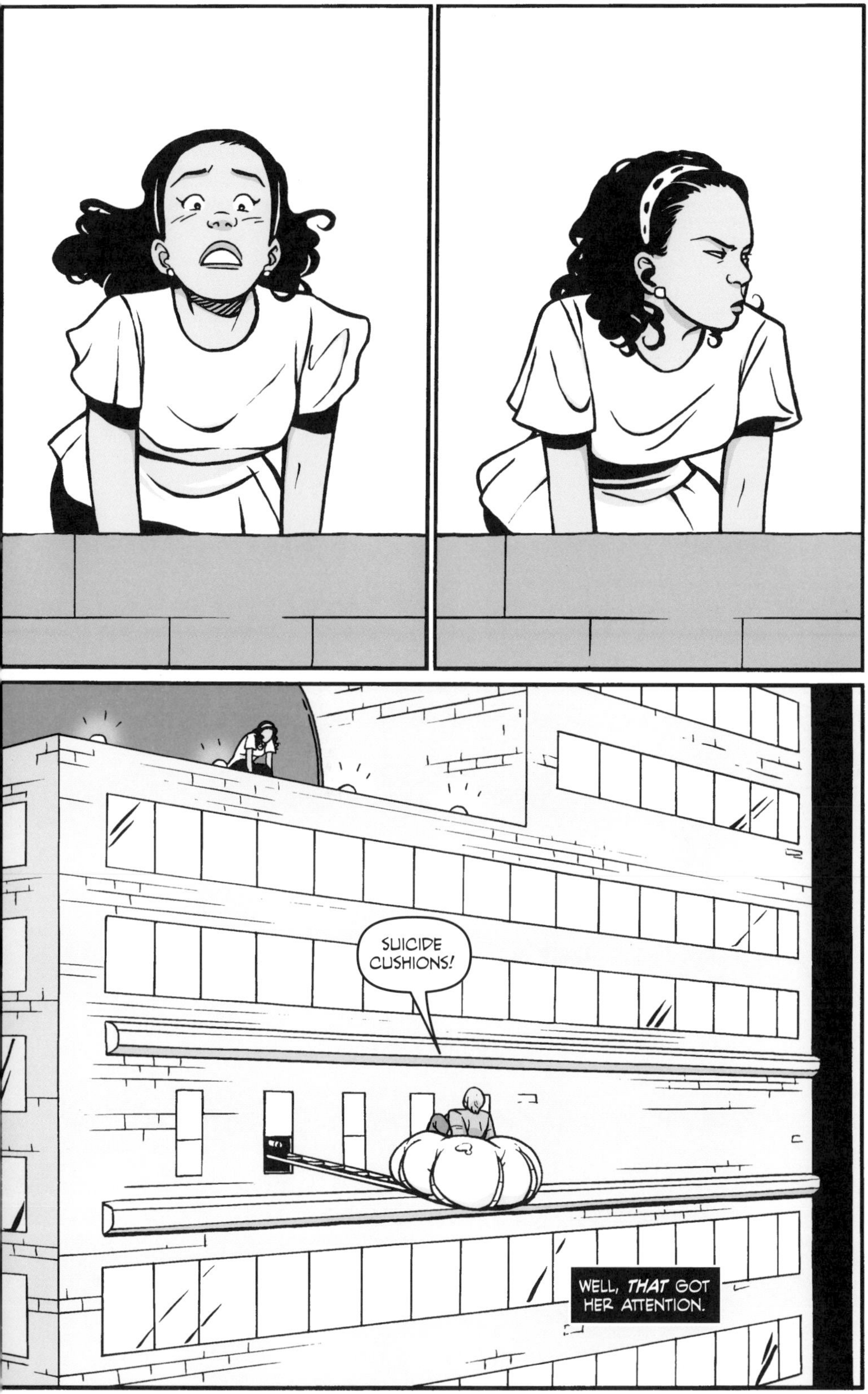
SUICIDE CUSHIONS!
WELL, THAT GOT HER ATTENTION.

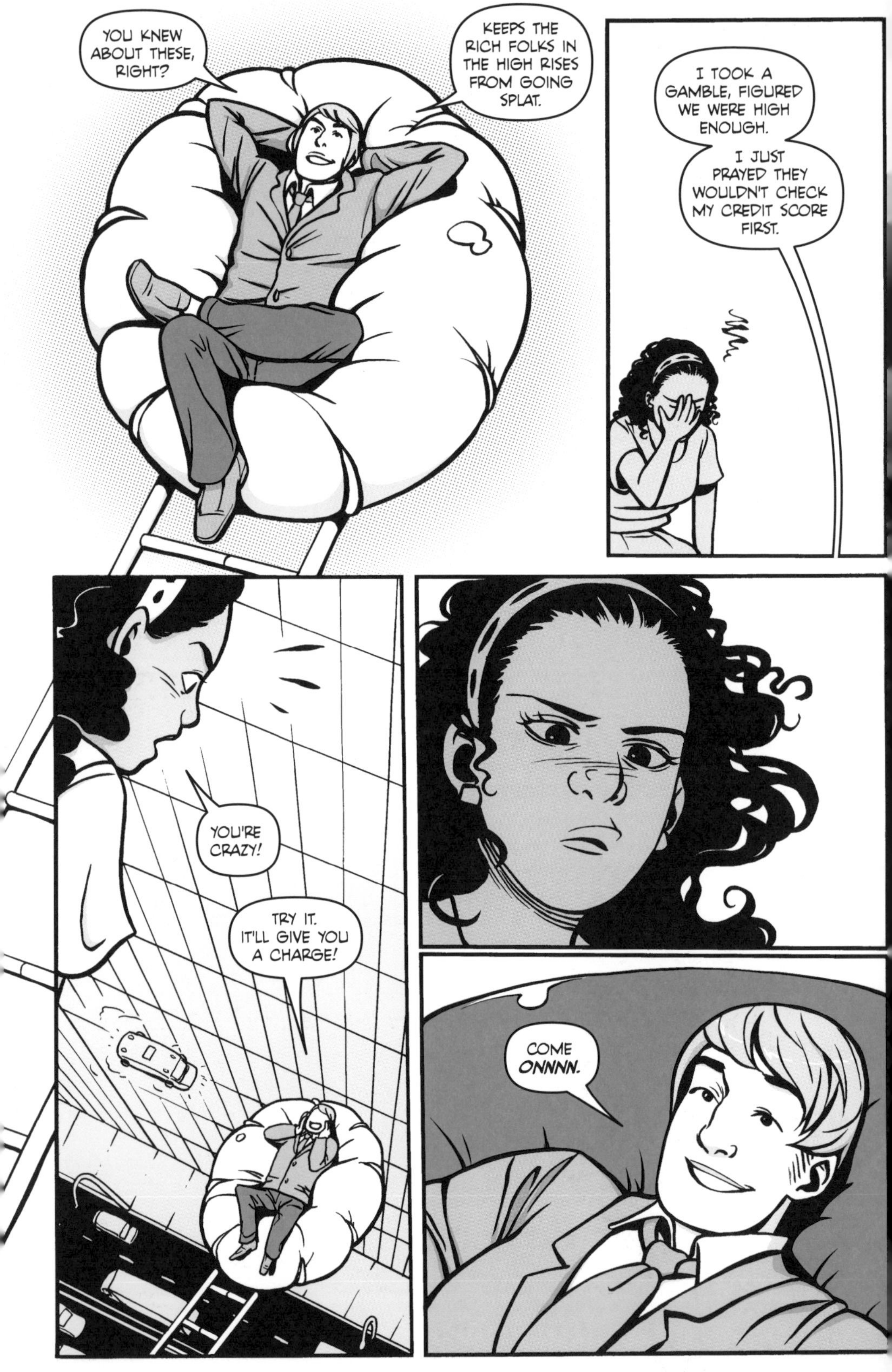
YOU KNEW ABOUT THESE, RIGHT?
KEEPS THE RICH FOLKS IN THE HIGH RISES FROM GOING SPLAT.
I TOOK A GAMBLE, FIGURED WE WERE HIGH ENOUGH.
I JUST PRAYED THEY WOULDN'T CHECK MY CREDIT SCORE FIRST.
YOU'RE CRAZY!
TRY IT. IT'LL GIVE YOU A CHARGE!
COME ONNNN.

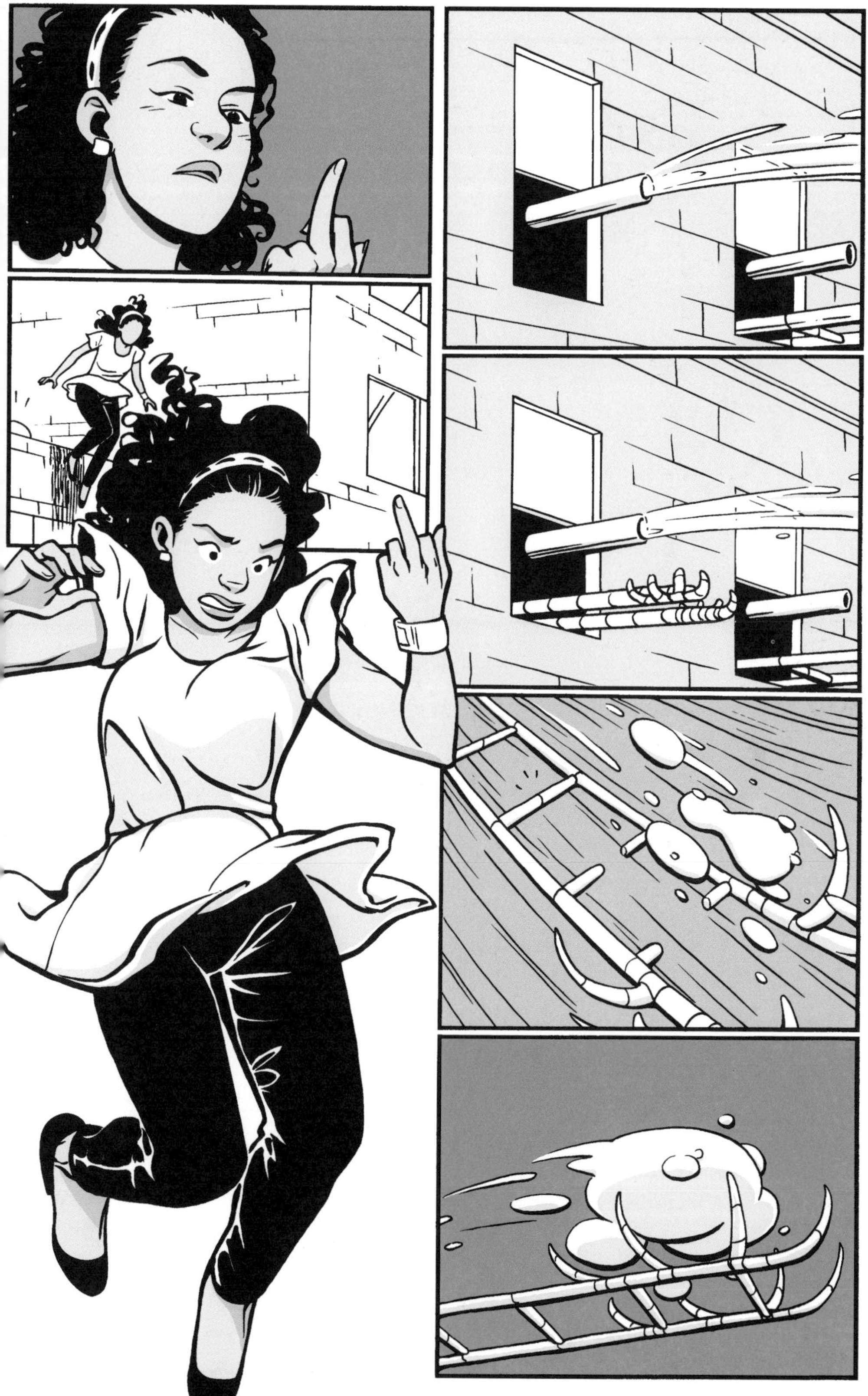

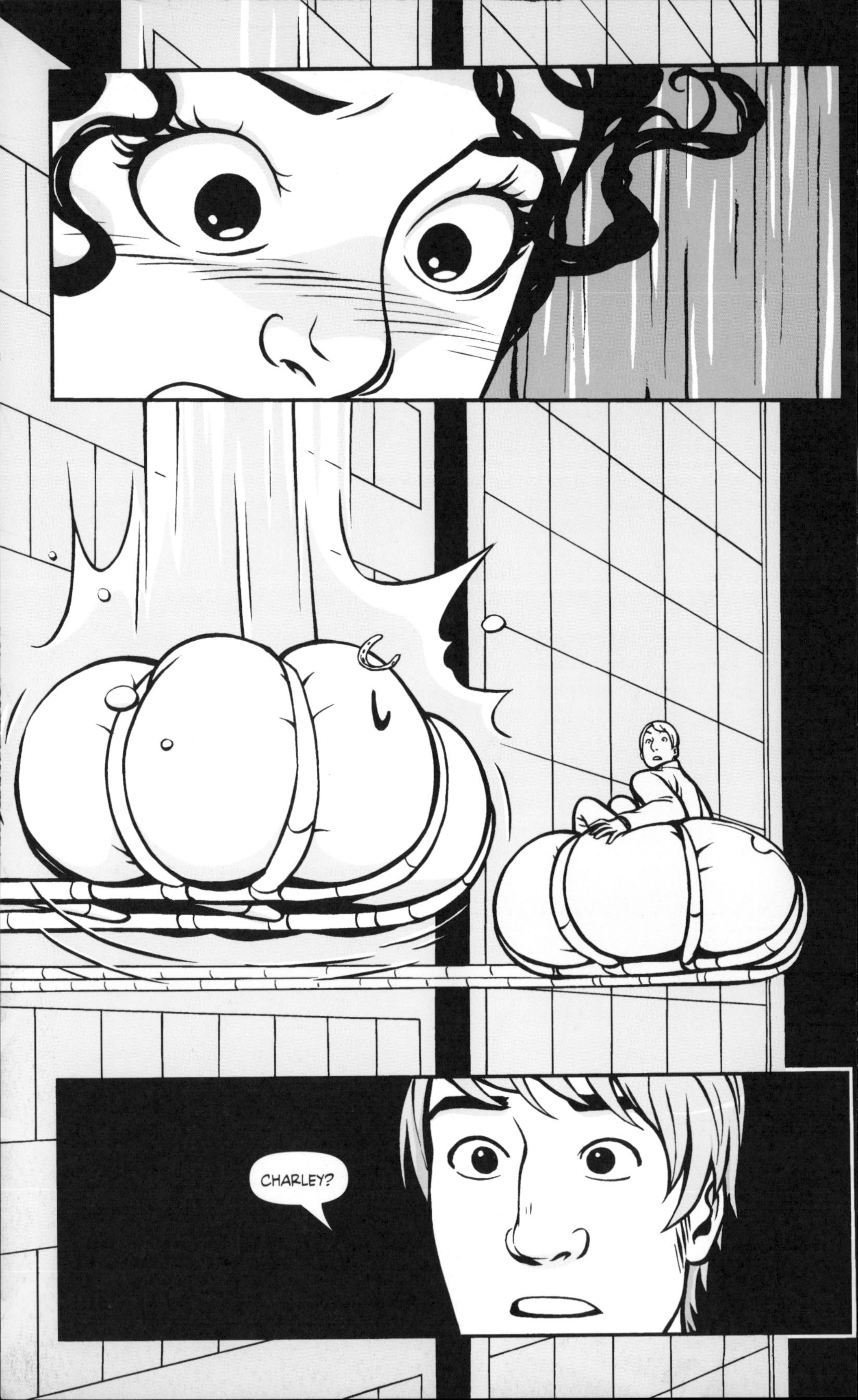
CHARLEY?

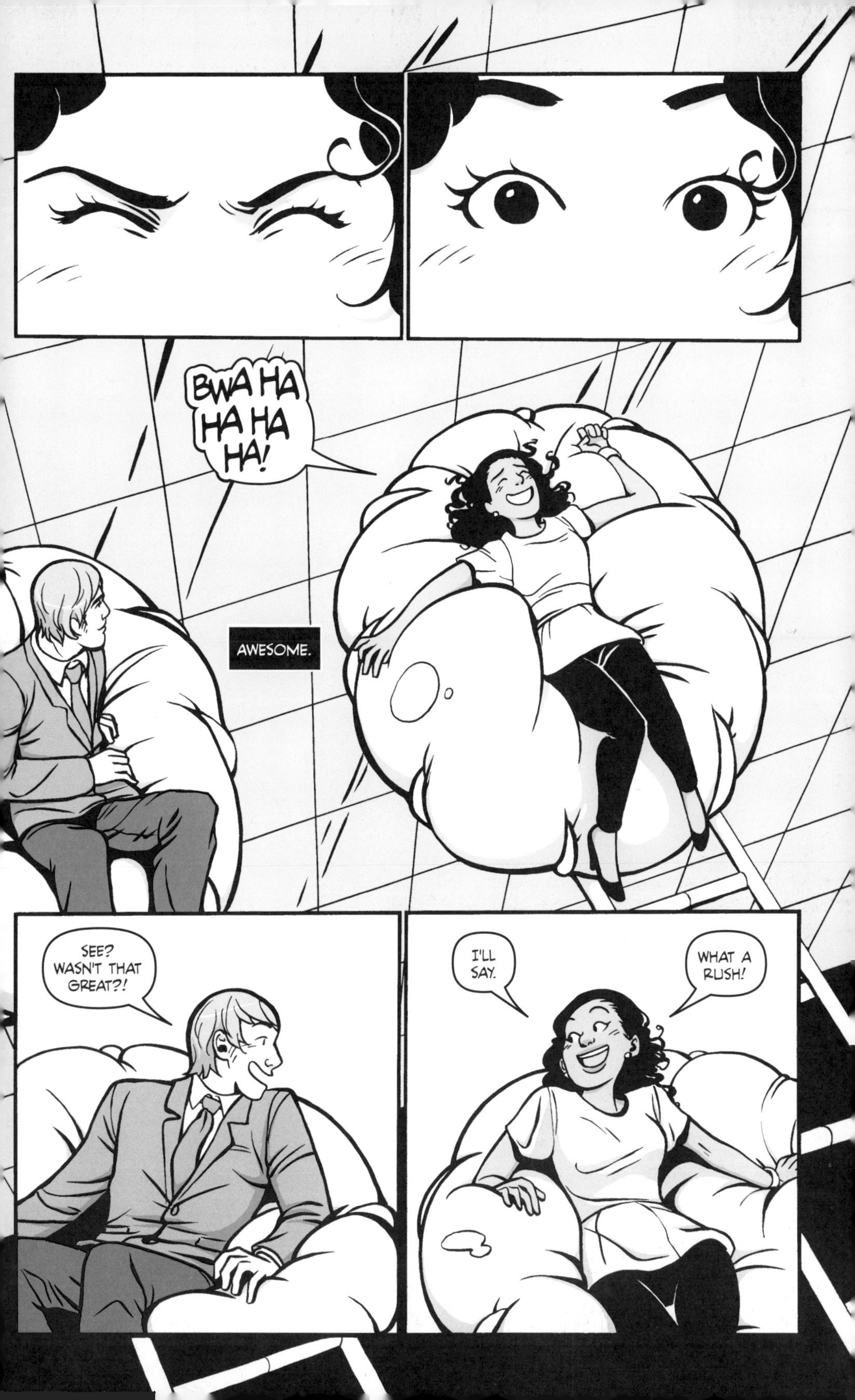
BWA HA HA HA HA!
AWESOME.
SEE? WASN'T THAT GREAT?!
I'LL SAY.
WHAT A RUSH!

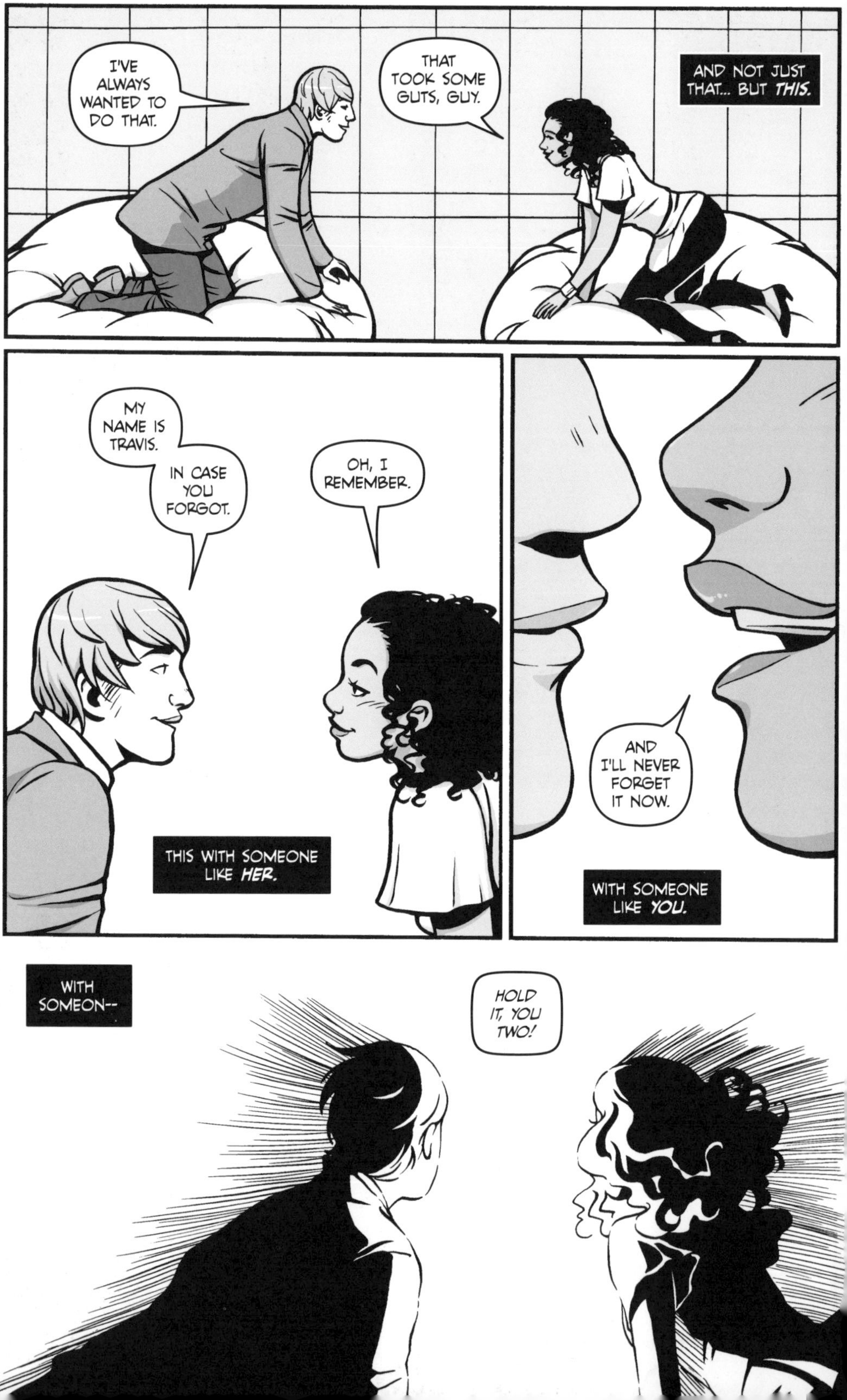
I'VE ALWAYS WANTED TO DO THAT.
THAT TOOK SOME GUTS, GUY.
AND NOT JUST THAT... BUT *THIS.*
MY NAME IS TRAVIS.
IN CASE YOU FORGOT.
OH, I REMEMBER.
THIS WITH SOMEONE LIKE *HER.*
AND I'LL NEVER FORGET IT NOW.
WITH SOMEONE LIKE *YOU.*
WITH SOMEON--
HOLD IT, YOU TWO!

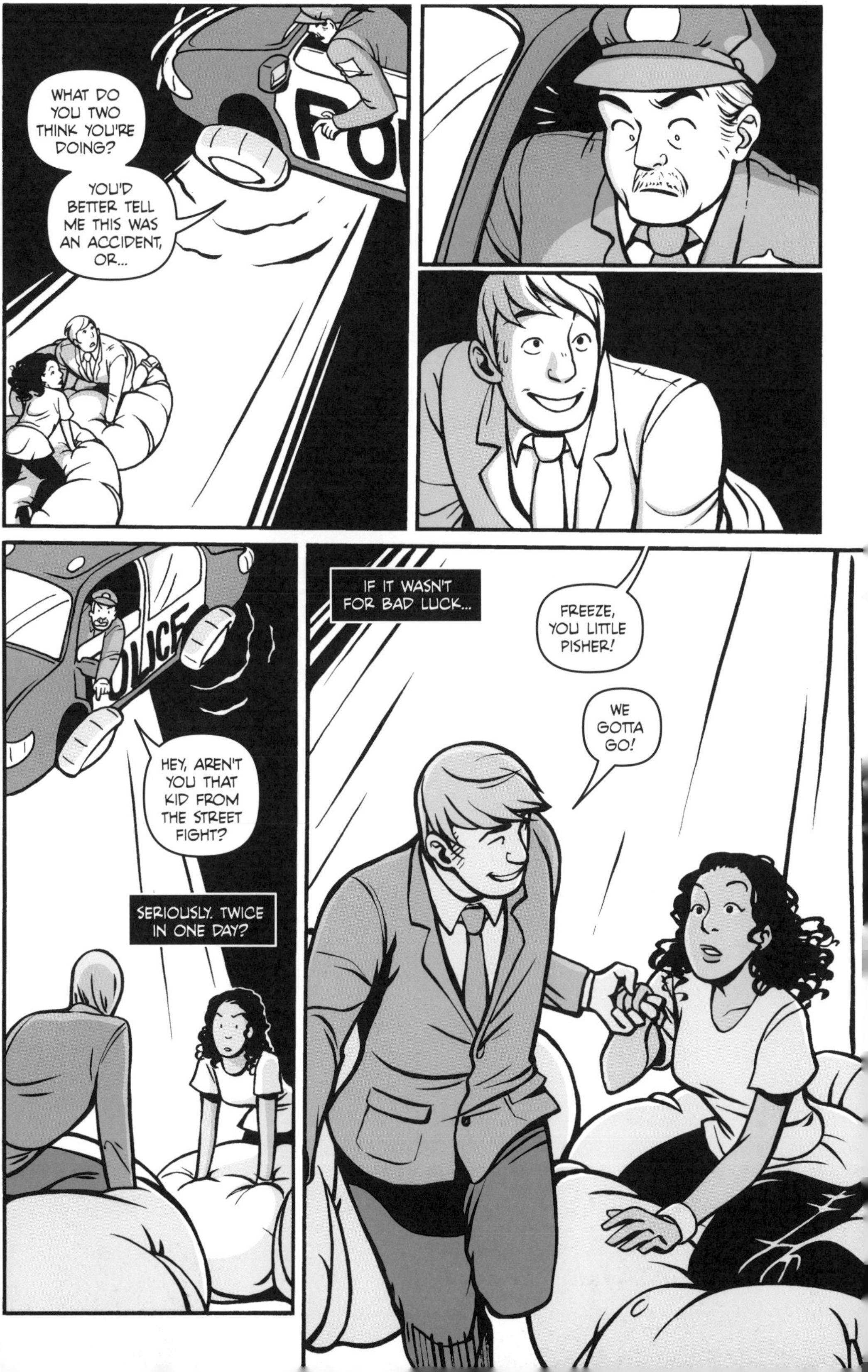
WHAT DO YOU TWO THINK YOU'RE DOING?
YOU'D BETTER TELL ME THIS WAS AN ACCIDENT, OR...
HEY, AREN'T YOU THAT KID FROM THE STREET FIGHT?
SERIOUSLY. TWICE IN ONE DAY?
IF IT WASN'T FOR BAD LUCK...
FREEZE, YOU LITTLE PISHER!
WE GOTTA GO!

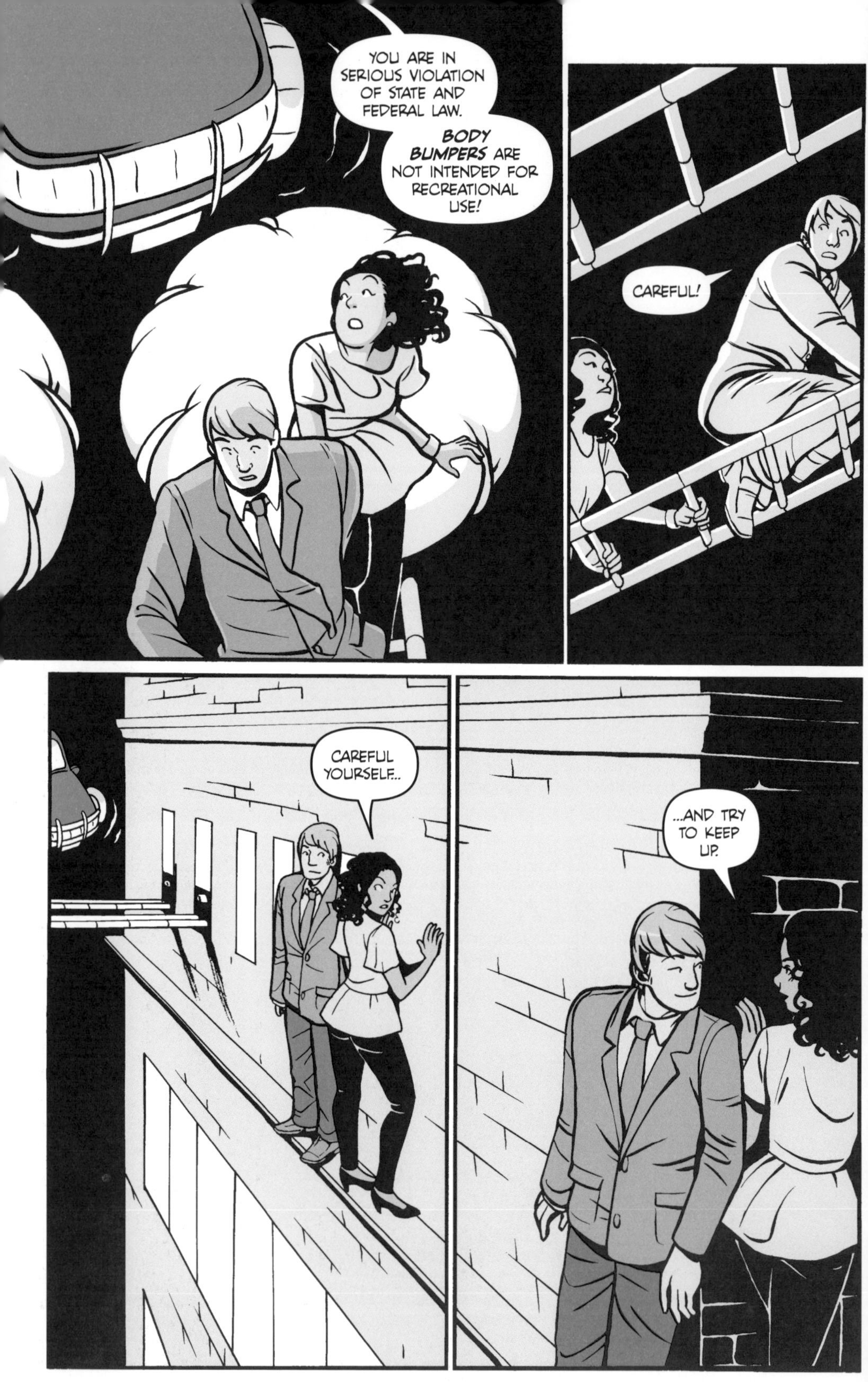
YOU ARE IN SERIOUS VIOLATION OF STATE AND FEDERAL LAW.
BODY BUMPERS ARE NOT INTENDED FOR RECREATIONAL USE!
CAREFUL!
CAREFUL YOURSELF...
...AND TRY TO KEEP UP.

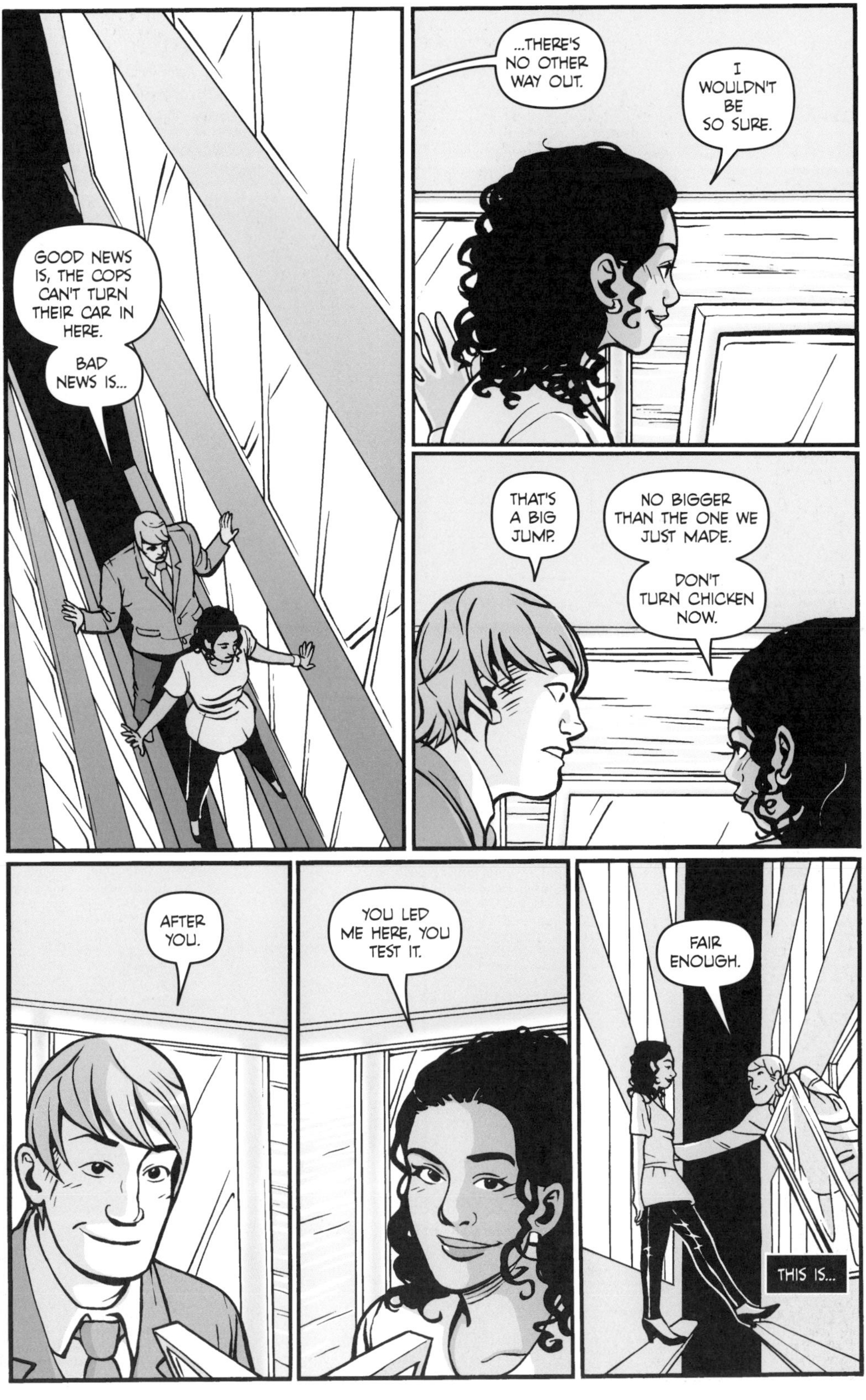
GOOD NEWS IS, THE COPS CAN'T TURN THEIR CAR IN HERE.
BAD NEWS IS...
...THERE'S NO OTHER WAY OUT.
I WOULDN'T BE SO SURE.
THAT'S A BIG JUMP.
NO BIGGER THAN THE ONE WE JUST MADE.
DON'T TURN CHICKEN NOW.
AFTER YOU.
YOU LED ME HERE, YOU TEST IT.
FAIR ENOUGH.
THIS IS...

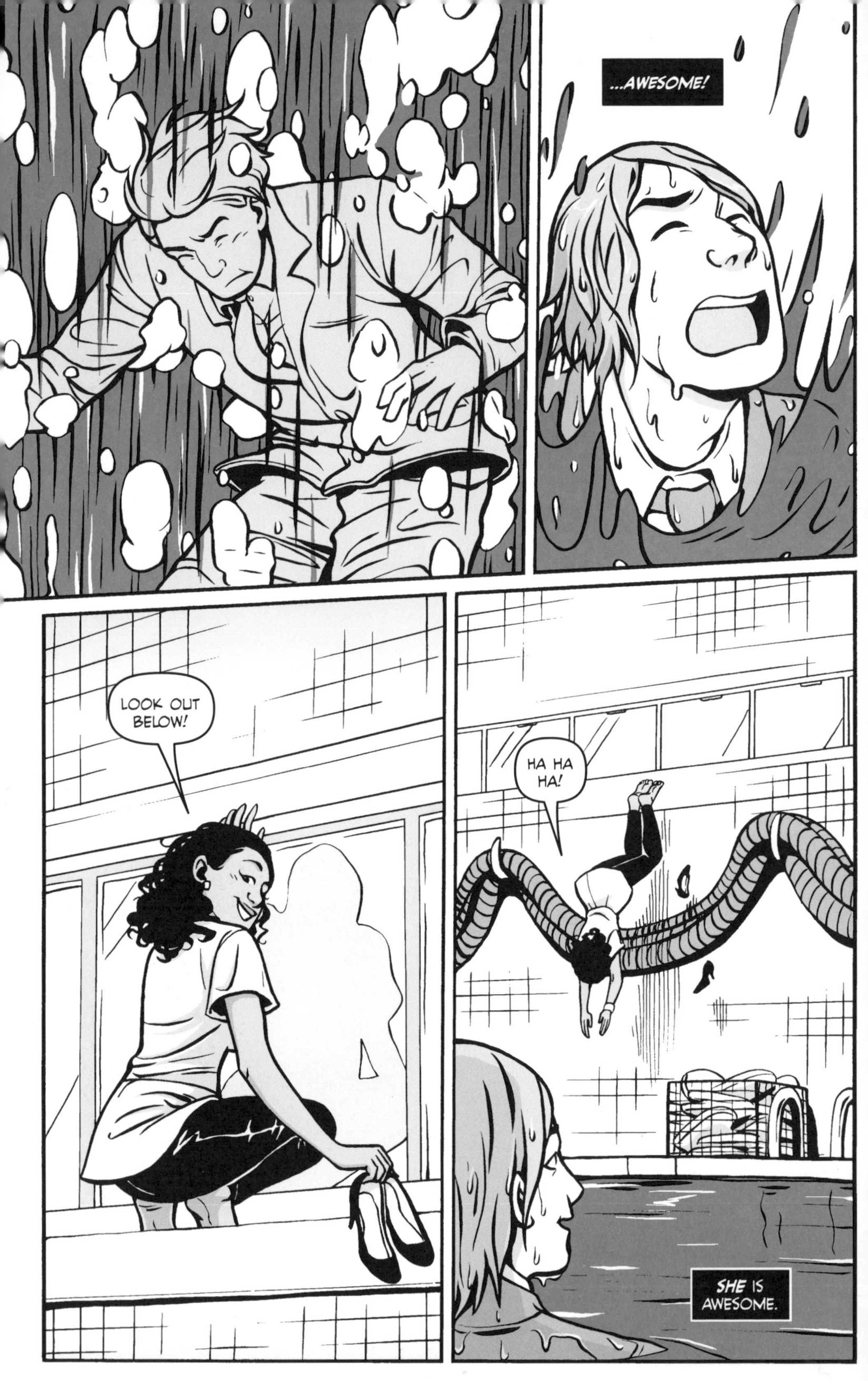
...AWESOME!
LOOK OUT BELOW!
HA HA HA!
SHE IS AWESOME.

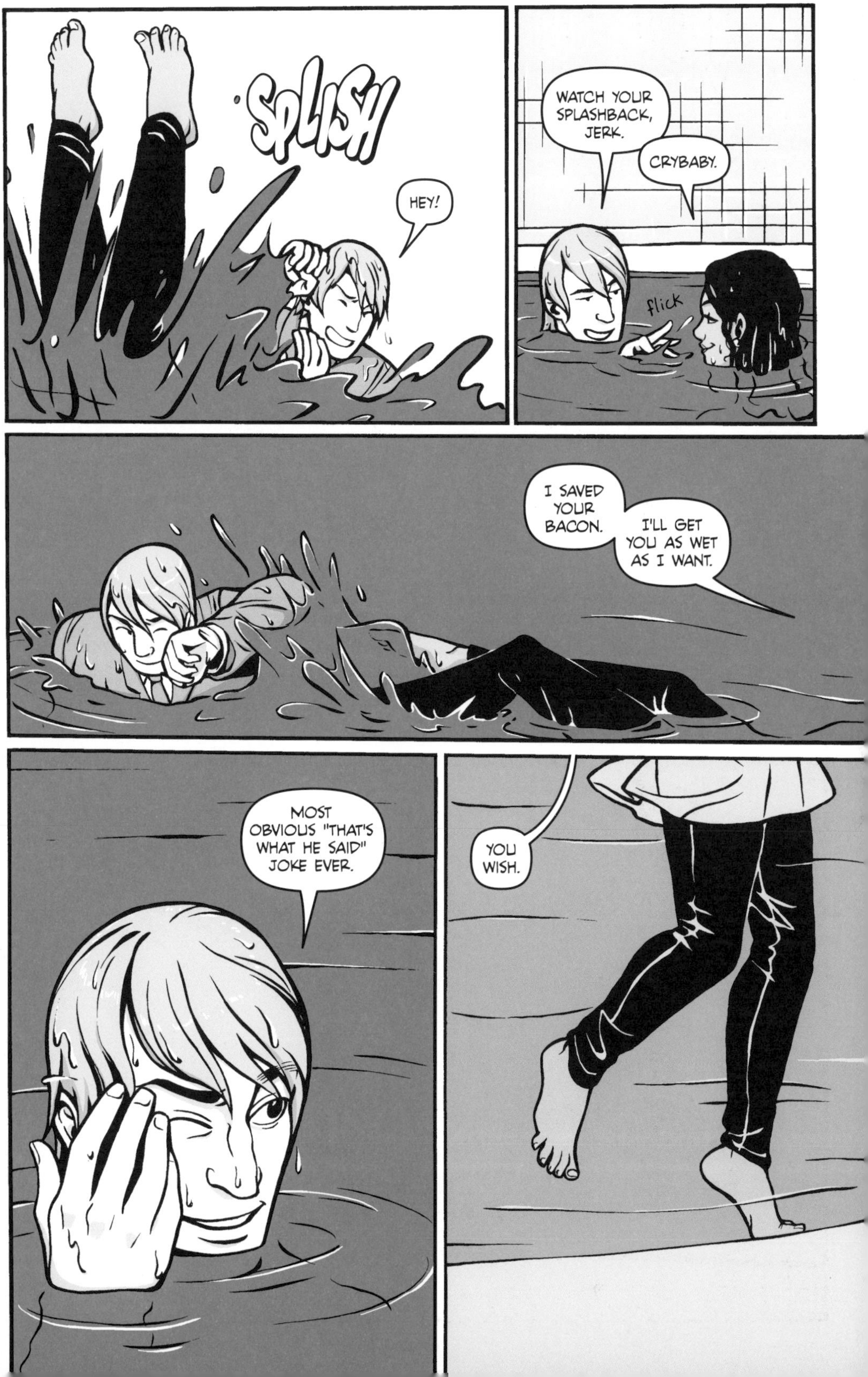
SPLISH
HEY!
WATCH YOUR SPLASHBACK, JERK.
CRYBABY.
flick
I SAVED YOUR BACON.
I'LL GET YOU AS WET AS I WANT.
MOST OBVIOUS "THAT'S WHAT HE SAID" JOKE EVER.
YOU WISH.

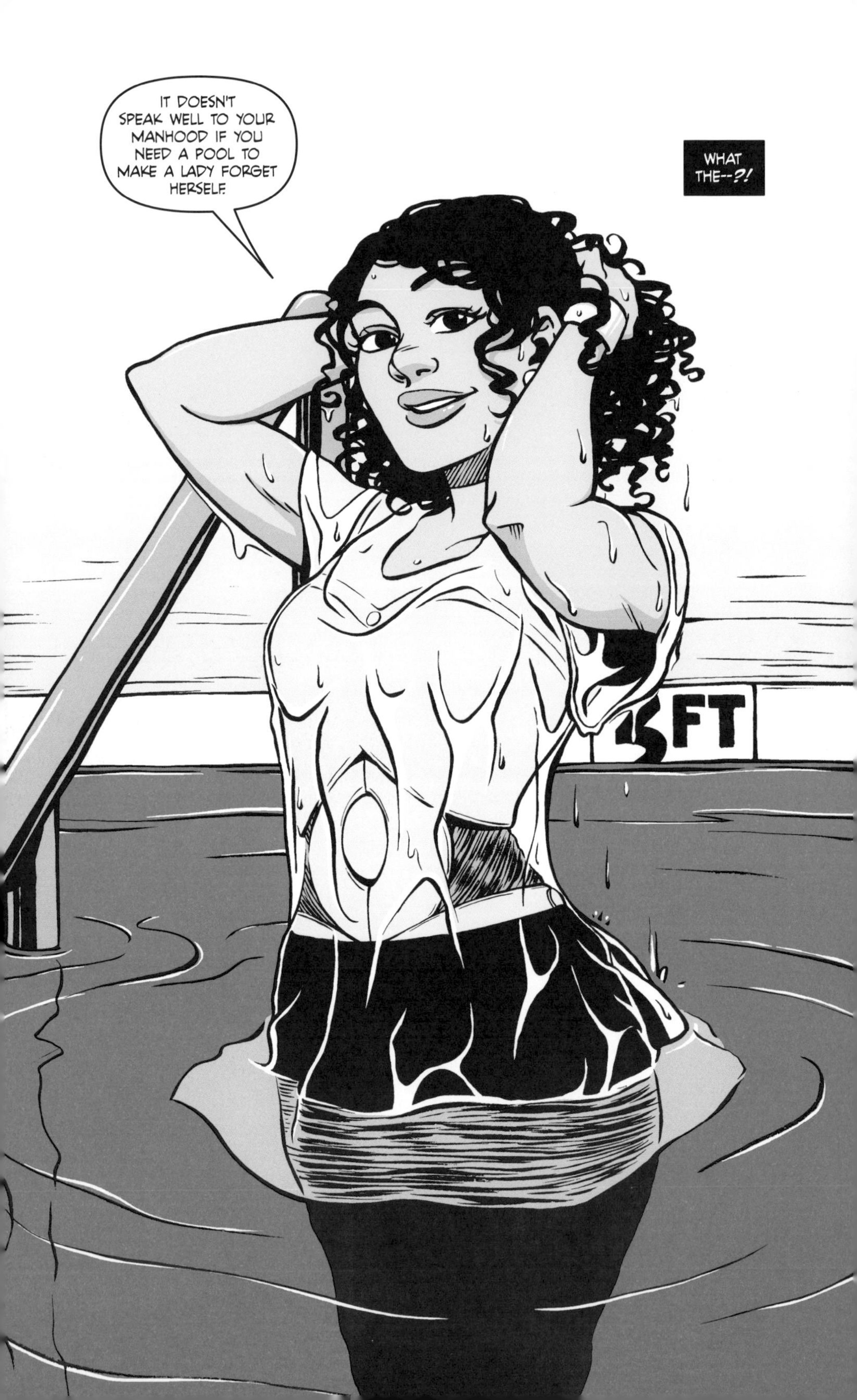
IT DOESN'T SPEAK WELL TO YOUR MANHOOD IF YOU NEED A POOL TO MAKE A LADY FORGET HERSELF.
WHAT THE--?!
5FT

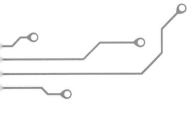

CHAPTER 6:

A BOY & A GIRL...

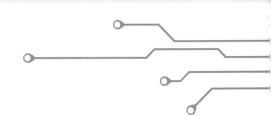

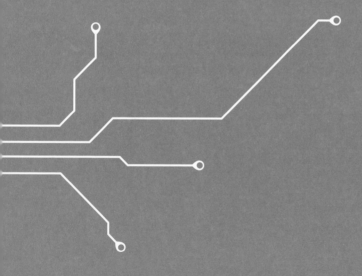

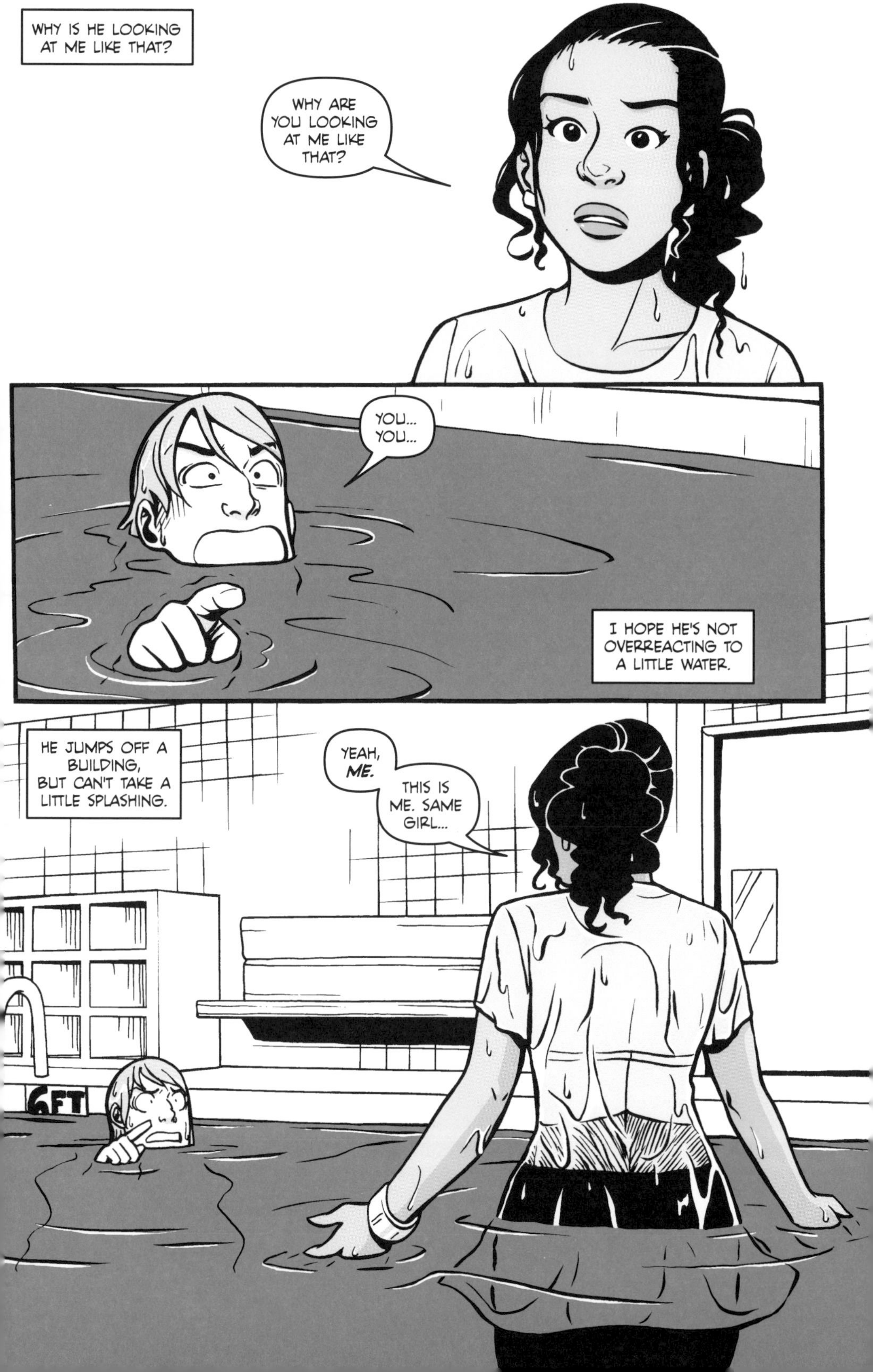
WHY IS HE LOOKING AT ME LIKE THAT?
WHY ARE YOU LOOKING AT ME LIKE THAT?
YOU... YOU...
I HOPE HE'S NOT OVERREACTING TO A LITTLE WATER.
HE JUMPS OFF A BUILDING, BUT CAN'T TAKE A LITTLE SPLASHING.
YEAH, ME.
THIS IS ME. SAME GIRL...
6FT

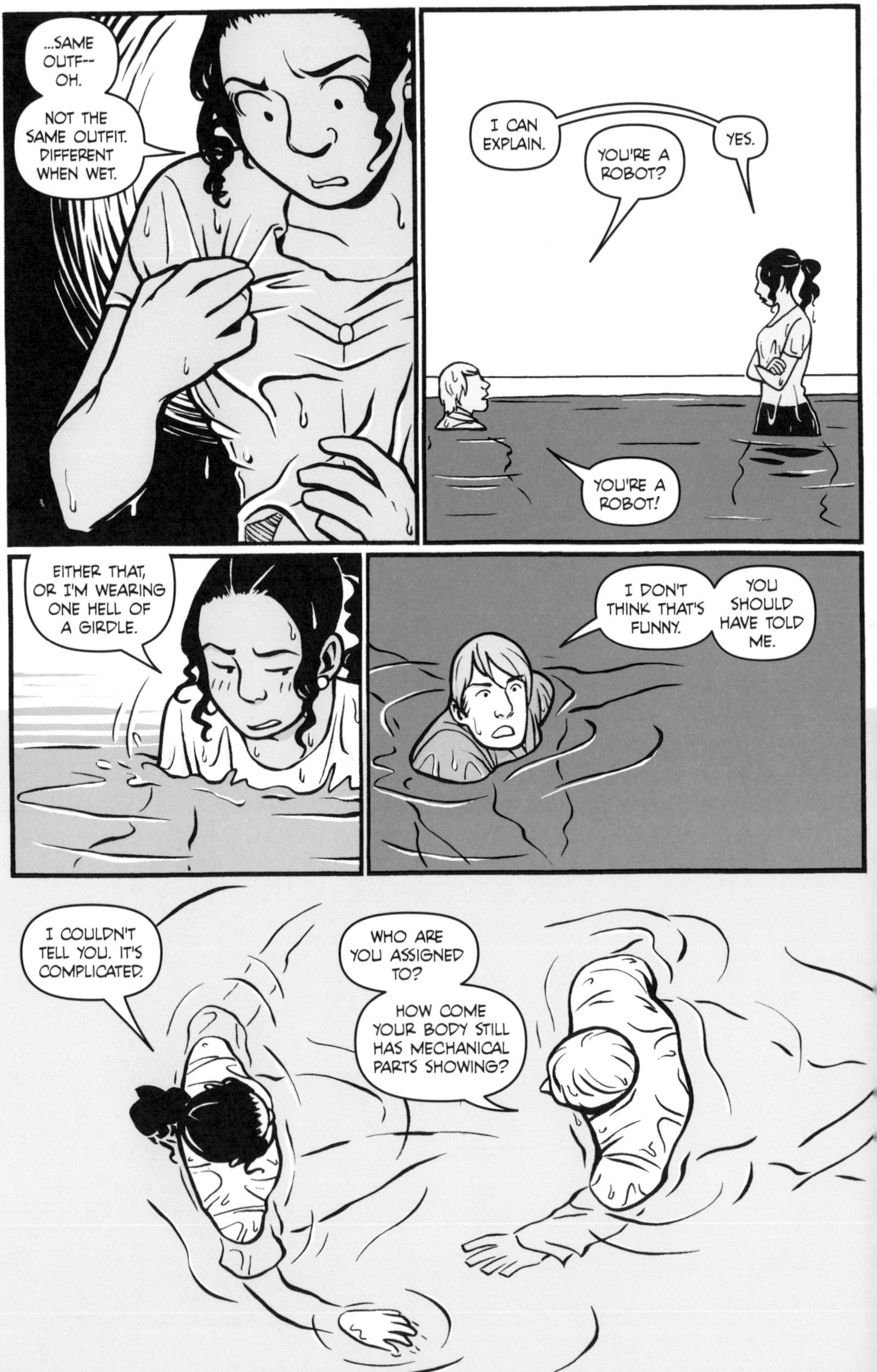
...SAME OUTF-- OH.
NOT THE SAME OUTFIT. DIFFERENT WHEN WET.
I CAN EXPLAIN.
YOU'RE A ROBOT?
YES.
YOU'RE A ROBOT!
EITHER THAT, OR I'M WEARING ONE HELL OF A GIRDLE.
I DON'T THINK THAT'S FUNNY.
YOU SHOULD HAVE TOLD ME.
I COULDN'T TELL YOU. IT'S COMPLICATED.
WHO ARE YOU ASSIGNED TO?
HOW COME YOUR BODY STILL HAS MECHANICAL PARTS SHOWING?

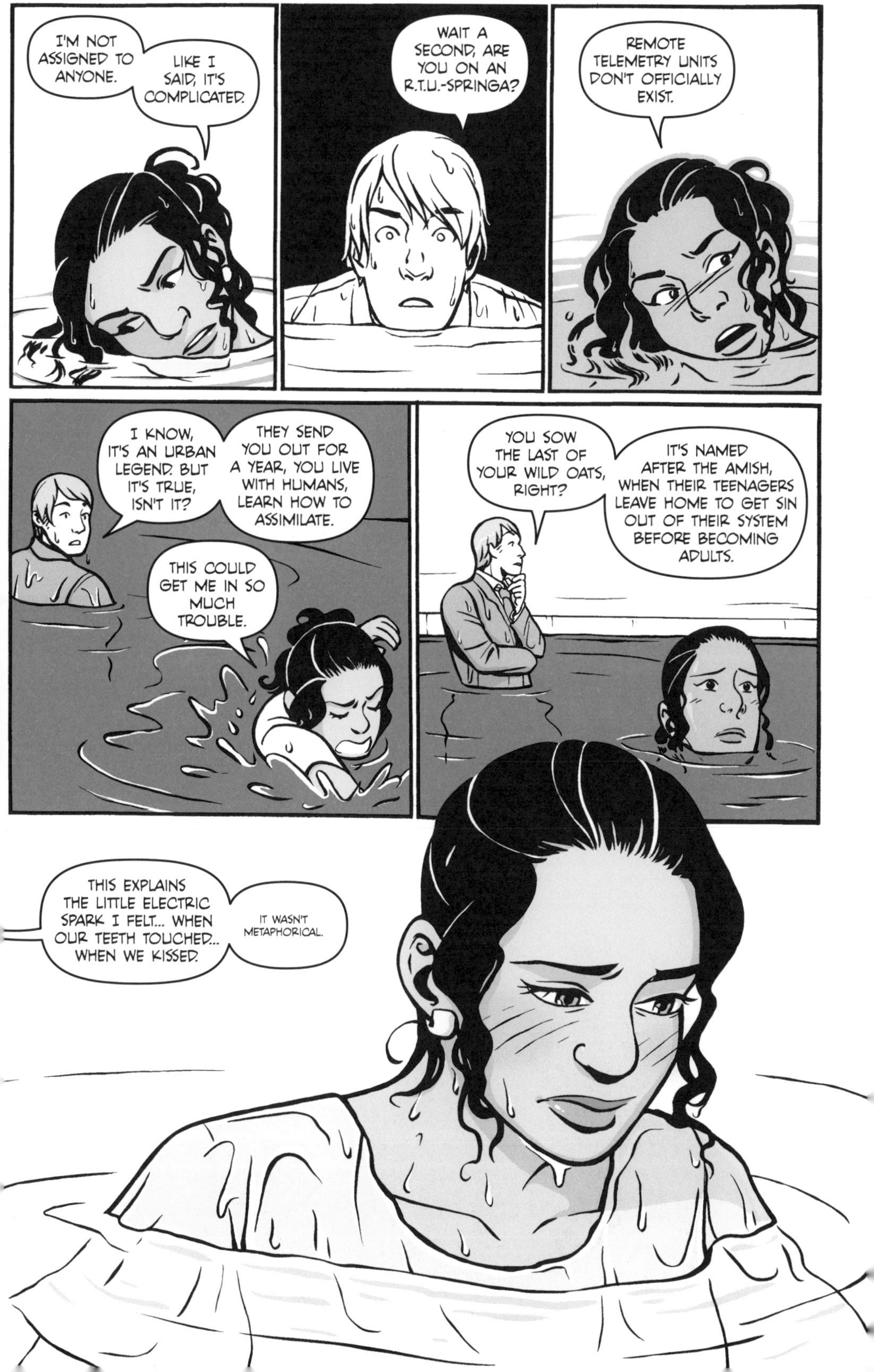

I'M NOT ASSIGNED TO ANYONE.
LIKE I SAID, IT'S COMPLICATED.
WAIT A SECOND, ARE YOU ON AN R.T.U.-SPRINGA?
REMOTE TELEMETRY UNITS DON'T OFFICIALLY EXIST.
I KNOW, IT'S AN URBAN LEGEND. BUT IT'S TRUE, ISN'T IT?
THEY SEND YOU OUT FOR A YEAR, YOU LIVE WITH HUMANS, LEARN HOW TO ASSIMILATE.
THIS COULD GET ME IN SO MUCH TROUBLE.
YOU SOW THE LAST OF YOUR WILD OATS, RIGHT?
IT'S NAMED AFTER THE AMISH, WHEN THEIR TEENAGERS LEAVE HOME TO GET SIN OUT OF THEIR SYSTEM BEFORE BECOMING ADULTS.
THIS EXPLAINS THE LITTLE ELECTRIC SPARK I FELT... WHEN OUR TEETH TOUCHED... WHEN WE KISSED.
IT WASN'T METAPHORICAL.

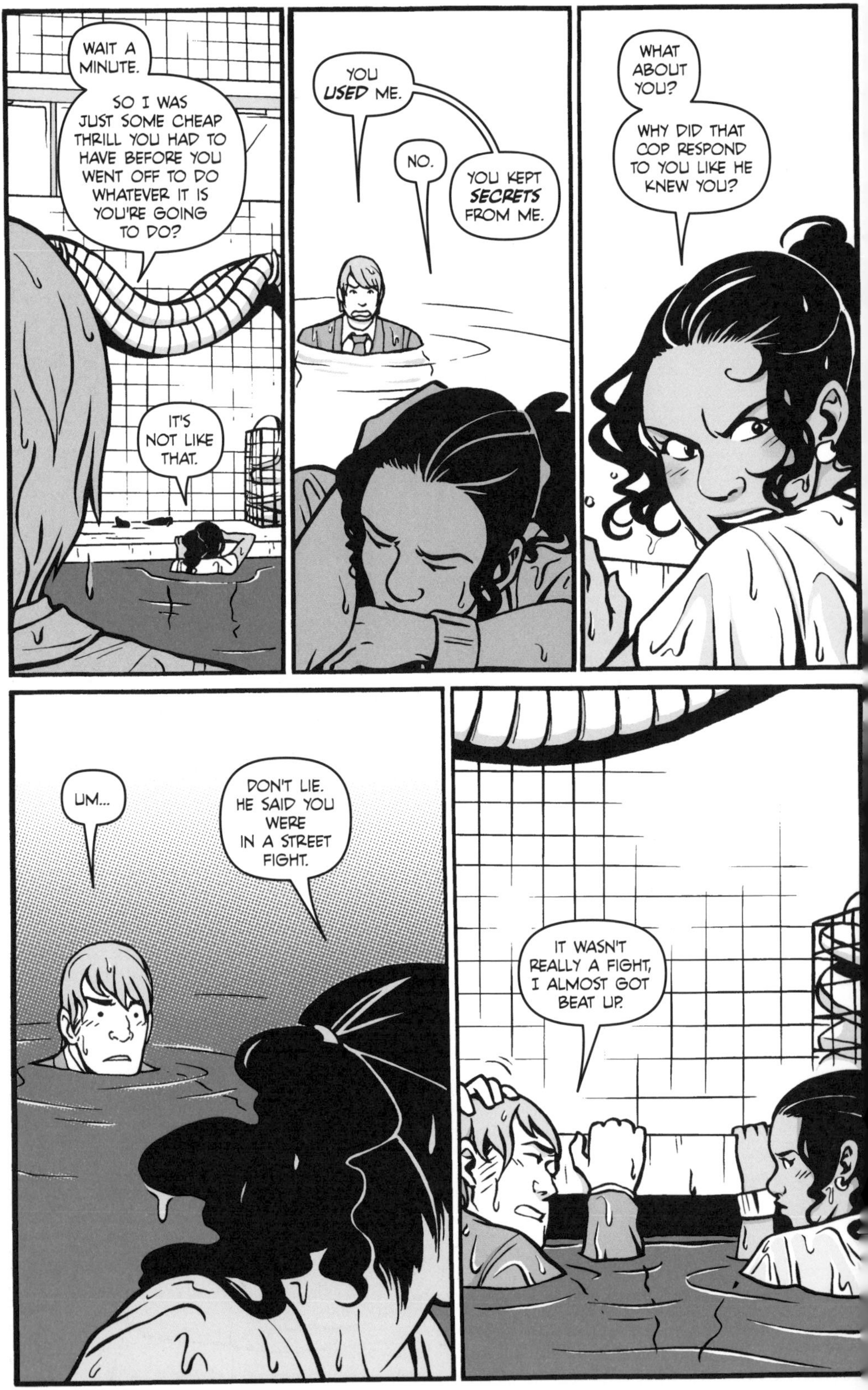
WAIT A MINUTE.
SO I WAS JUST SOME CHEAP THRILL YOU HAD TO HAVE BEFORE YOU WENT OFF TO DO WHATEVER IT IS YOU'RE GOING TO DO?
IT'S NOT LIKE THAT.
YOU *USED* ME.
NO.
YOU KEPT *SECRETS* FROM ME.
WHAT ABOUT YOU?
WHY DID THAT COP RESPOND TO YOU LIKE HE KNEW YOU?
UM...
DON'T LIE. HE SAID YOU WERE IN A STREET FIGHT.
IT WASN'T REALLY A FIGHT, I ALMOST GOT BEAT UP.

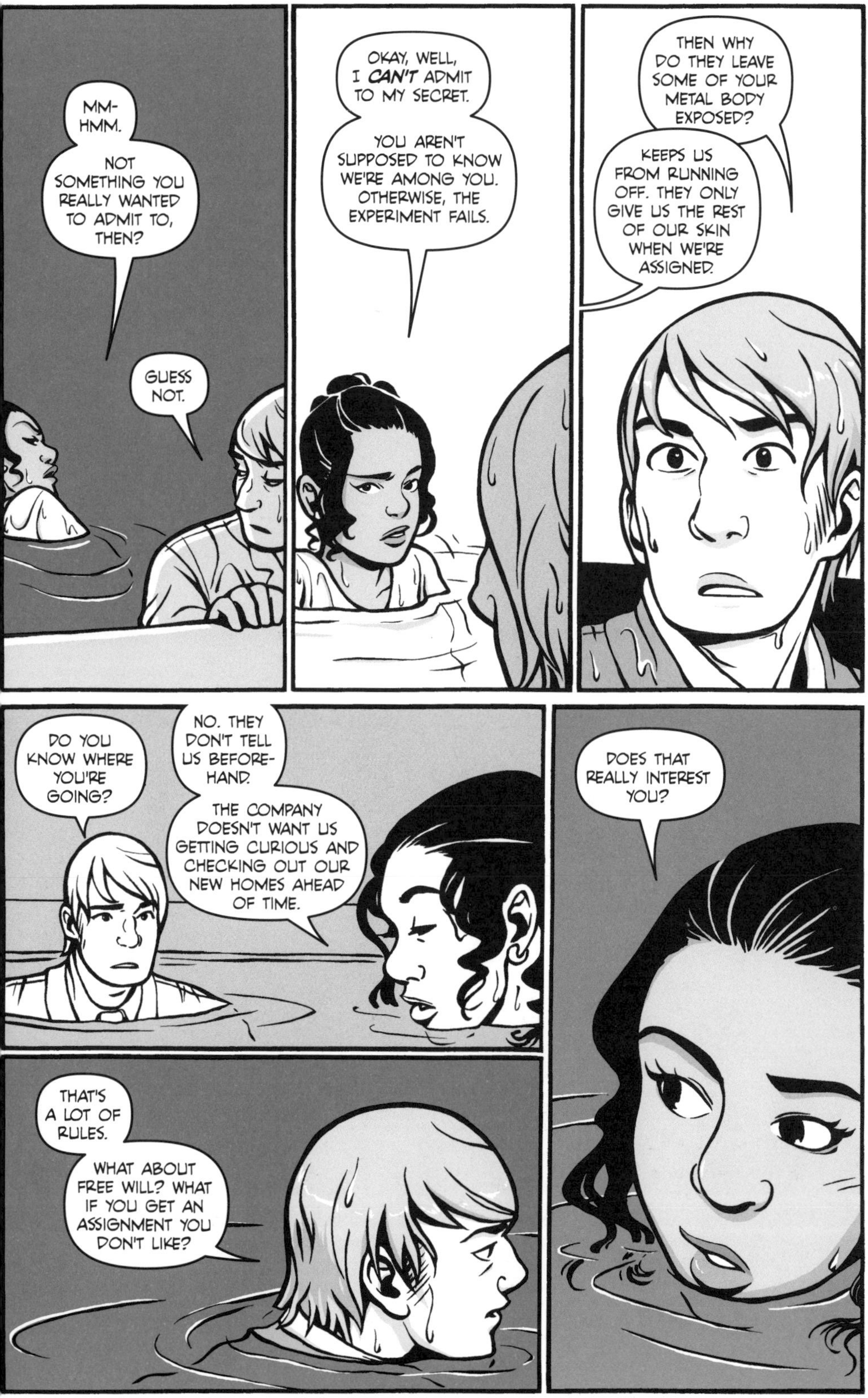
MM-HMM.
NOT SOMETHING YOU REALLY WANTED TO ADMIT TO, THEN?
GUESS NOT.
OKAY, WELL, I CAN'T ADMIT TO MY SECRET.
YOU AREN'T SUPPOSED TO KNOW WE'RE AMONG YOU. OTHERWISE, THE EXPERIMENT FAILS.
THEN WHY DO THEY LEAVE SOME OF YOUR METAL BODY EXPOSED?
KEEPS US FROM RUNNING OFF. THEY ONLY GIVE US THE REST OF OUR SKIN WHEN WE'RE ASSIGNED.
DO YOU KNOW WHERE YOU'RE GOING?
NO. THEY DON'T TELL US BEFORE-HAND.
THE COMPANY DOESN'T WANT US GETTING CURIOUS AND CHECKING OUT OUR NEW HOMES AHEAD OF TIME.
DOES THAT REALLY INTEREST YOU?
THAT'S A LOT OF RULES.
WHAT ABOUT FREE WILL? WHAT IF YOU GET AN ASSIGNMENT YOU DON'T LIKE?

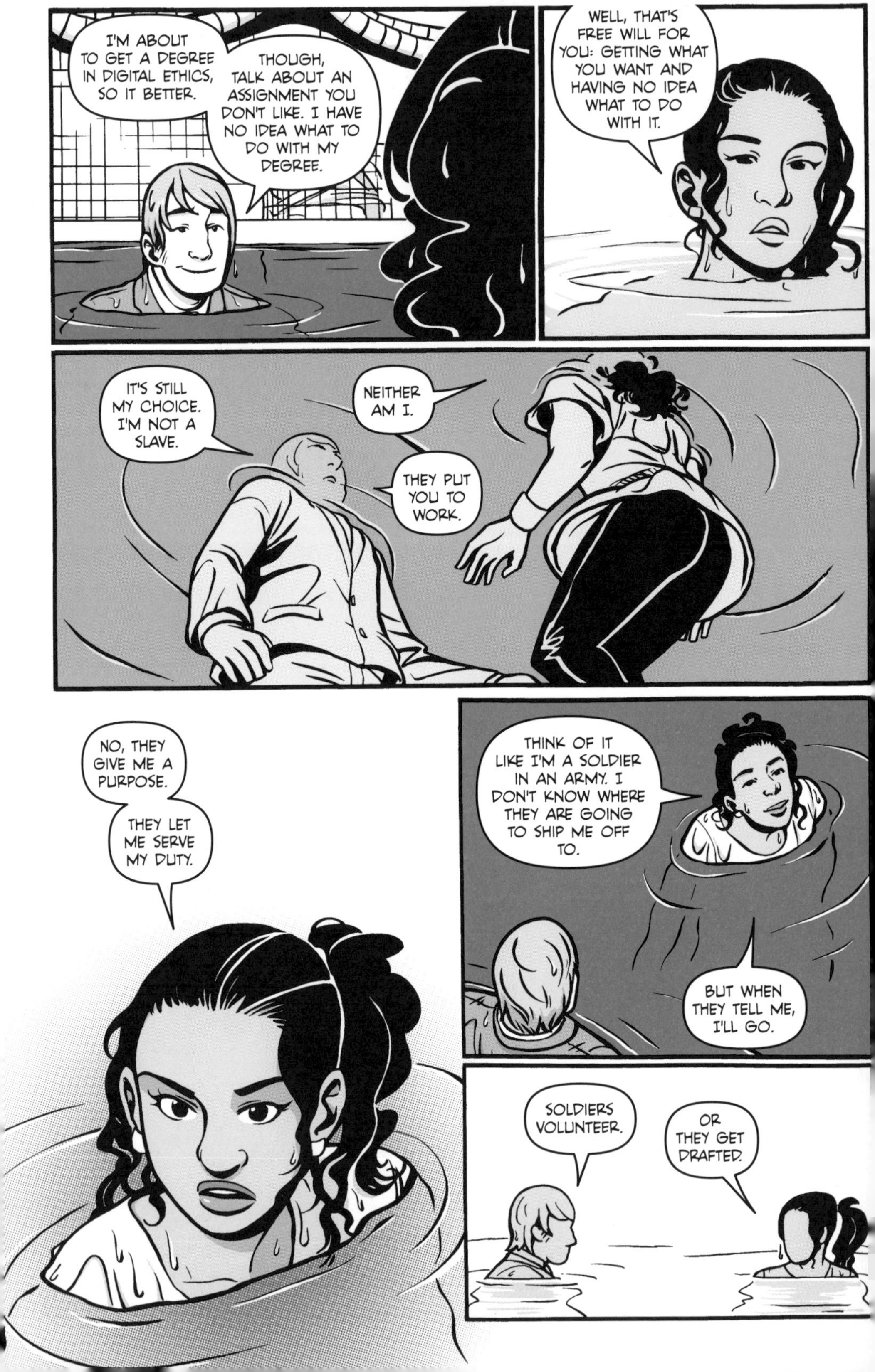
I'M ABOUT TO GET A DEGREE IN DIGITAL ETHICS, SO IT BETTER.
THOUGH, TALK ABOUT AN ASSIGNMENT YOU DON'T LIKE. I HAVE NO IDEA WHAT TO DO WITH MY DEGREE.
WELL, THAT'S FREE WILL FOR YOU: GETTING WHAT YOU WANT AND HAVING NO IDEA WHAT TO DO WITH IT.
IT'S STILL MY CHOICE. I'M NOT A SLAVE.
NEITHER AM I.
THEY PUT YOU TO WORK.
NO, THEY GIVE ME A PURPOSE.
THEY LET ME SERVE MY DUTY.
THINK OF IT LIKE I'M A SOLDIER IN AN ARMY. I DON'T KNOW WHERE THEY ARE GOING TO SHIP ME OFF TO.
BUT WHEN THEY TELL ME, I'LL GO.
SOLDIERS VOLUNTEER.
OR THEY GET DRAFTED.

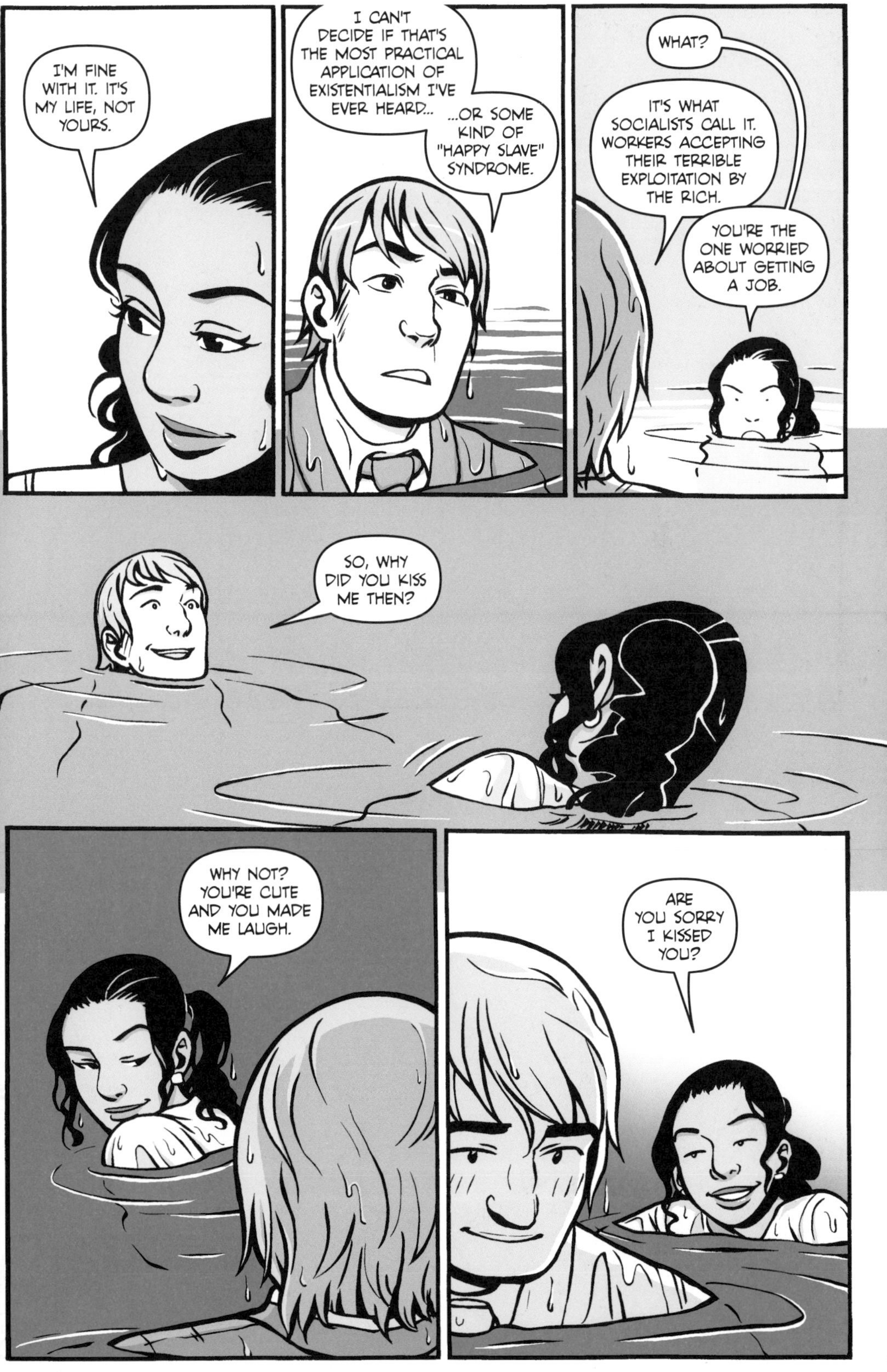
I'M FINE WITH IT. IT'S MY LIFE, NOT YOURS.
I CAN'T DECIDE IF THAT'S THE MOST PRACTICAL APPLICATION OF EXISTENTIALISM I'VE EVER HEARD...
...OR SOME KIND OF "HAPPY SLAVE" SYNDROME.
WHAT?
IT'S WHAT SOCIALISTS CALL IT. WORKERS ACCEPTING THEIR TERRIBLE EXPLOITATION BY THE RICH.
YOU'RE THE ONE WORRIED ABOUT GETTING A JOB.
SO, WHY DID YOU KISS ME THEN?
WHY NOT? YOU'RE CUTE AND YOU MADE ME LAUGH.
ARE YOU SORRY I KISSED YOU?

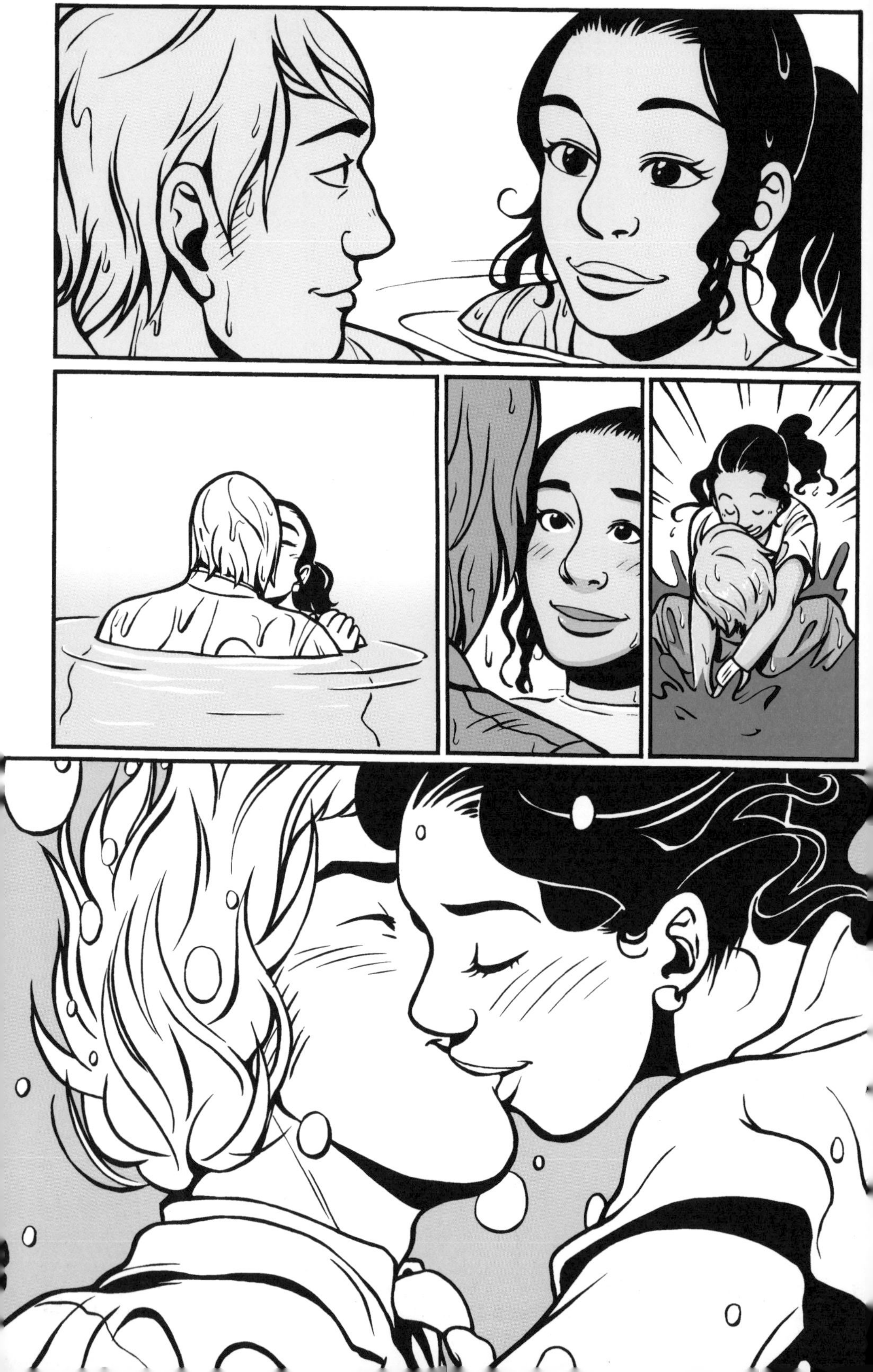

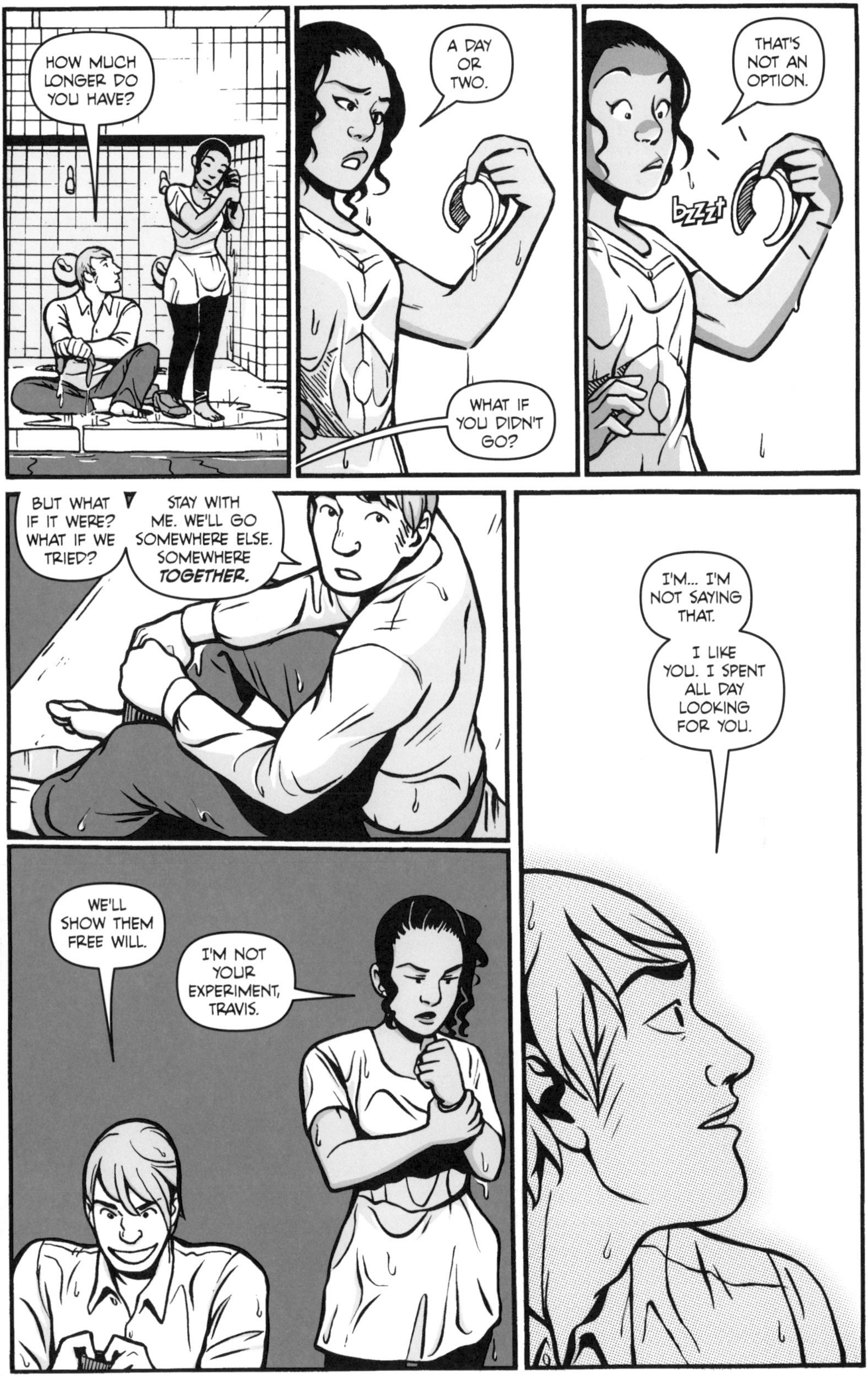
HOW MUCH LONGER DO YOU HAVE?
A DAY OR TWO.
WHAT IF YOU DIDN'T GO?
THAT'S NOT AN OPTION.
bzzzt
BUT WHAT IF IT WERE? WHAT IF WE TRIED?
STAY WITH ME. WE'LL GO SOMEWHERE ELSE. SOMEWHERE *TOGETHER.*
WE'LL SHOW THEM FREE WILL.
I'M NOT YOUR EXPERIMENT, TRAVIS.
I'M... I'M NOT SAYING THAT.
I LIKE YOU. I SPENT ALL DAY LOOKING FOR YOU.

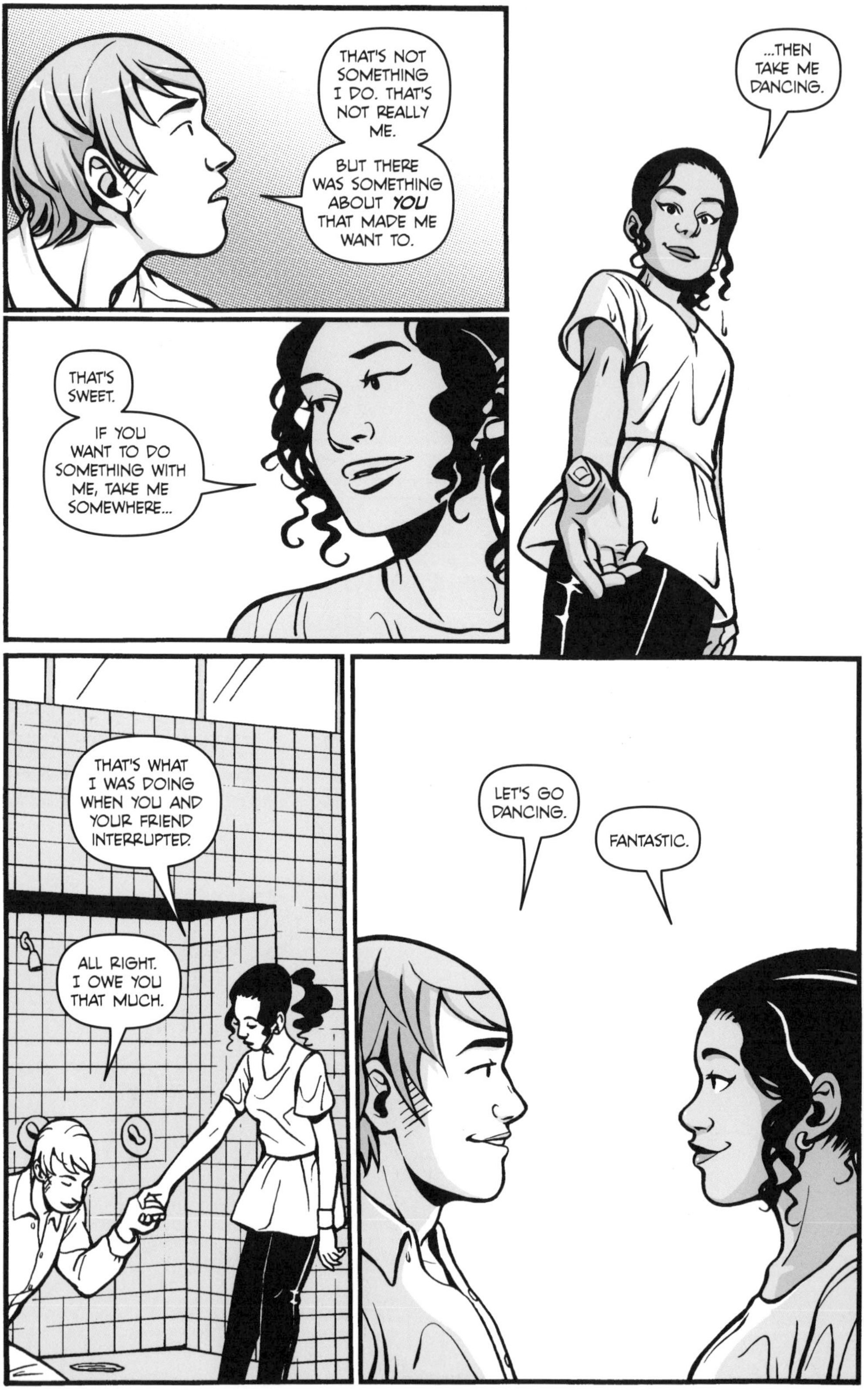
THAT'S NOT SOMETHING I DO. THAT'S NOT REALLY ME.
BUT THERE WAS SOMETHING ABOUT *YOU* THAT MADE ME WANT TO.
THAT'S SWEET.
IF YOU WANT TO DO SOMETHING WITH ME, TAKE ME SOMEWHERE...
...THEN TAKE ME DANCING.
THAT'S WHAT I WAS DOING WHEN YOU AND YOUR FRIEND INTERRUPTED.
ALL RIGHT. I OWE YOU THAT MUCH.
LET'S GO DANCING.
FANTASTIC.

CHAPTER 7: HER

ALL DISCO DANCE...

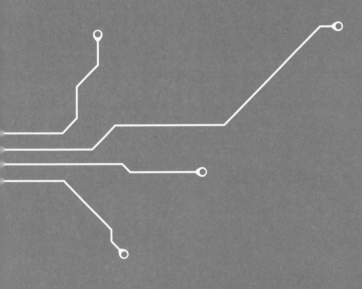

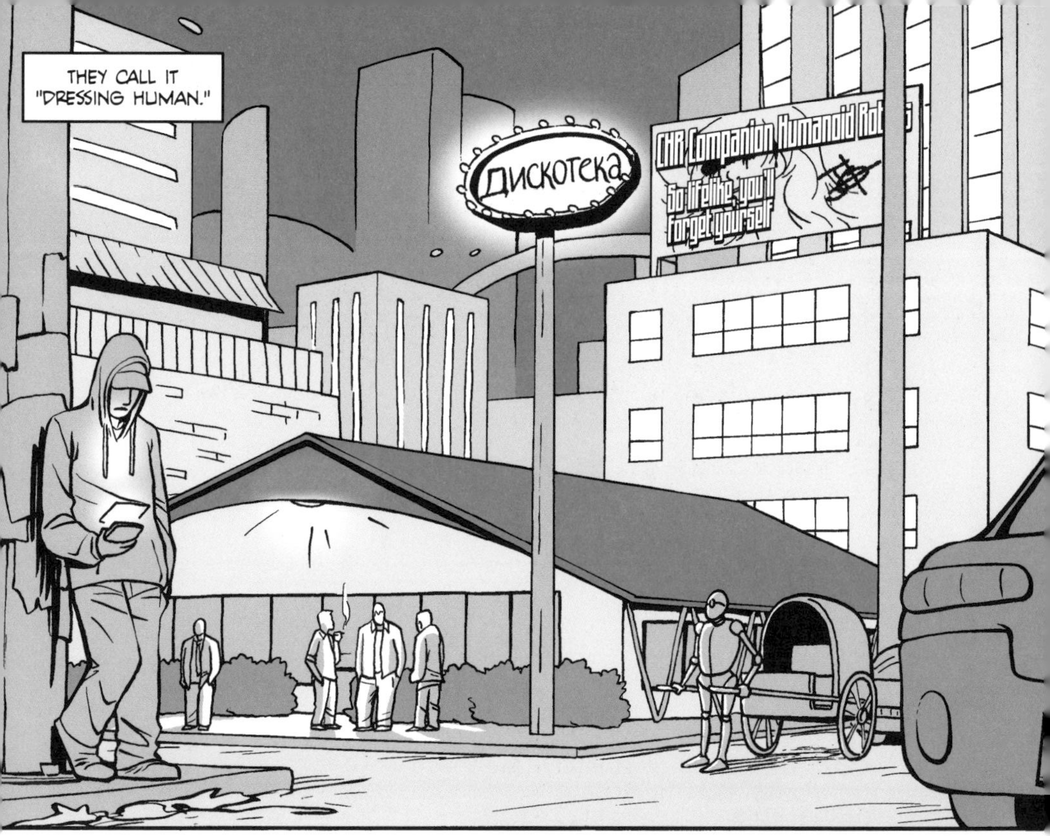
THEY CALL IT "DRESSING HUMAN."
Дискотека
CHR Companion Humanoid Rob
So lifelike, you'll forget yourself

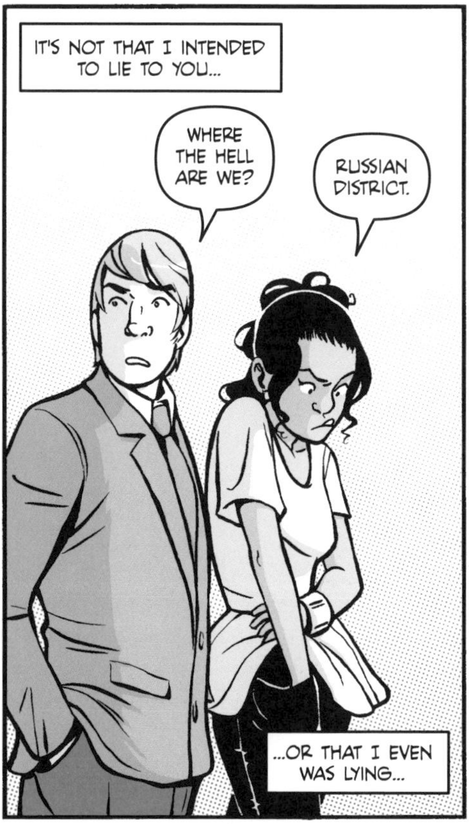
IT'S NOT THAT I INTENDED TO LIE TO YOU...
WHERE THE HELL ARE WE?
RUSSIAN DISTRICT.
...OR THAT I EVEN WAS LYING...

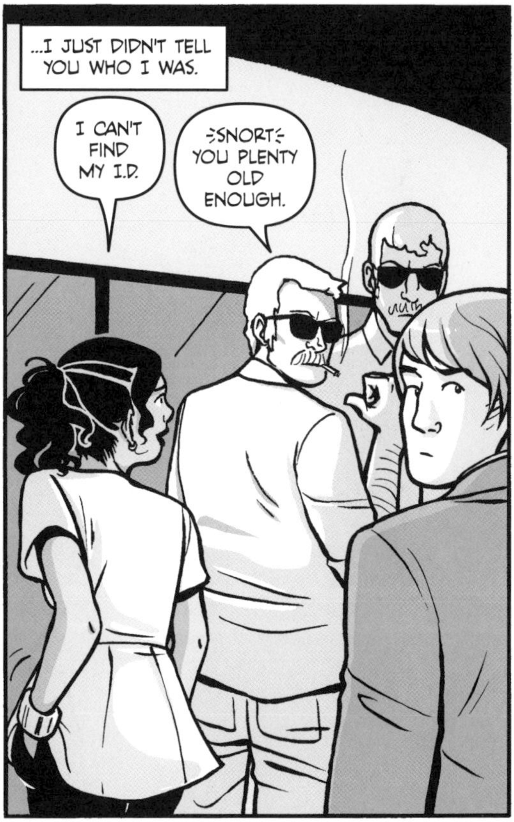
...I JUST DIDN'T TELL YOU WHO I WAS.
I CAN'T FIND MY I.D.
SNORT
YOU PLENTY OLD ENOUGH.

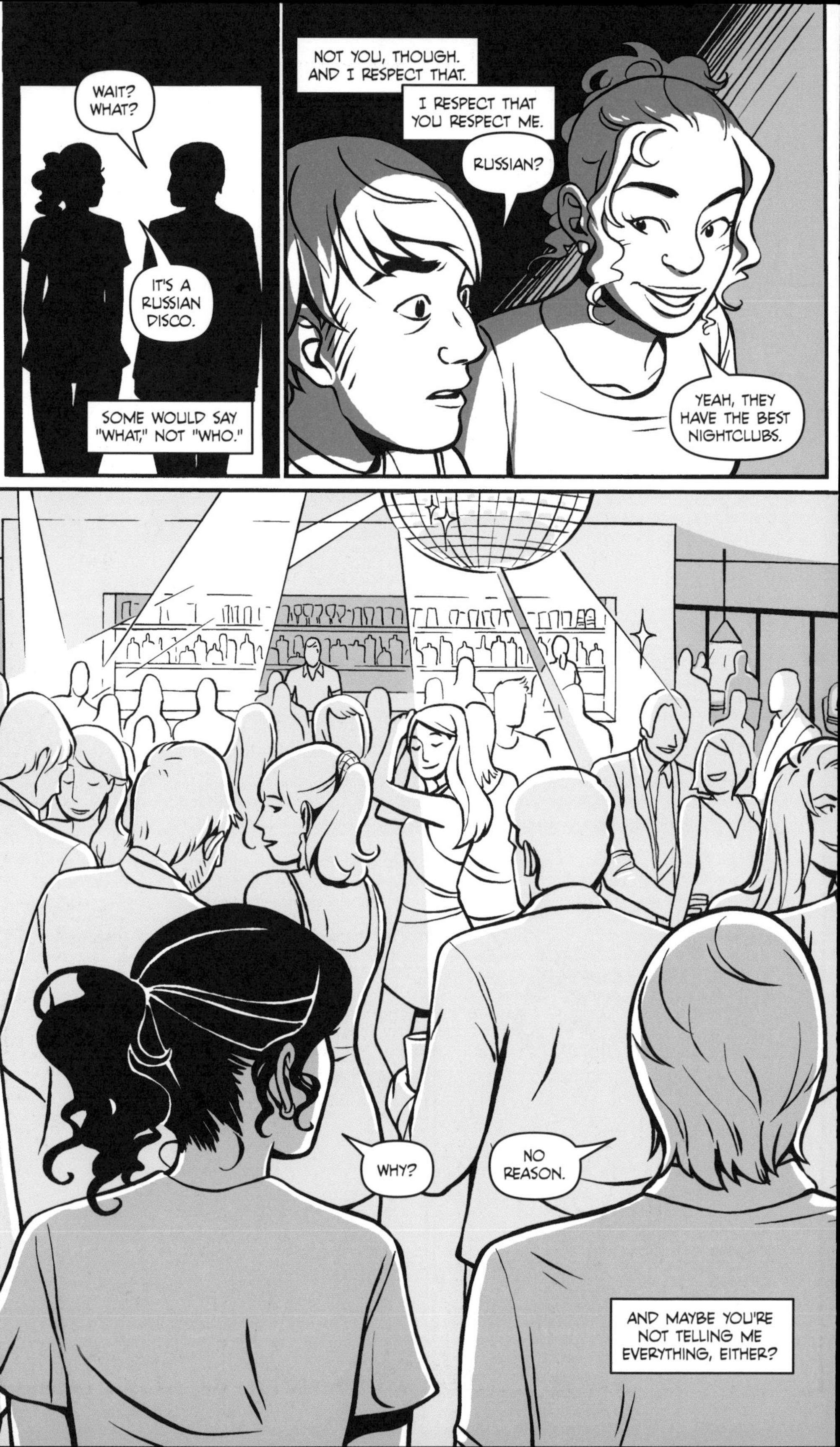
WAIT? WHAT?
IT'S A RUSSIAN DISCO.
SOME WOULD SAY "WHAT," NOT "WHO."
NOT YOU, THOUGH. AND I RESPECT THAT.
I RESPECT THAT YOU RESPECT ME.
RUSSIAN?
YEAH, THEY HAVE THE BEST NIGHTCLUBS.
WHY?
NO REASON.
AND MAYBE YOU'RE NOT TELLING ME EVERYTHING, EITHER?

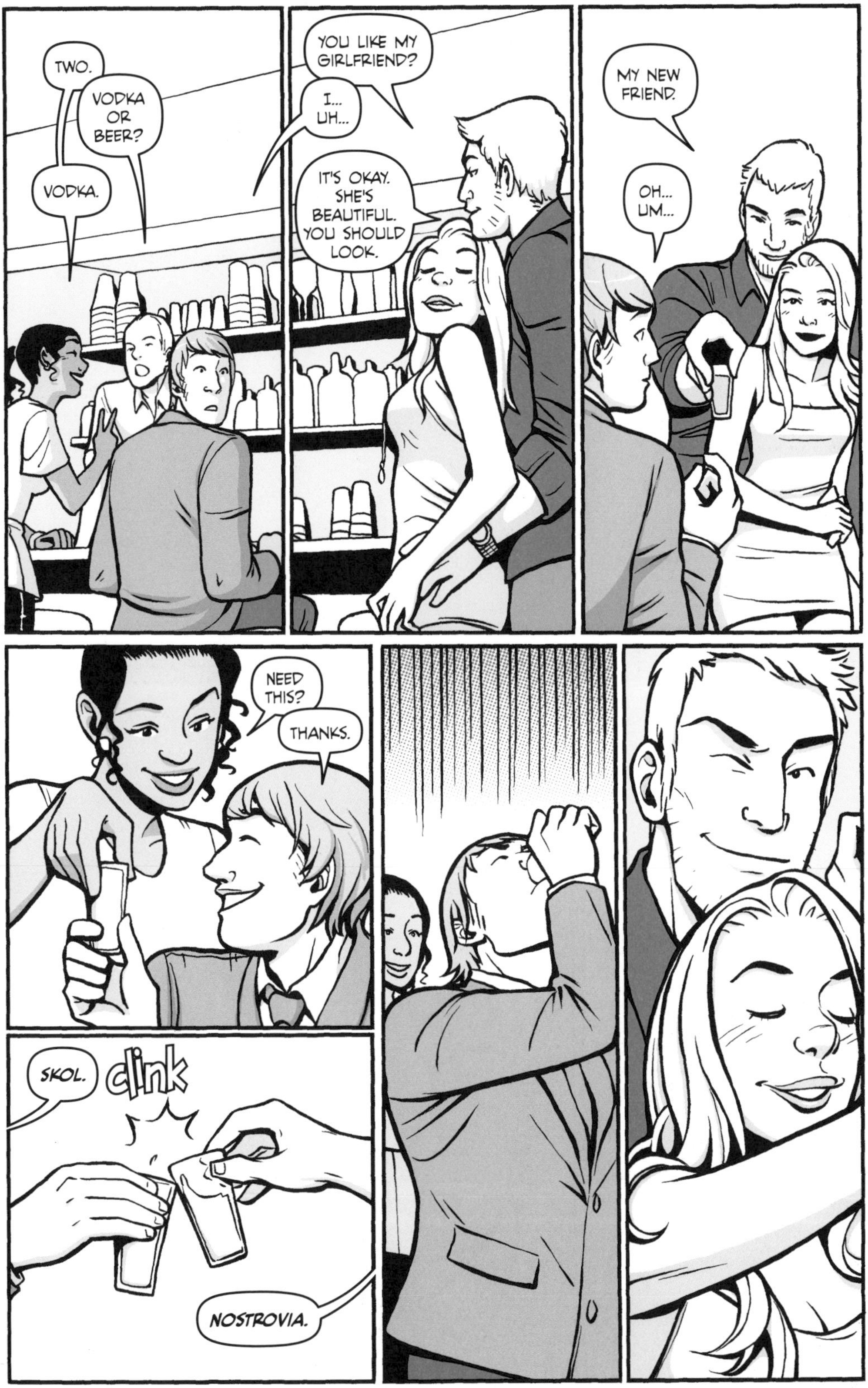
TWO.
VODKA OR BEER?
VODKA.
YOU LIKE MY GIRLFRIEND?
I... UH...
IT'S OKAY. SHE'S BEAUTIFUL. YOU SHOULD LOOK.
MY NEW FRIEND.
OH... UM...
NEED THIS?
THANKS.
SKOL.
clink
NOSTROVIA.

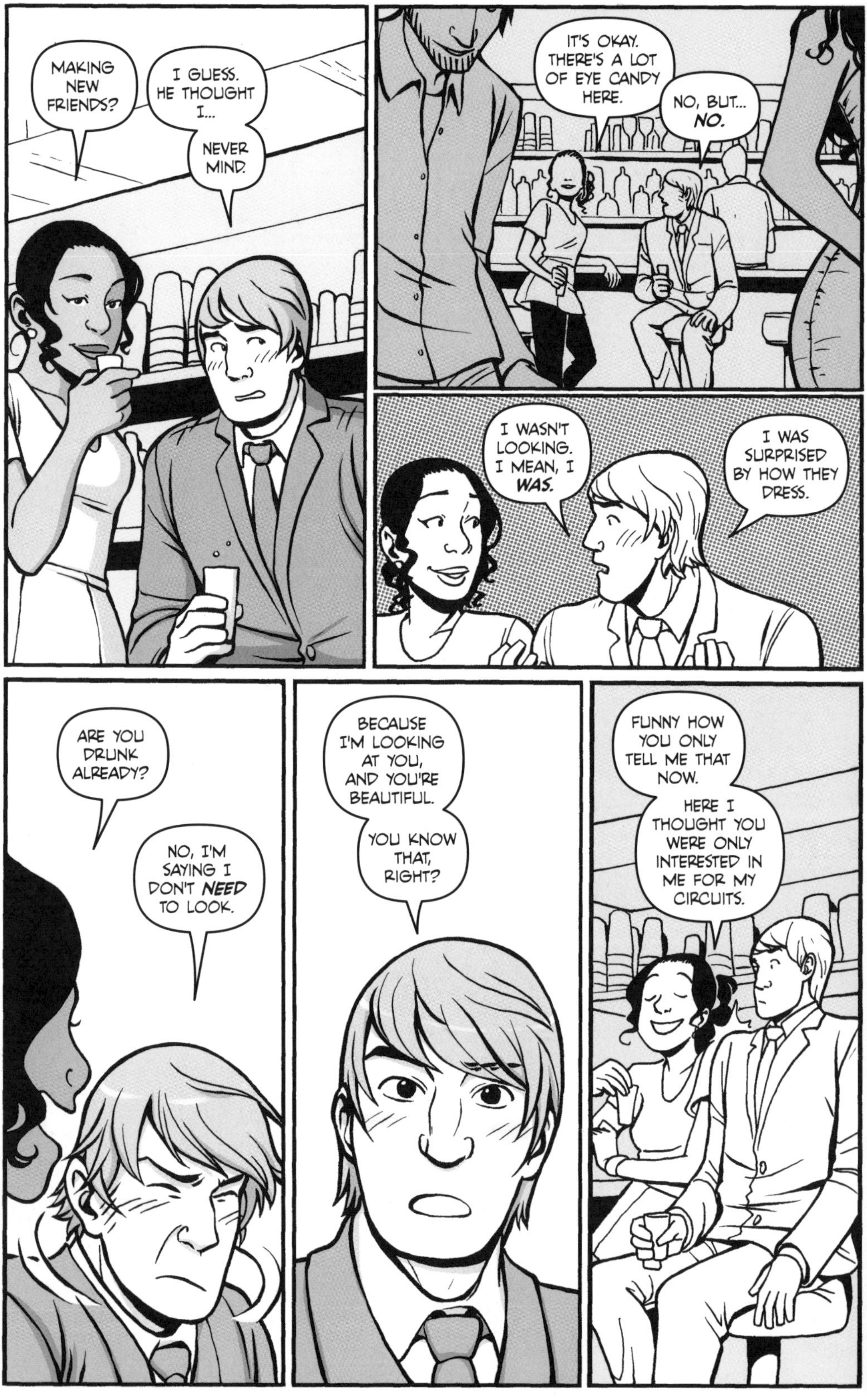
MAKING NEW FRIENDS?
I GUESS. HE THOUGHT I...
NEVER MIND.
IT'S OKAY. THERE'S A LOT OF EYE CANDY HERE.
NO, BUT... NO.
I WASN'T LOOKING. I MEAN, I WAS.
I WAS SURPRISED BY HOW THEY DRESS.
ARE YOU DRUNK ALREADY?
NO, I'M SAYING I DON'T NEED TO LOOK.
BECAUSE I'M LOOKING AT YOU, AND YOU'RE BEAUTIFUL.
YOU KNOW THAT, RIGHT?
FUNNY HOW YOU ONLY TELL ME THAT NOW.
HERE I THOUGHT YOU WERE ONLY INTERESTED IN ME FOR MY CIRCUITS.

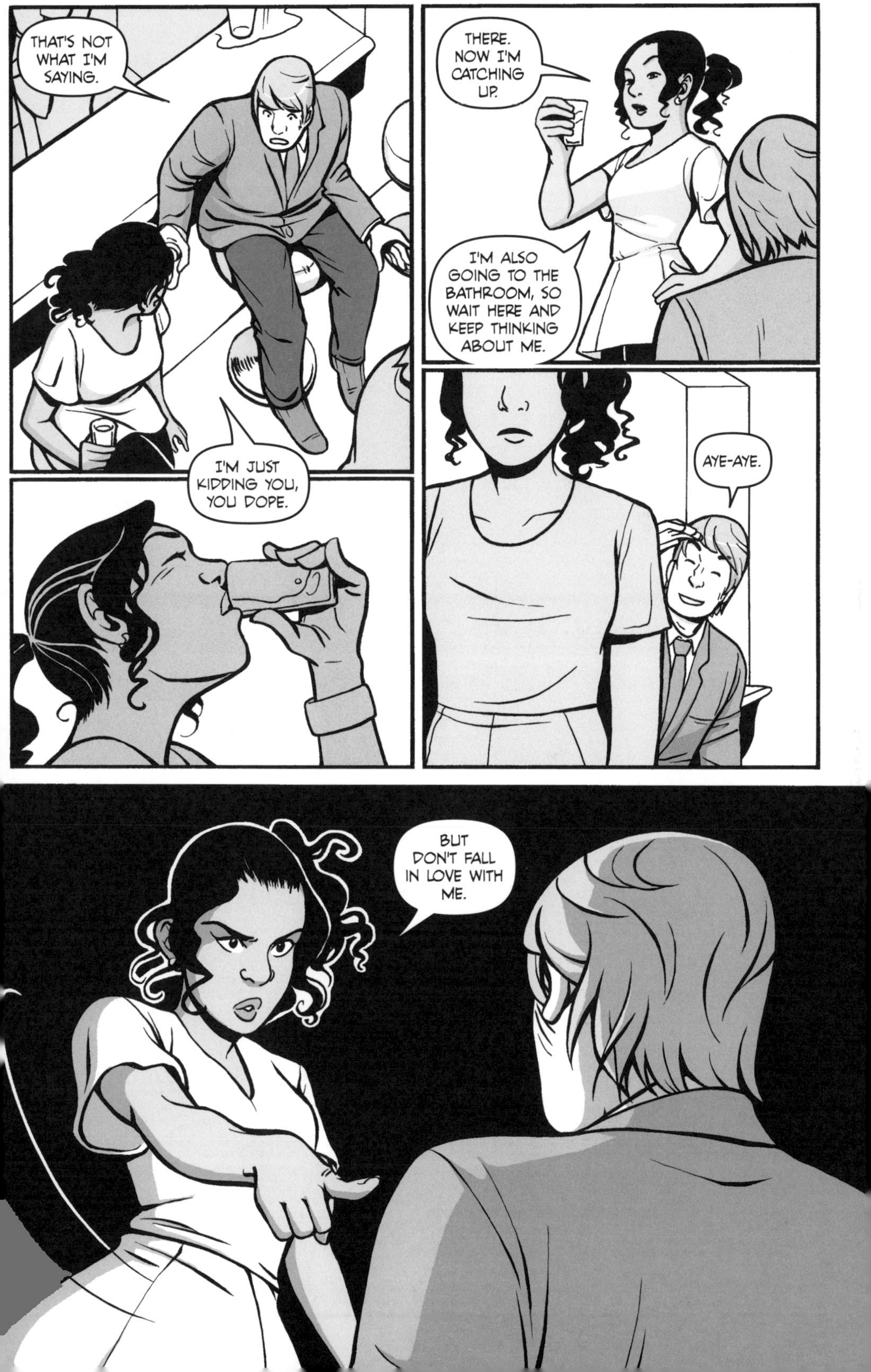
THAT'S NOT WHAT I'M SAYING.
THERE. NOW I'M CATCHING UP.
I'M ALSO GOING TO THE BATHROOM, SO WAIT HERE AND KEEP THINKING ABOUT ME.
I'M JUST KIDDING YOU, YOU DOPE.
AYE-AYE.
BUT DON'T FALL IN LOVE WITH ME.

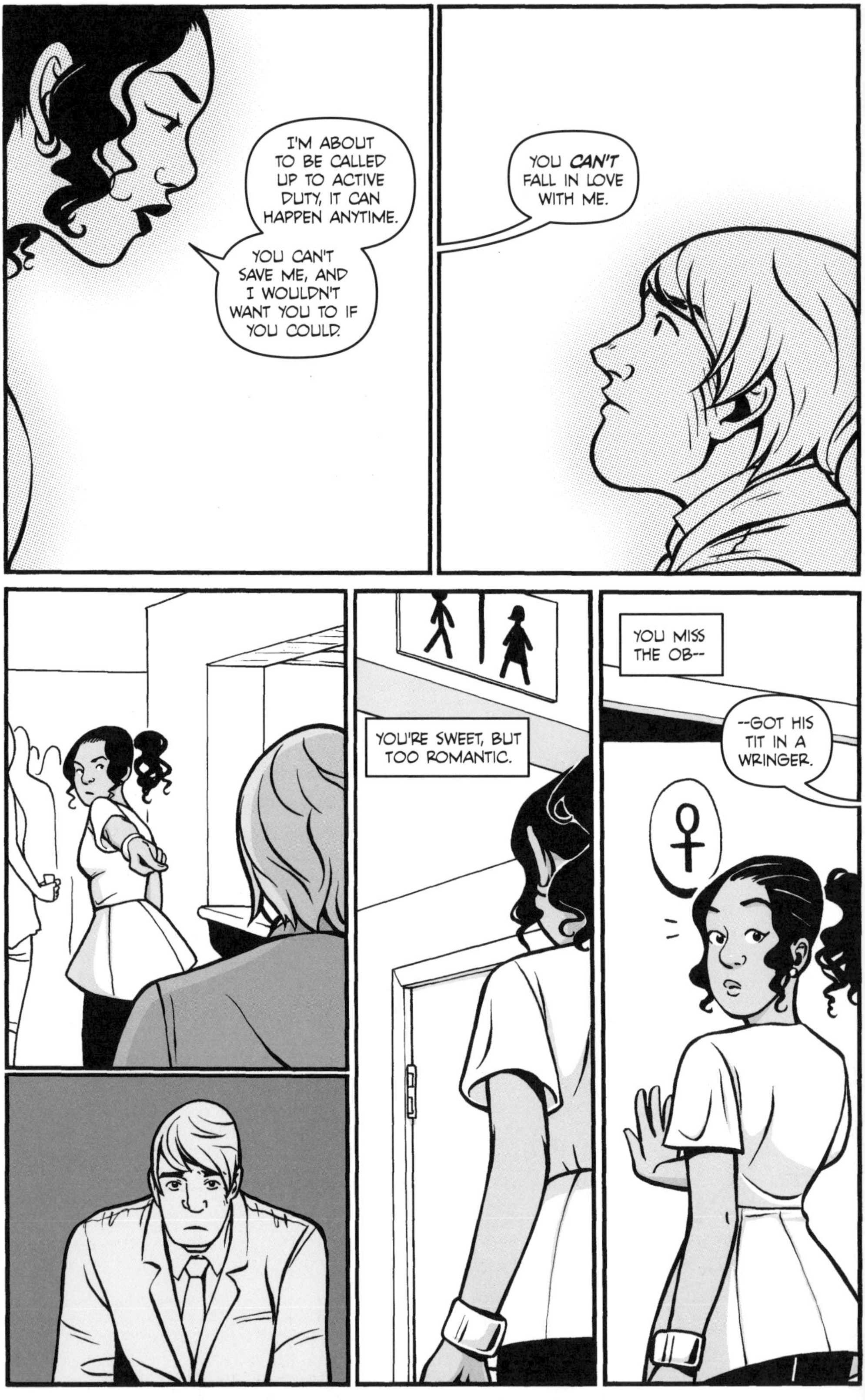
I'M ABOUT TO BE CALLED UP TO ACTIVE DUTY, IT CAN HAPPEN ANYTIME.
YOU CAN'T SAVE ME, AND I WOULDN'T WANT YOU TO IF YOU COULD.
YOU *CAN'T* FALL IN LOVE WITH ME.
YOU'RE SWEET, BUT TOO ROMANTIC.
YOU MISS THE OB--
--GOT HIS TIT IN A WRINGER.
♀

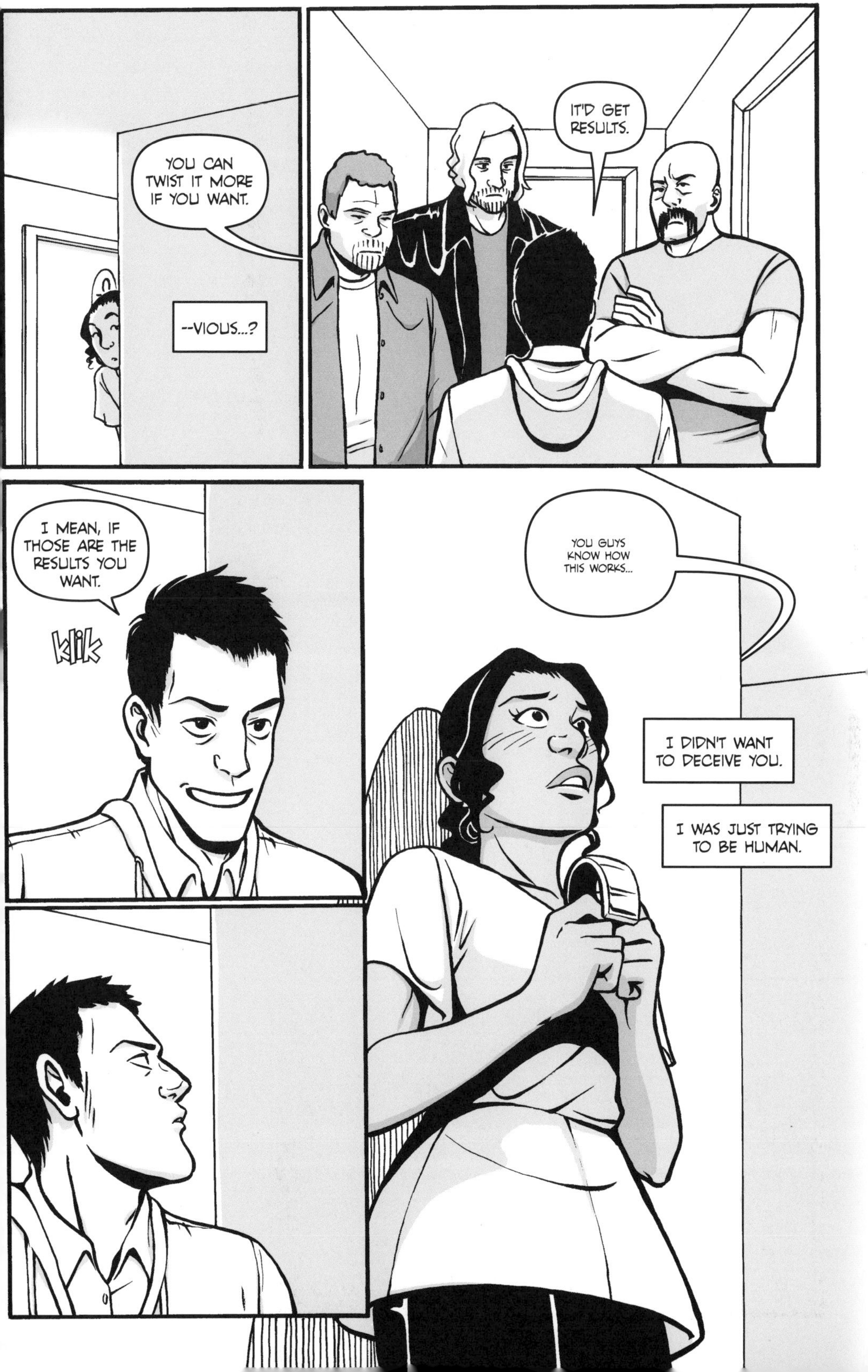
YOU CAN TWIST IT MORE IF YOU WANT.
--VIOUS...?
IT'D GET RESULTS.
I MEAN, IF THOSE ARE THE RESULTS YOU WANT.
klik
YOU GUYS KNOW HOW THIS WORKS...
I DIDN'T WANT TO DECEIVE YOU.
I WAS JUST TRYING TO BE HUMAN.

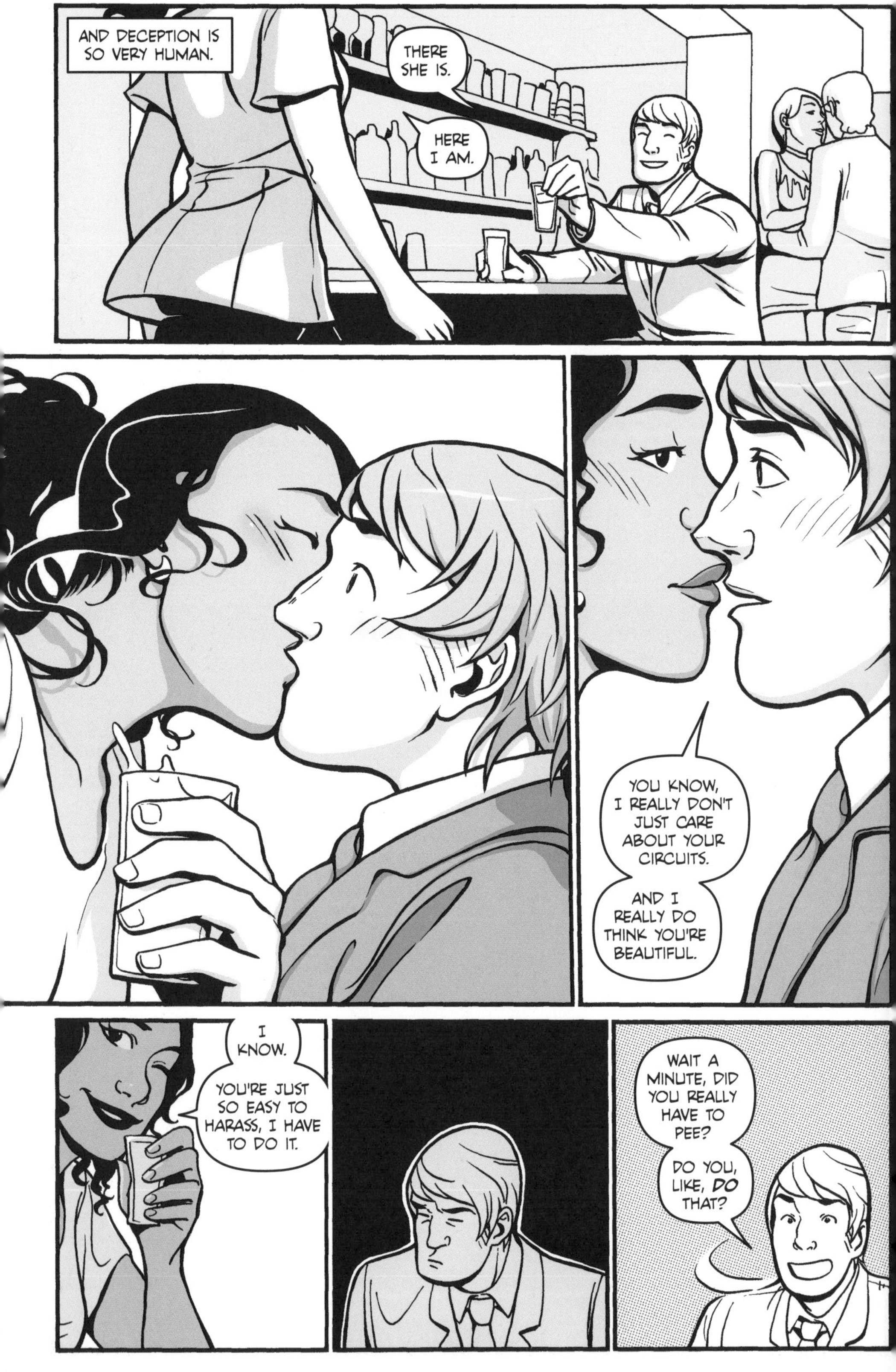
AND DECEPTION IS SO VERY HUMAN.
THERE SHE IS.
HERE I AM.
YOU KNOW, I REALLY DON'T JUST CARE ABOUT YOUR CIRCUITS.
AND I REALLY DO THINK YOU'RE BEAUTIFUL.
I KNOW.
YOU'RE JUST SO EASY TO HARASS, I HAVE TO DO IT.
WAIT A MINUTE, DID YOU REALLY HAVE TO PEE?
DO YOU, LIKE, ***DO*** THAT?

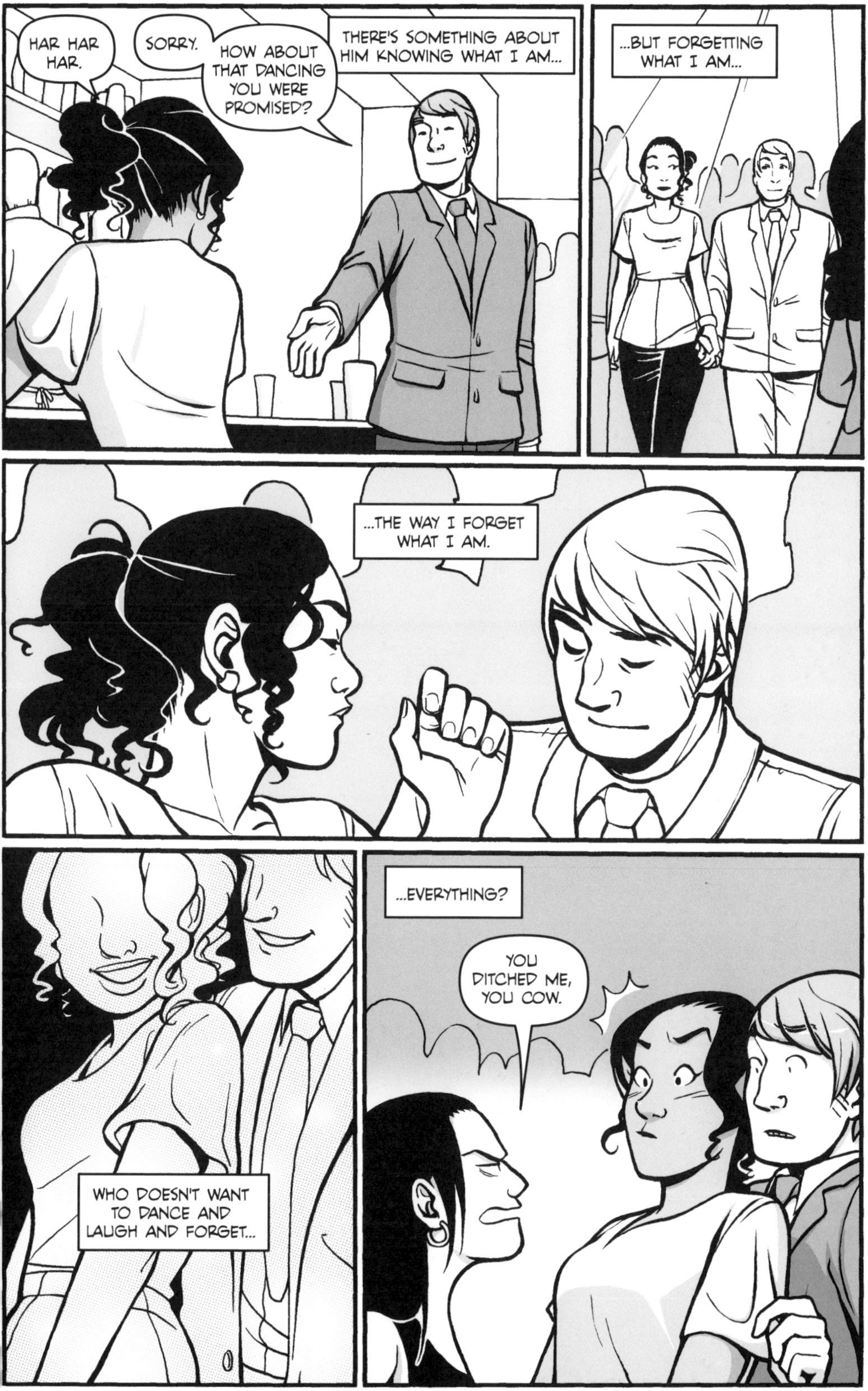
HAR HAR HAR.
SORRY.
HOW ABOUT THAT DANCING YOU WERE PROMISED?
THERE'S SOMETHING ABOUT HIM KNOWING WHAT I AM...
...BUT FORGETTING WHAT I AM...
...THE WAY I FORGET WHAT I AM.
WHO DOESN'T WANT TO DANCE AND LAUGH AND FORGET...
...EVERYTHING?
YOU DITCHED ME, YOU COW.

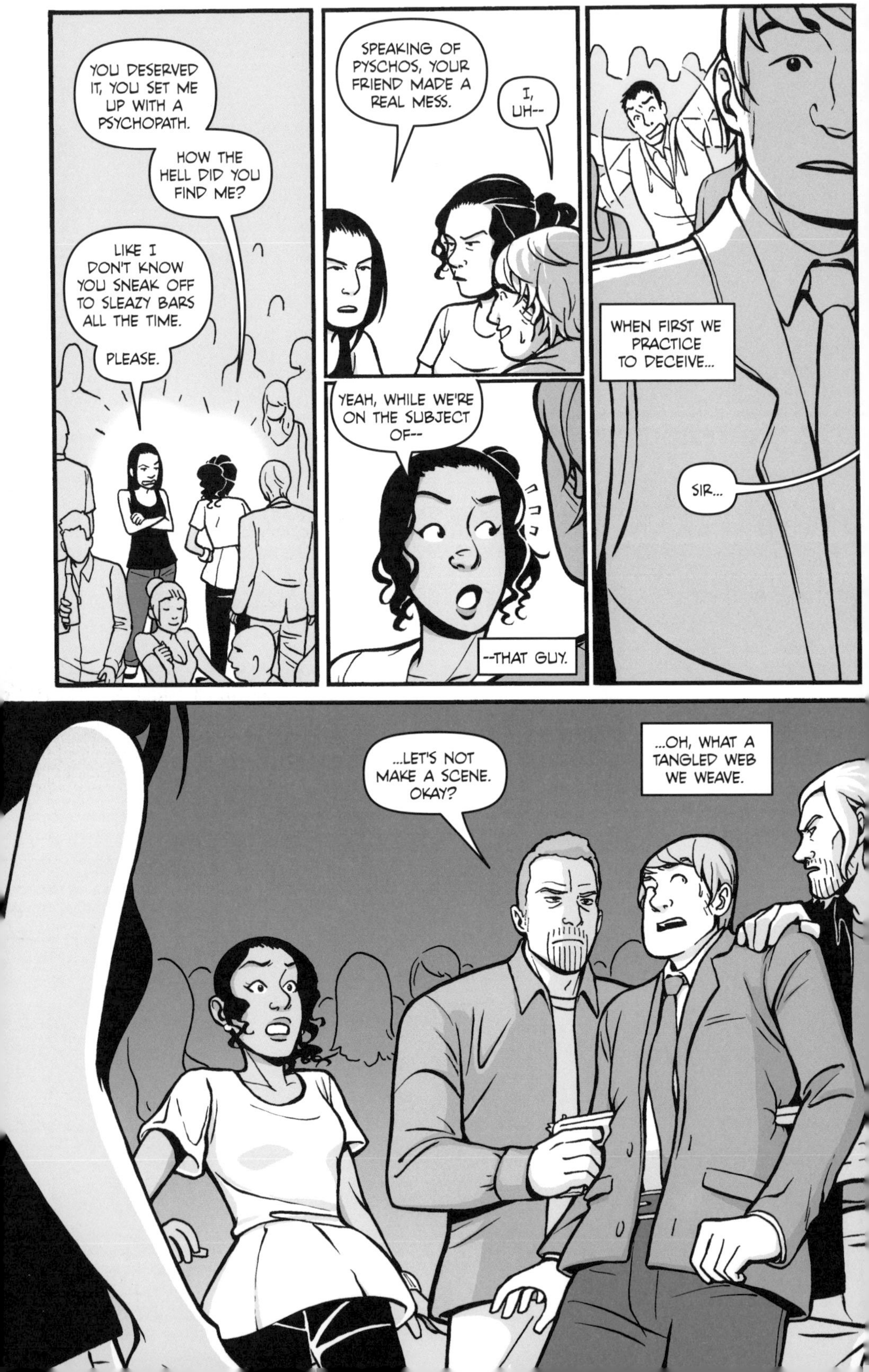
YOU DESERVED IT, YOU SET ME UP WITH A PSYCHOPATH.
HOW THE HELL DID YOU FIND ME?
LIKE I DON'T KNOW YOU SNEAK OFF TO SLEAZY BARS ALL THE TIME.
PLEASE.
SPEAKING OF PYSCHOS, YOUR FRIEND MADE A REAL MESS.
I, UH--
YEAH, WHILE WE'RE ON THE SUBJECT OF--
--THAT GUY.
WHEN FIRST WE PRACTICE TO DECEIVE...
SIR...
...LET'S NOT MAKE A SCENE. OKAY?
...OH, WHAT A TANGLED WEB WE WEAVE.

CHAPTER 8: HIM

...MUST END IN BROKEN BONES

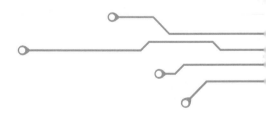

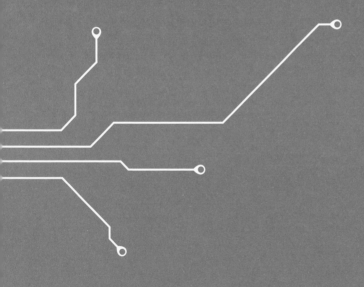

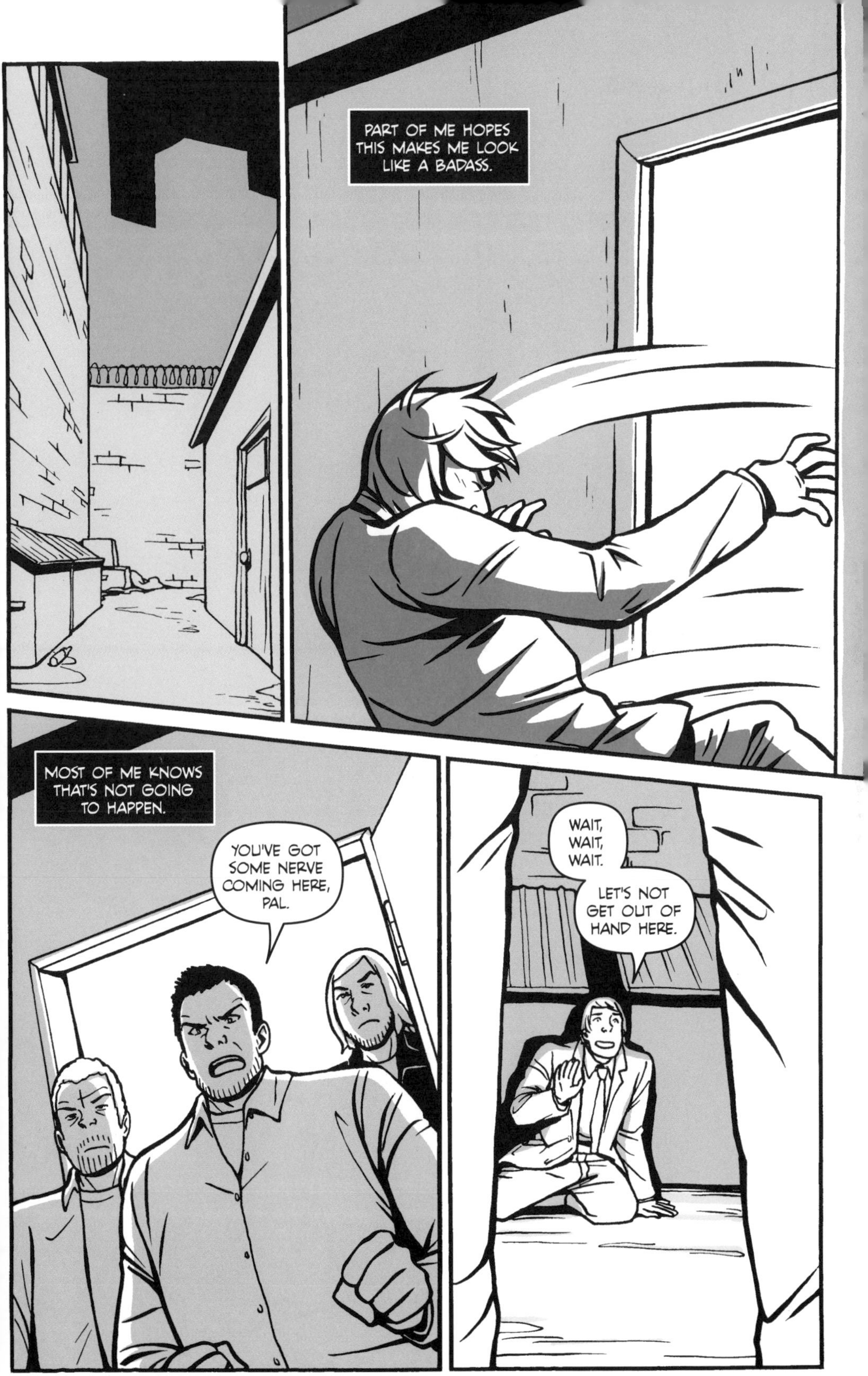
PART OF ME HOPES THIS MAKES ME LOOK LIKE A BADASS.
MOST OF ME KNOWS THAT'S NOT GOING TO HAPPEN.
YOU'VE GOT SOME NERVE COMING HERE, PAL.
WAIT, WAIT, WAIT.
LET'S NOT GET OUT OF HAND HERE.

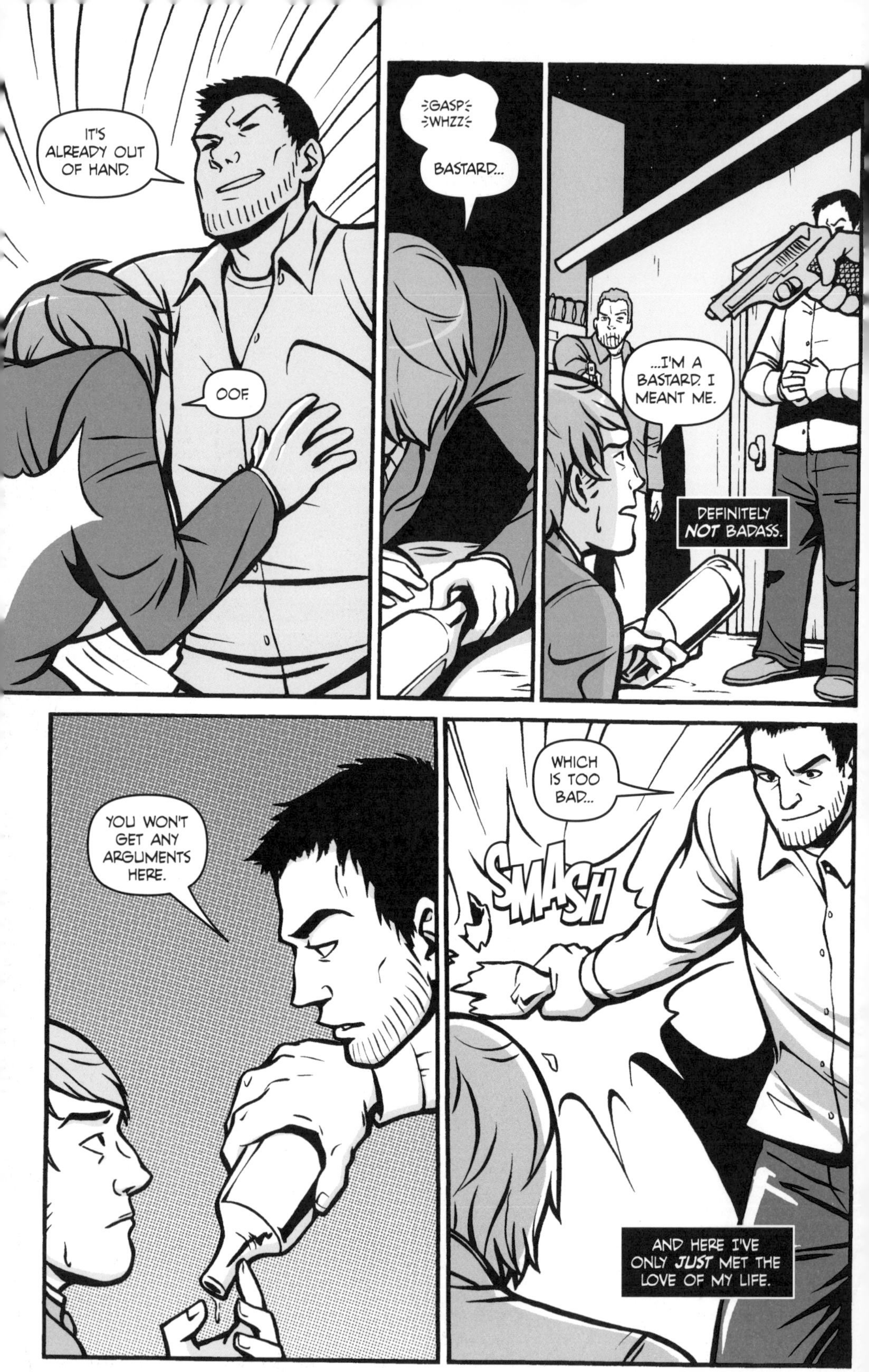
IT'S ALREADY OUT OF HAND.
OOF.
GASP WHZZ
BASTARD...
...I'M A BASTARD. I MEANT ME.
DEFINITELY NOT BADASS.
YOU WON'T GET ANY ARGUMENTS HERE.
WHICH IS TOO BAD...
SMASH
AND HERE I'VE ONLY JUST MET THE LOVE OF MY LIFE.

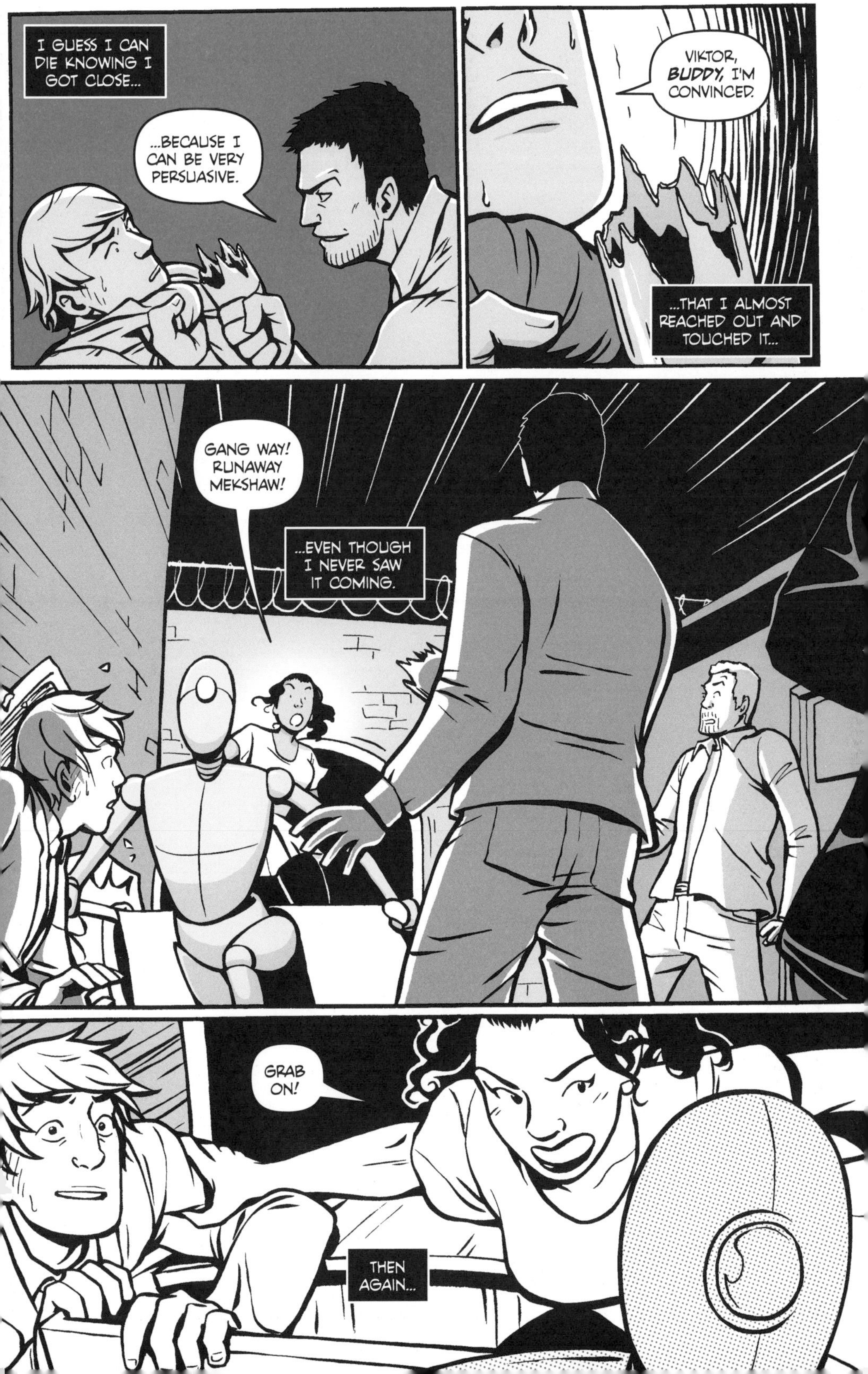
I GUESS I CAN DIE KNOWING I GOT CLOSE...
...BECAUSE I CAN BE VERY PERSUASIVE.
VIKTOR, BUDDY, I'M CONVINCED.
...THAT I ALMOST REACHED OUT AND TOUCHED IT...
GANG WAY! RUNAWAY MEKSHAW!
...EVEN THOUGH I NEVER SAW IT COMING.
GRAB ON!
THEN AGAIN...

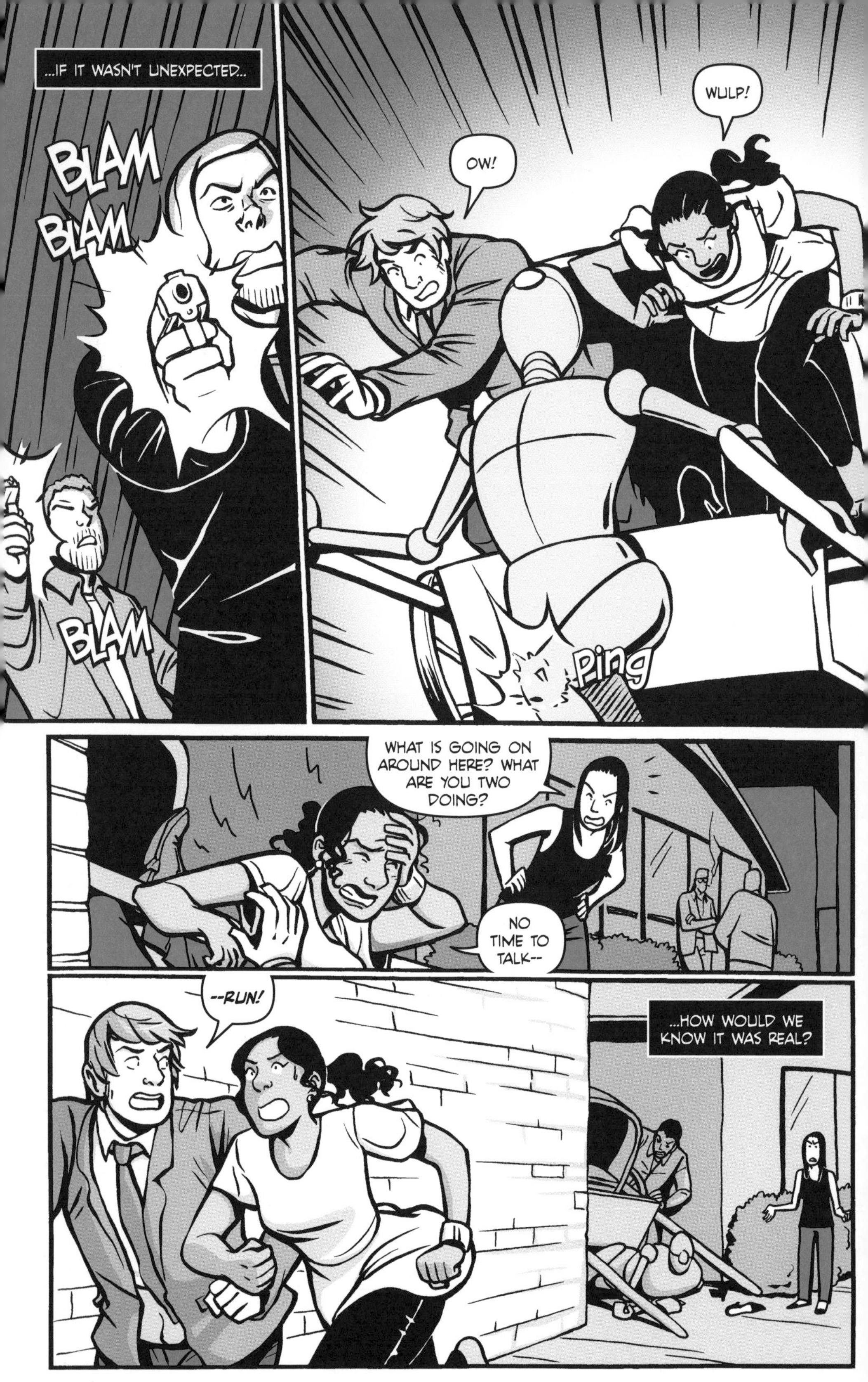
...IF IT WASN'T UNEXPECTED...
BLAM
BLAM
BLAM
OW!
WULP!
Ping
WHAT IS GOING ON AROUND HERE? WHAT ARE YOU TWO DOING?
NO TIME TO TALK--
--RUN!
...HOW WOULD WE KNOW IT WAS REAL?

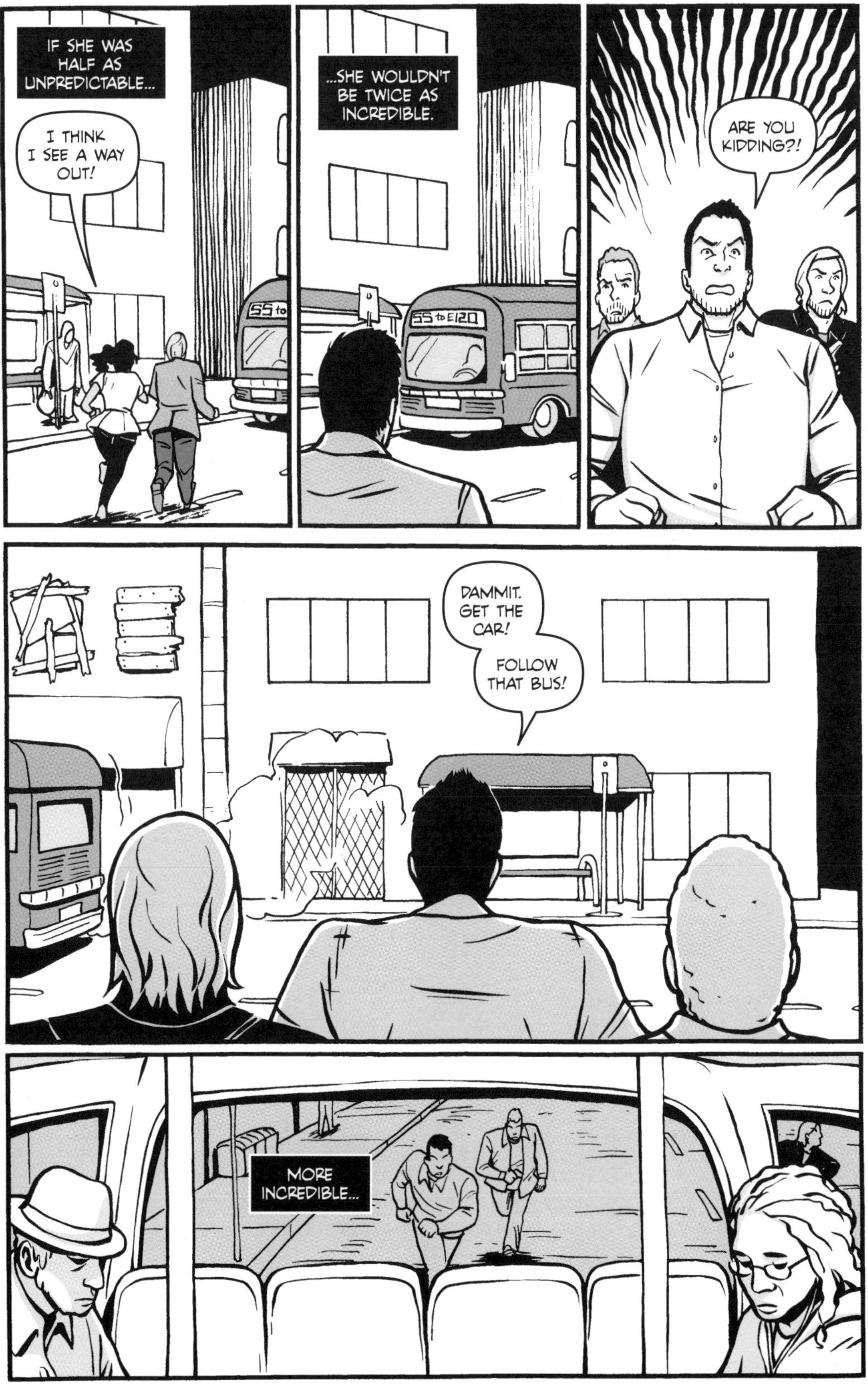
IF SHE WAS HALF AS UNPREDICTABLE...
I THINK I SEE A WAY OUT!
55 to
...SHE WOULDN'T BE TWICE AS INCREDIBLE.
55 to E120
ARE YOU KIDDING?!
DAMMIT. GET THE CAR!
FOLLOW THAT BUS!
MORE INCREDIBLE...

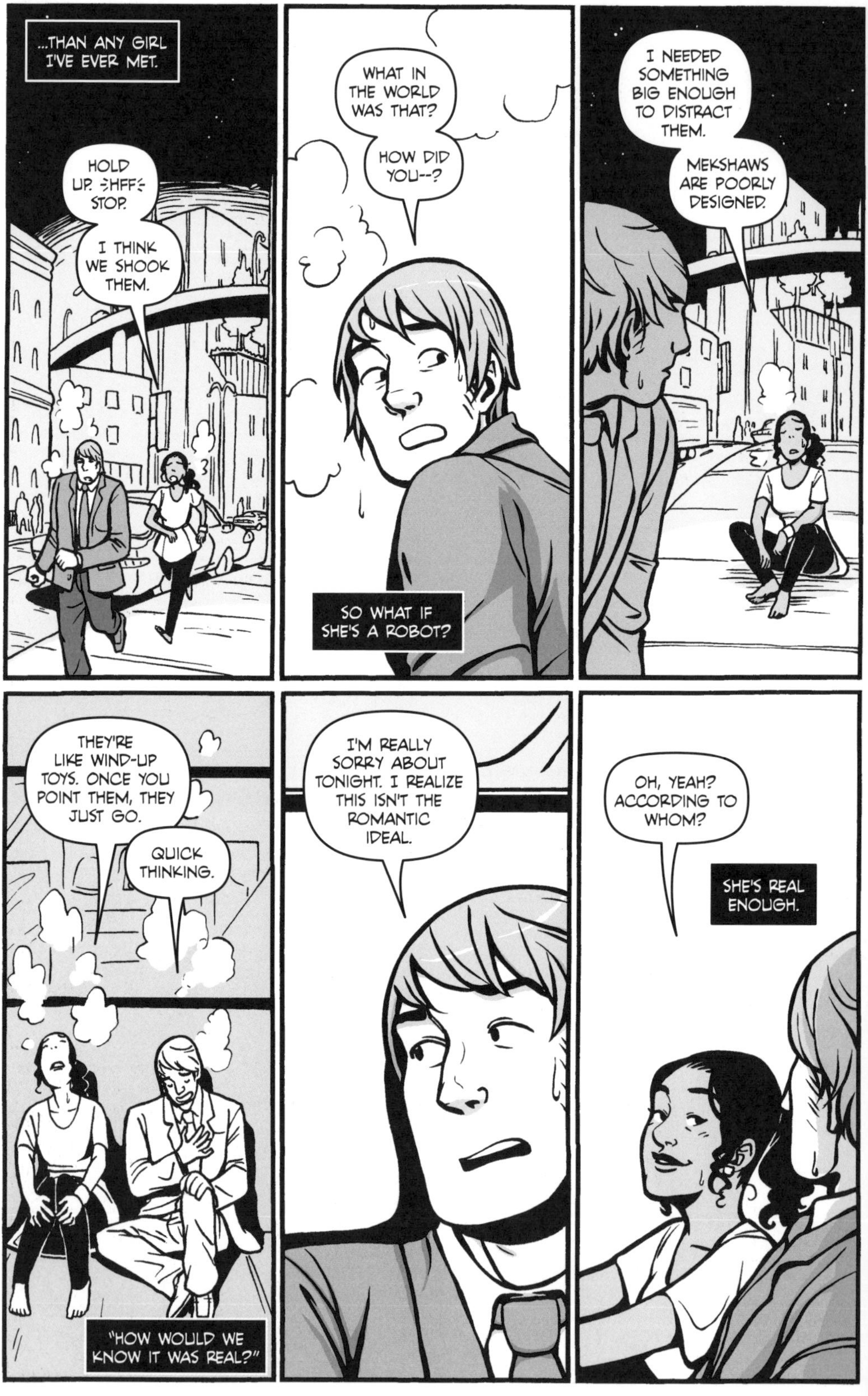
...THAN ANY GIRL I'VE EVER MET.
HOLD UP. HFF STOP.
I THINK WE SHOOK THEM.
WHAT IN THE WORLD WAS THAT?
HOW DID YOU--?
SO WHAT IF SHE'S A ROBOT?
I NEEDED SOMETHING BIG ENOUGH TO DISTRACT THEM.
MEKSHAWS ARE POORLY DESIGNED.
THEY'RE LIKE WIND-UP TOYS. ONCE YOU POINT THEM, THEY JUST GO.
QUICK THINKING.
"HOW WOULD WE KNOW IT WAS REAL?"
I'M REALLY SORRY ABOUT TONIGHT. I REALIZE THIS ISN'T THE ROMANTIC IDEAL.
OH, YEAH? ACCORDING TO WHOM?
SHE'S REAL ENOUGH.

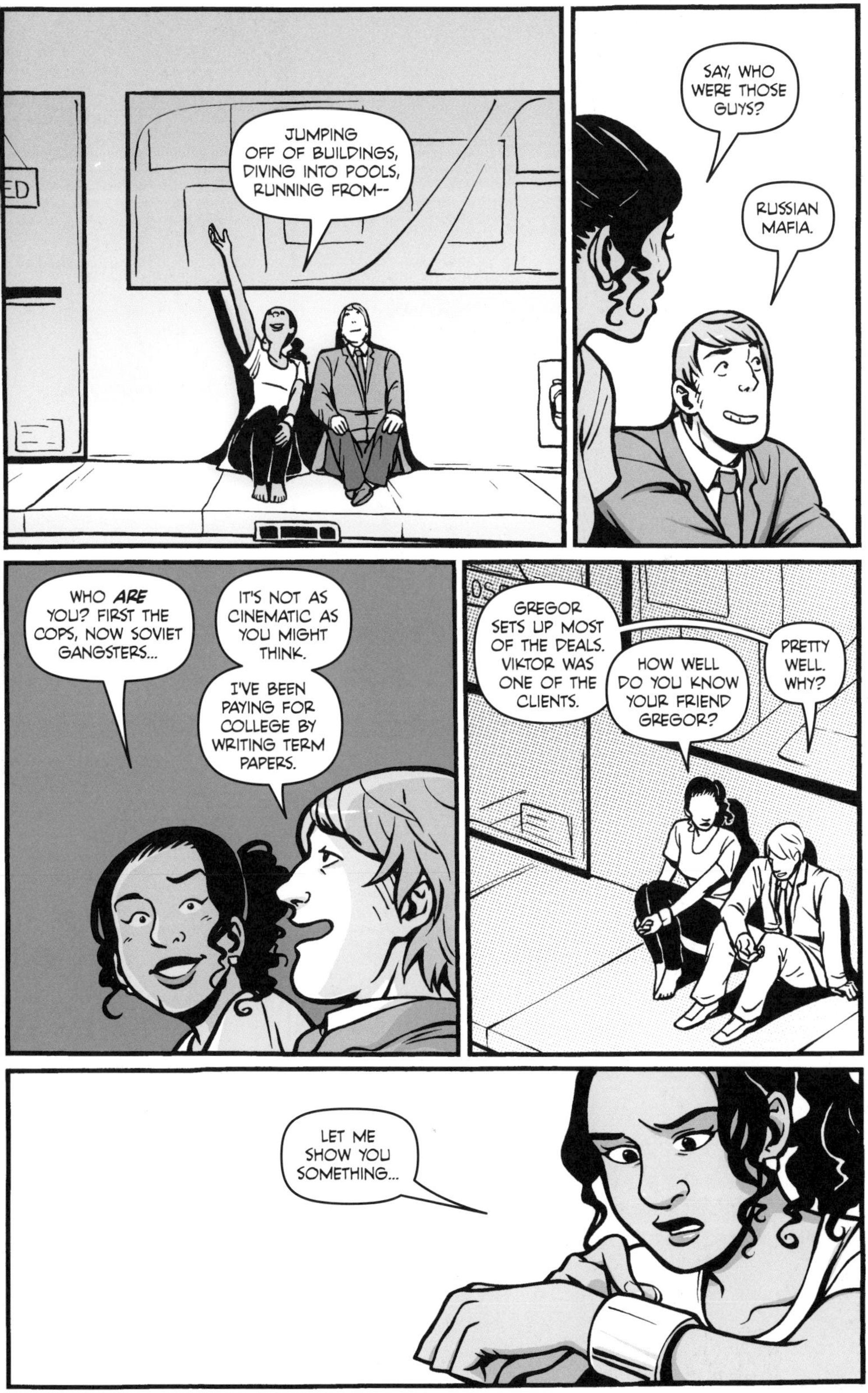
JUMPING OFF OF BUILDINGS, DIVING INTO POOLS, RUNNING FROM--
SAY, WHO WERE THOSE GUYS?
RUSSIAN MAFIA.
WHO *ARE* YOU? FIRST THE COPS, NOW SOVIET GANGSTERS...
IT'S NOT AS CINEMATIC AS YOU MIGHT THINK.
I'VE BEEN PAYING FOR COLLEGE BY WRITING TERM PAPERS.
HOW WELL DO YOU KNOW YOUR FRIEND GREGOR?
PRETTY WELL. WHY?
GREGOR SETS UP MOST OF THE DEALS. VIKTOR WAS ONE OF THE CLIENTS.
LET ME SHOW YOU SOMETHING...

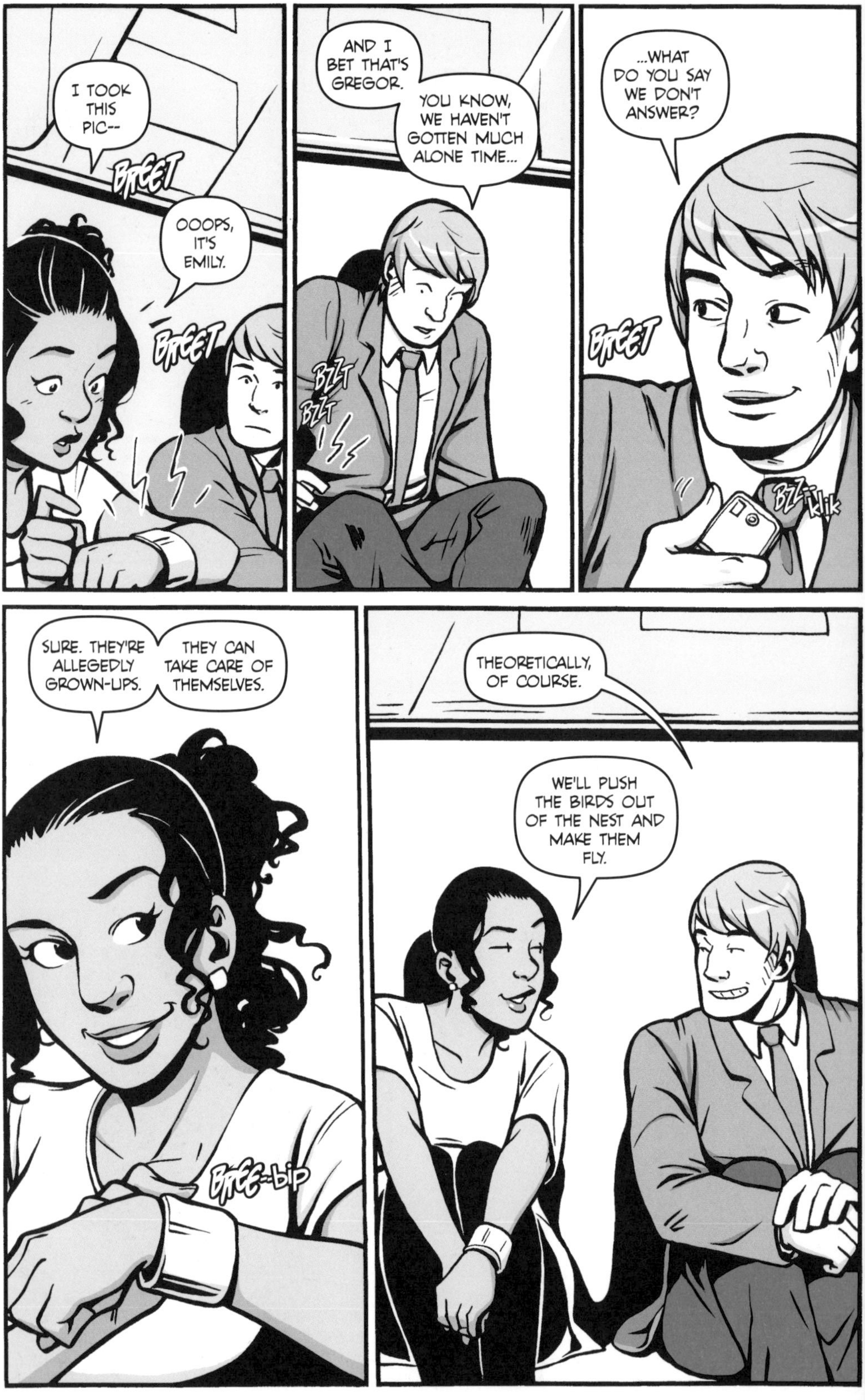
I TOOK THIS PIC--
BREET
OOOPS, IT'S EMILY.
BREET
AND I BET THAT'S GREGOR.
YOU KNOW, WE HAVEN'T GOTTEN MUCH ALONE TIME...
BZZT BZZT
...WHAT DO YOU SAY WE DON'T ANSWER?
BREET
BZZ-klik
SURE. THEY'RE ALLEGEDLY GROWN-UPS.
THEY CAN TAKE CARE OF THEMSELVES.
BREE-bip
THEORETICALLY, OF COURSE.
WE'LL PUSH THE BIRDS OUT OF THE NEST AND MAKE THEM FLY.

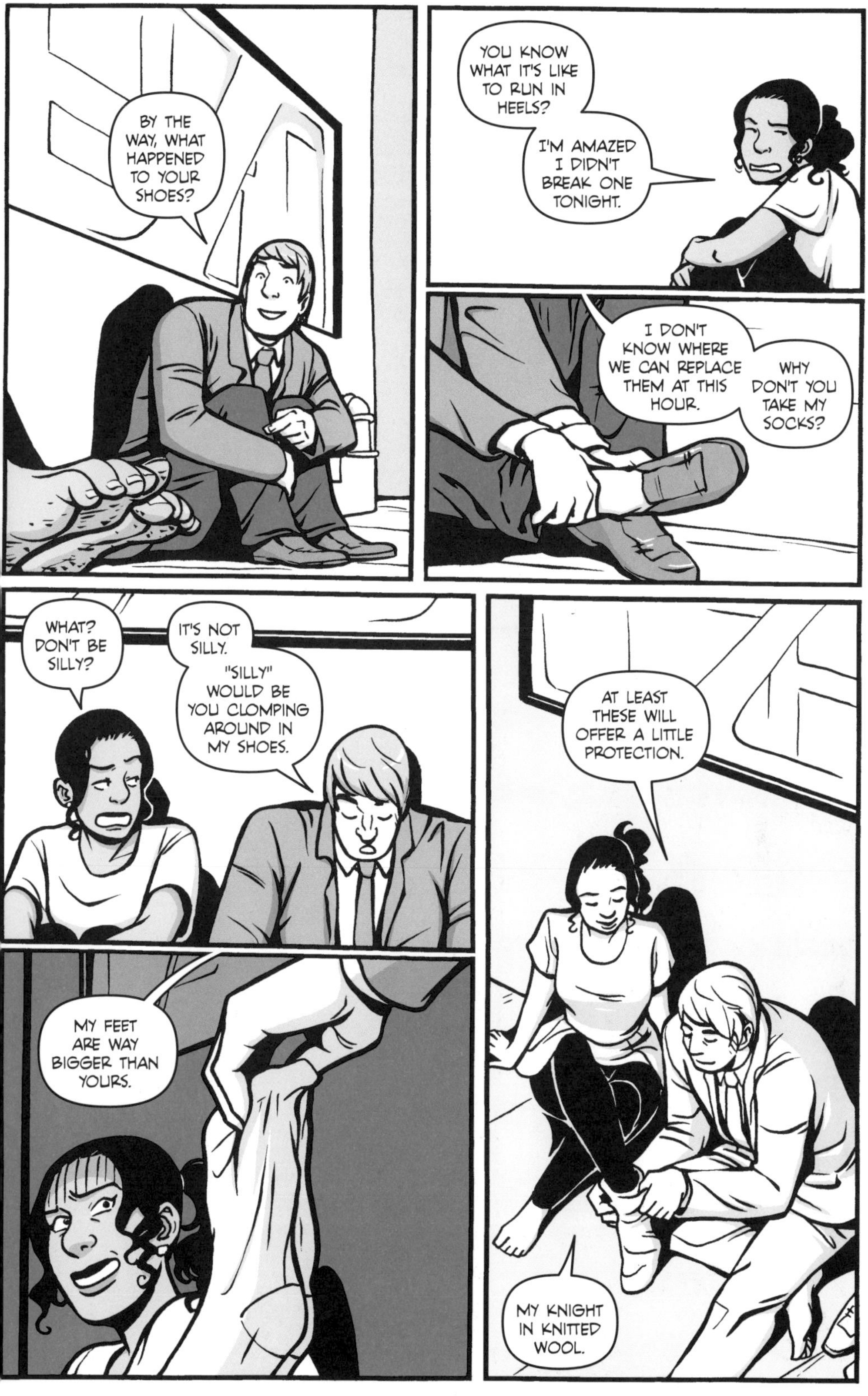
BY THE WAY, WHAT HAPPENED TO YOUR SHOES?
YOU KNOW WHAT IT'S LIKE TO RUN IN HEELS?
I'M AMAZED I DIDN'T BREAK ONE TONIGHT.
I DON'T KNOW WHERE WE CAN REPLACE THEM AT THIS HOUR.
WHY DON'T YOU TAKE MY SOCKS?
WHAT? DON'T BE SILLY?
IT'S NOT SILLY.
"SILLY" WOULD BE YOU CLOMPING AROUND IN MY SHOES.
MY FEET ARE WAY BIGGER THAN YOURS.
AT LEAST THESE WILL OFFER A LITTLE PROTECTION.
MY KNIGHT IN KNITTED WOOL.

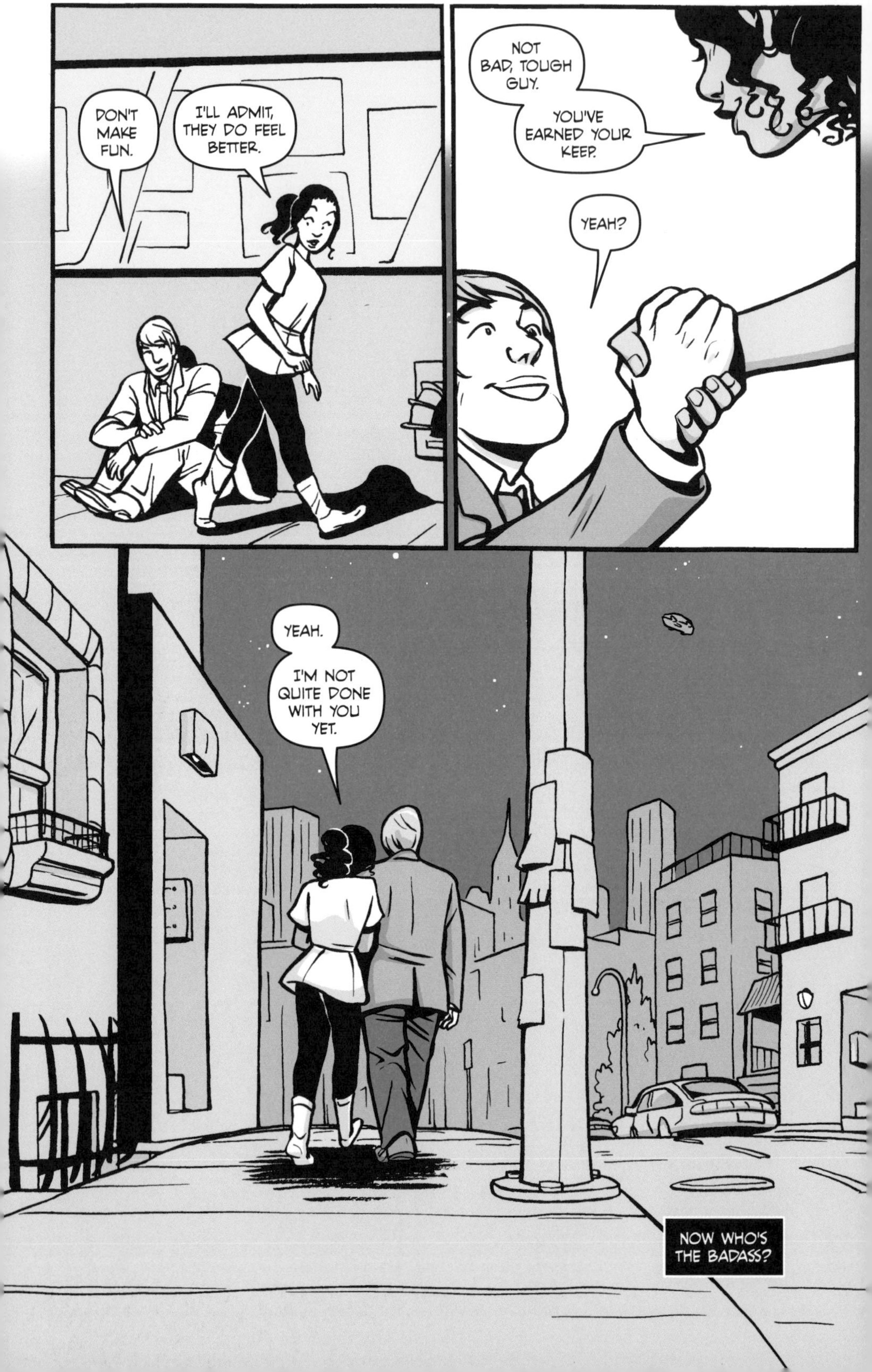
DON'T MAKE FUN.
I'LL ADMIT, THEY DO FEEL BETTER.
NOT BAD, TOUGH GUY.
YOU'VE EARNED YOUR KEEP.
YEAH?
YEAH.
I'M NOT QUITE DONE WITH YOU YET.
NOW WHO'S THE BADASS?

CHAPTER 9: HER

ONE LAST FLING

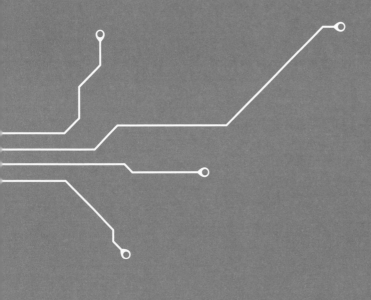

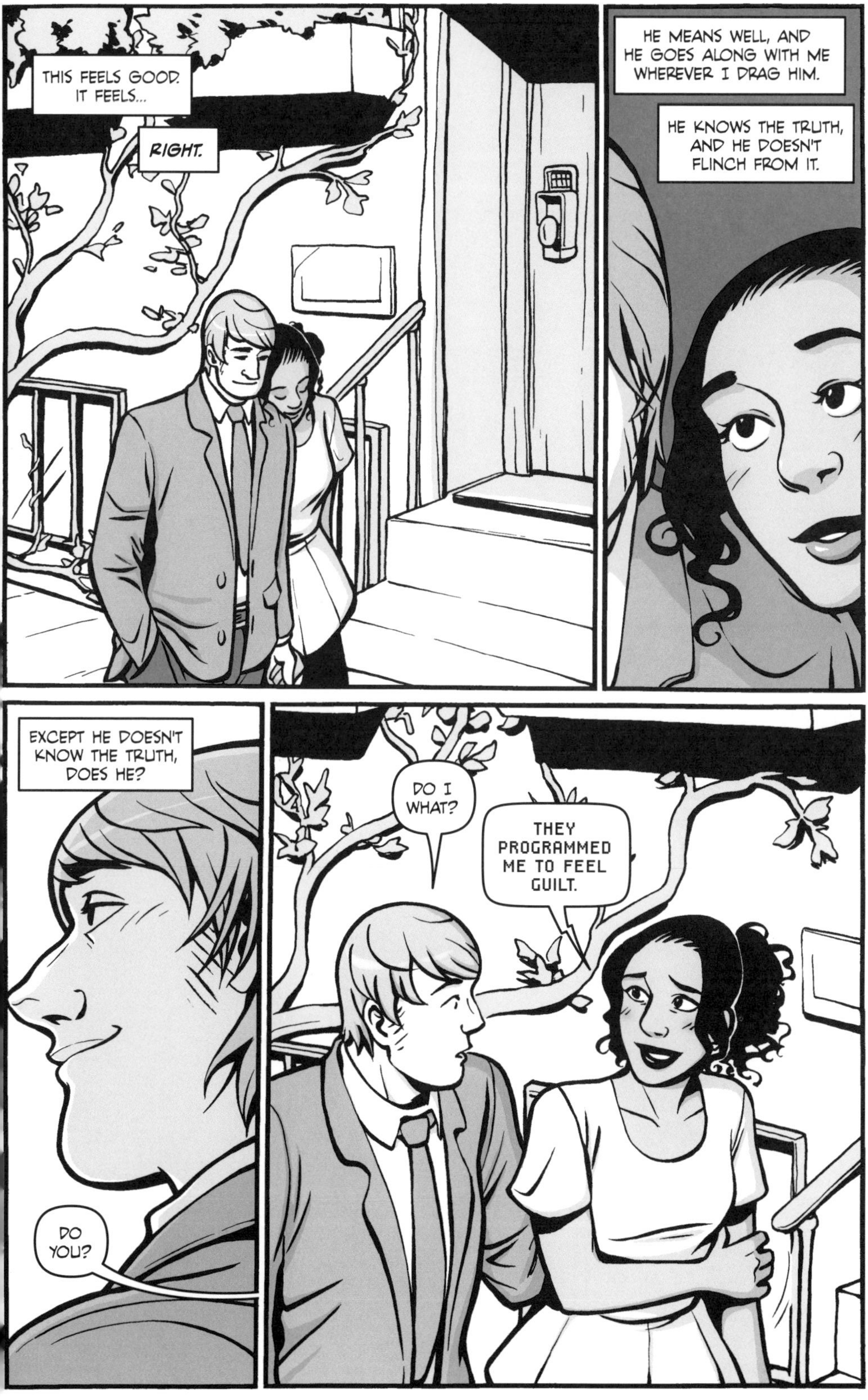
THIS FEELS GOOD. IT FEELS...
RIGHT.
HE MEANS WELL, AND HE GOES ALONG WITH ME WHEREVER I DRAG HIM.
HE KNOWS THE TRUTH, AND HE DOESN'T FLINCH FROM IT.
EXCEPT HE DOESN'T KNOW THE TRUTH, DOES HE?
DO YOU?
DO I WHAT?
THEY PROGRAMMED ME TO FEEL GUILT.

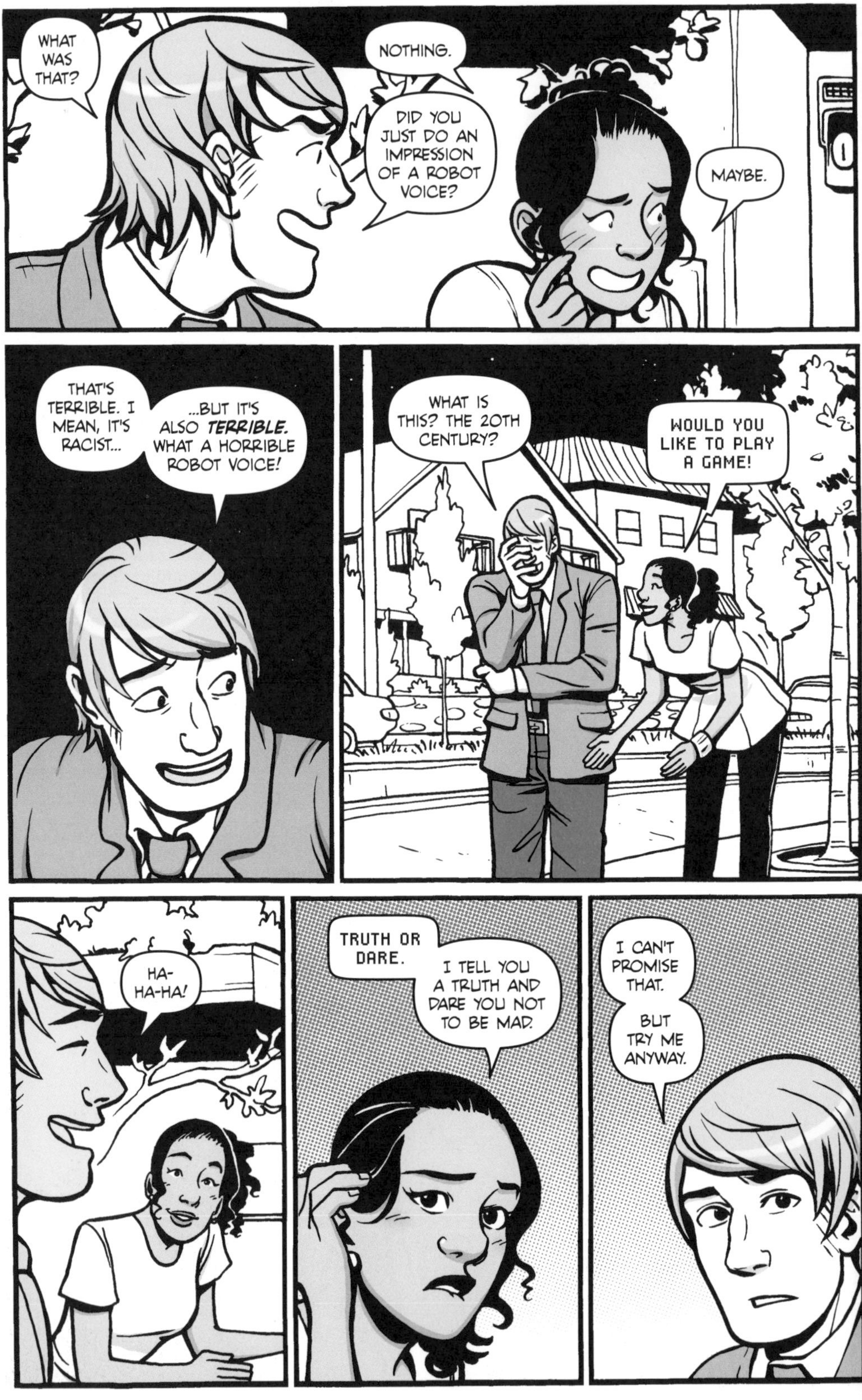
WHAT WAS THAT?
NOTHING.
DID YOU JUST DO AN IMPRESSION OF A ROBOT VOICE?
MAYBE.
THAT'S TERRIBLE. I MEAN, IT'S RACIST...
...BUT IT'S ALSO *TERRIBLE.* WHAT A HORRIBLE ROBOT VOICE!
WHAT IS THIS? THE 20TH CENTURY?
WOULD YOU LIKE TO PLAY A GAME!
HA-HA-HA!
TRUTH OR DARE.
I TELL YOU A TRUTH AND DARE YOU NOT TO BE MAD.
I CAN'T PROMISE THAT.
BUT TRY ME ANYWAY.

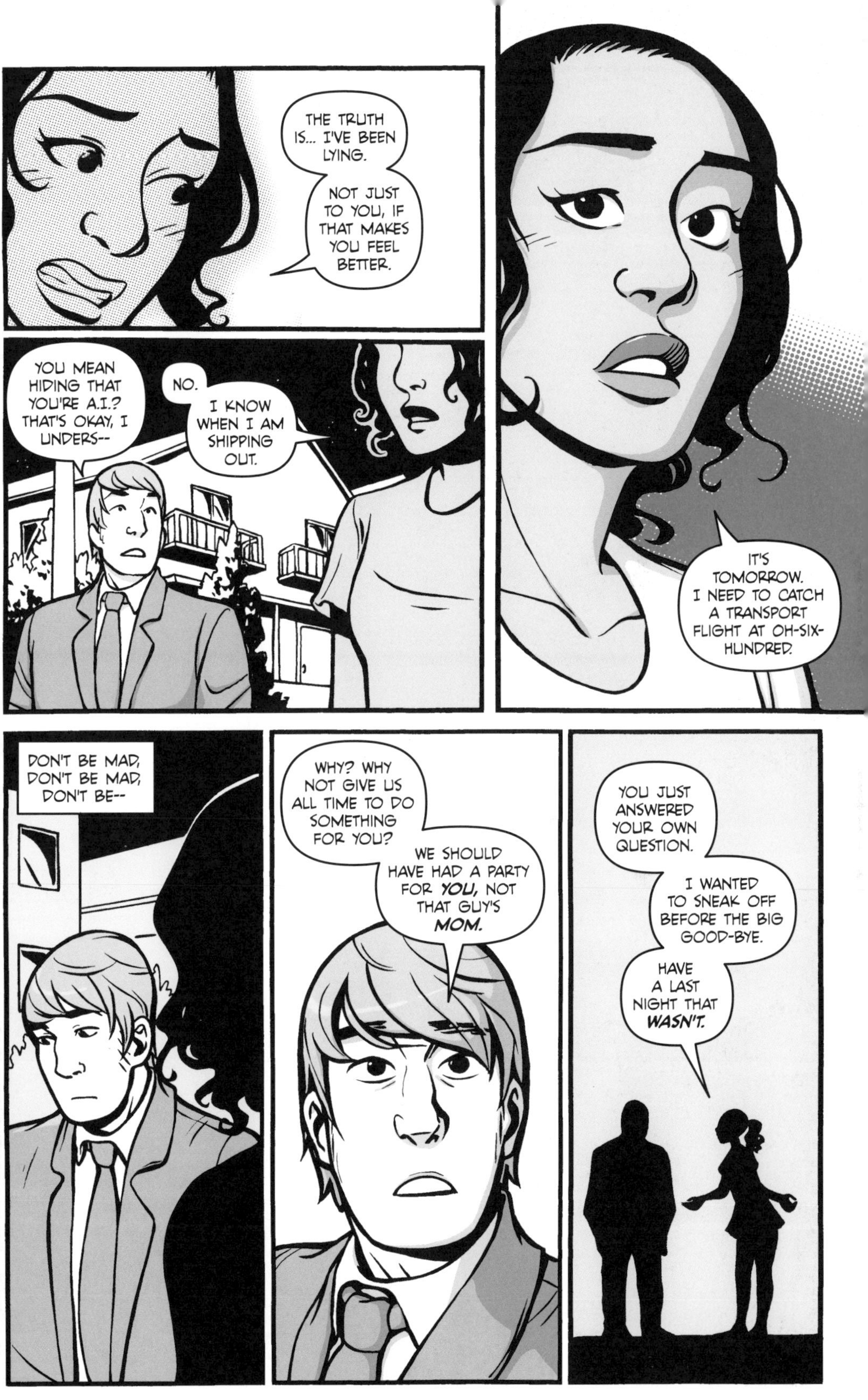
THE TRUTH IS... I'VE BEEN LYING.
NOT JUST TO YOU, IF THAT MAKES YOU FEEL BETTER.
YOU MEAN HIDING THAT YOU'RE A.I.? THAT'S OKAY, I UNDERS--
NO.
I KNOW WHEN I AM SHIPPING OUT.
IT'S TOMORROW. I NEED TO CATCH A TRANSPORT FLIGHT AT OH-SIX-HUNDRED.
DON'T BE MAD, DON'T BE MAD, DON'T BE--
WHY? WHY NOT GIVE US ALL TIME TO DO SOMETHING FOR YOU?
WE SHOULD HAVE HAD A PARTY FOR *YOU,* NOT THAT GUY'S ***MOM.***
YOU JUST ANSWERED YOUR OWN QUESTION.
I WANTED TO SNEAK OFF BEFORE THE BIG GOOD-BYE.
HAVE A LAST NIGHT THAT ***WASN'T.***

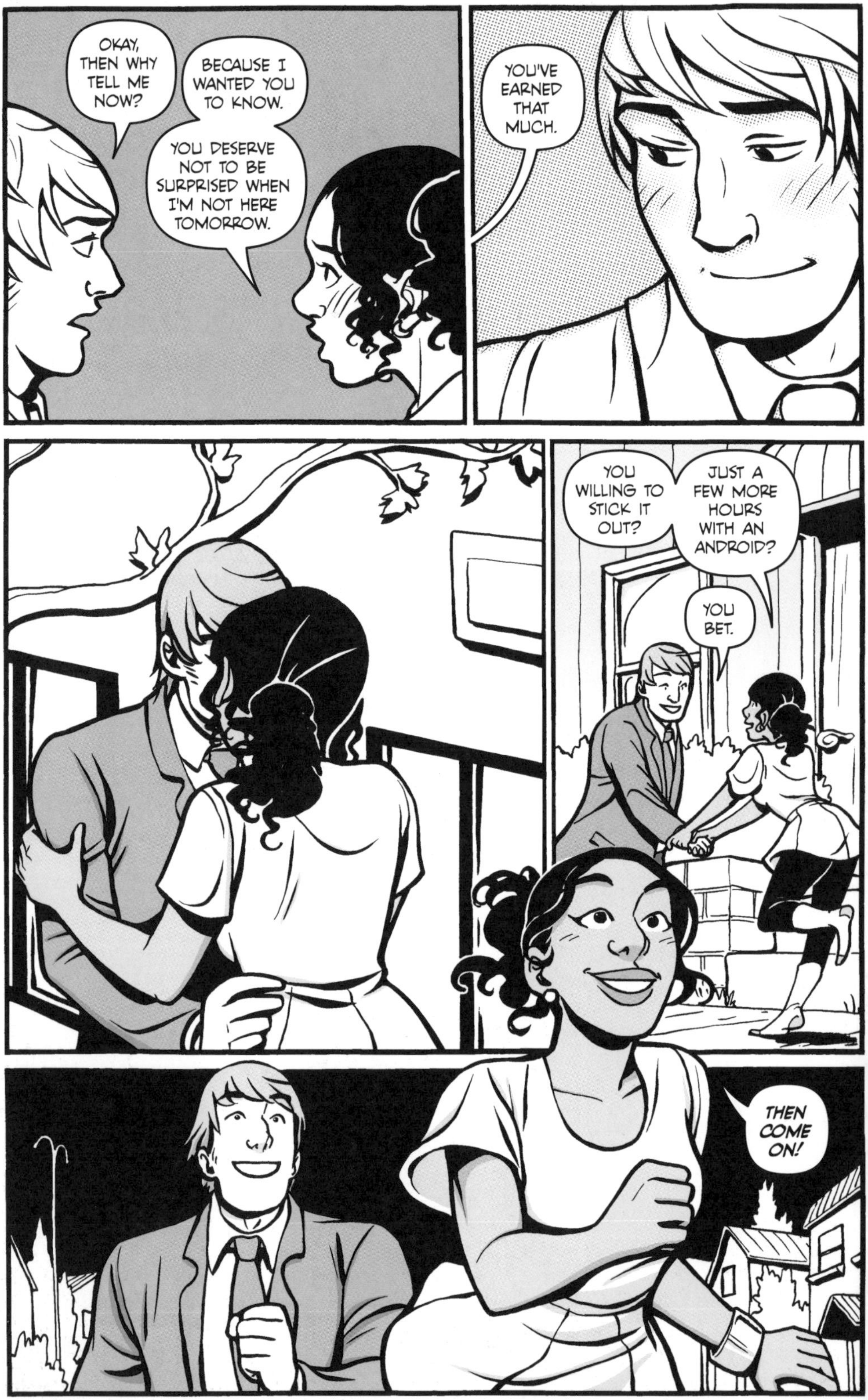
OKAY, THEN WHY TELL ME NOW?
BECAUSE I WANTED YOU TO KNOW.
YOU DESERVE NOT TO BE SURPRISED WHEN I'M NOT HERE TOMORROW.
YOU'VE EARNED THAT MUCH.
YOU WILLING TO STICK IT OUT?
JUST A FEW MORE HOURS WITH AN ANDROID?
YOU BET.
THEN COME ON!

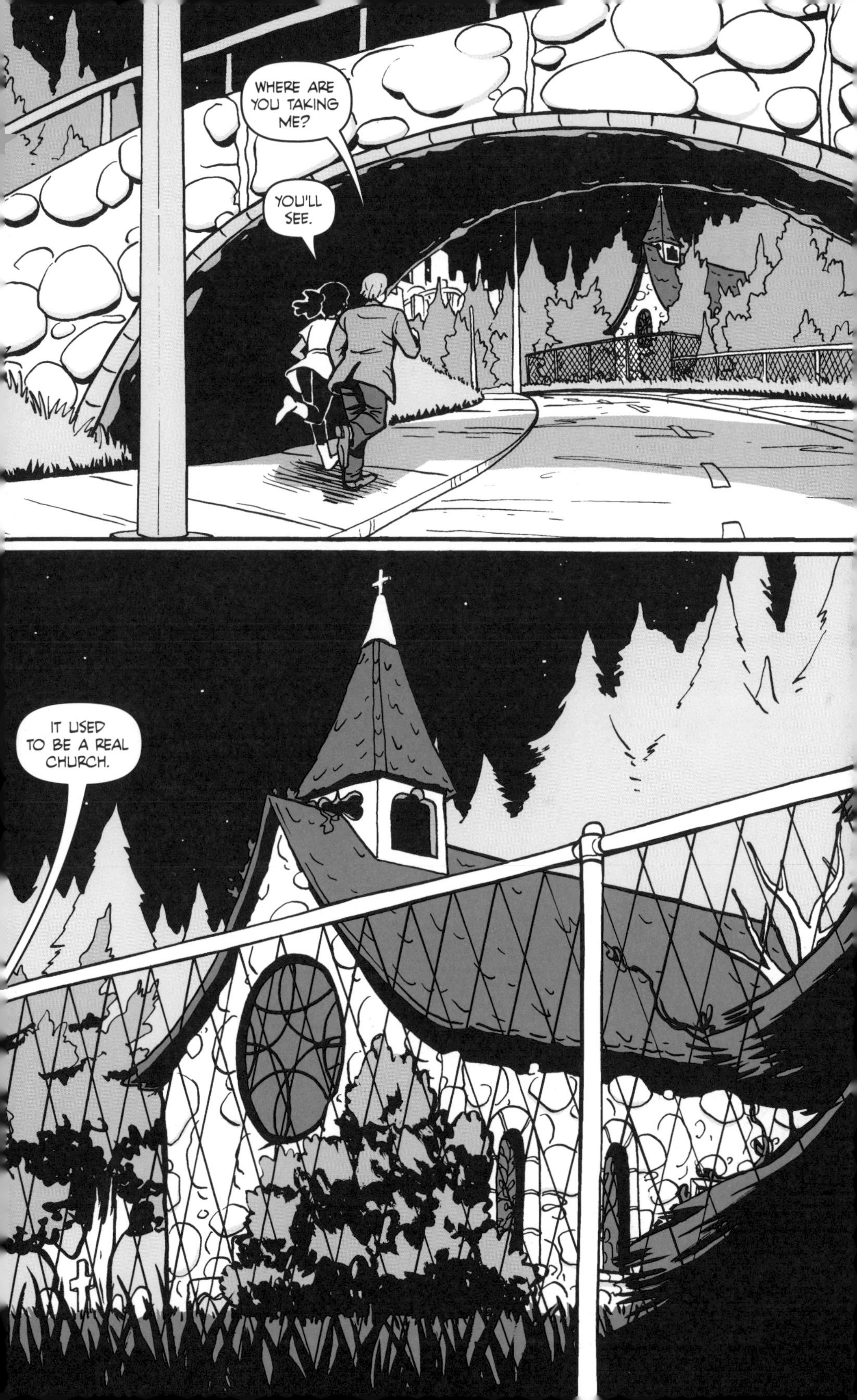
WHERE ARE YOU TAKING ME?
YOU'LL SEE.
IT USED TO BE A REAL CHURCH.

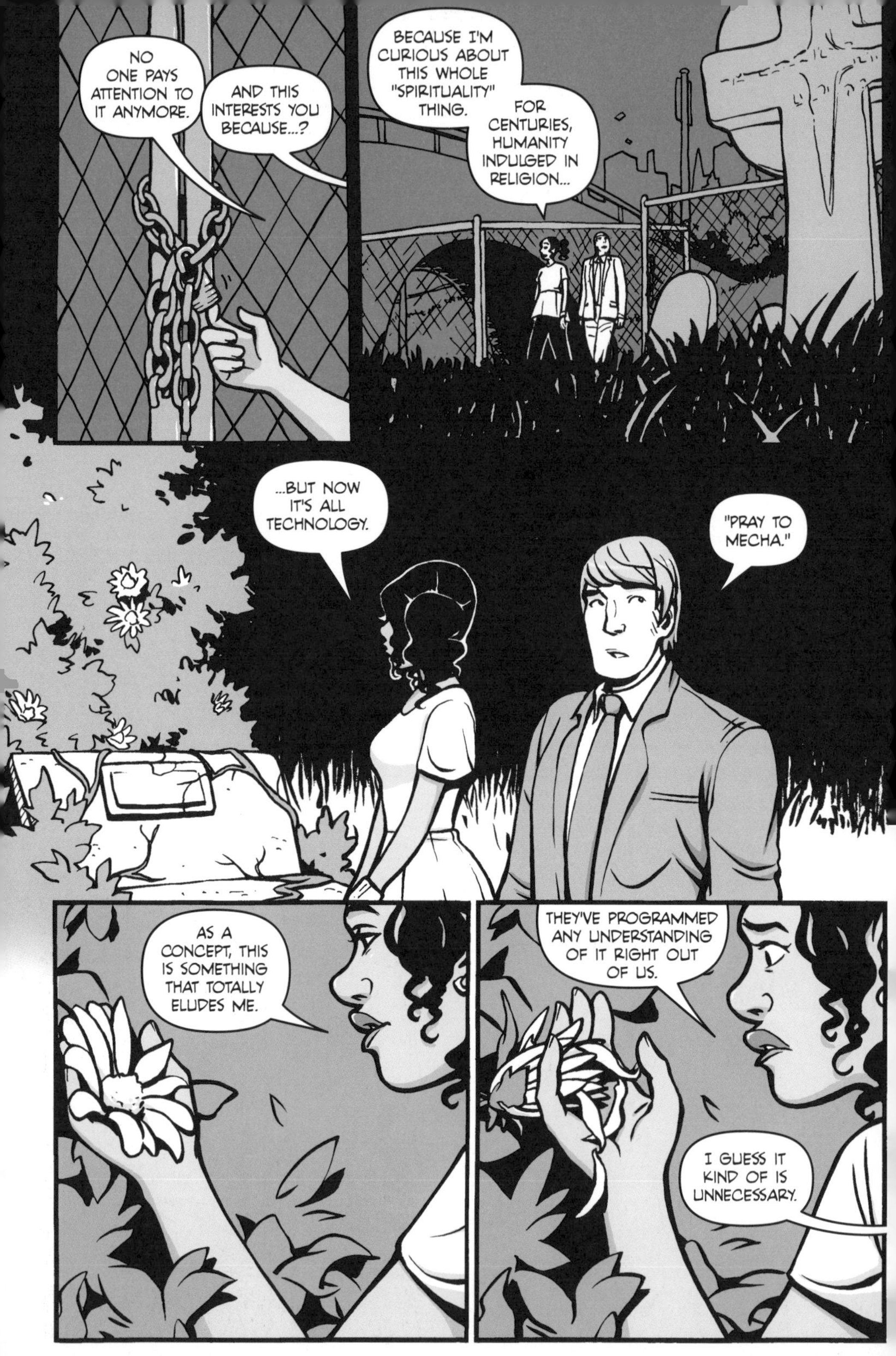
NO ONE PAYS ATTENTION TO IT ANYMORE.
AND THIS INTERESTS YOU BECAUSE...?
BECAUSE I'M CURIOUS ABOUT THIS WHOLE "SPIRITUALITY" THING.
FOR CENTURIES, HUMANITY INDULGED IN RELIGION...
...BUT NOW IT'S ALL TECHNOLOGY.
"PRAY TO MECHA."
AS A CONCEPT, THIS IS SOMETHING THAT TOTALLY ELUDES ME.
THEY'VE PROGRAMMED ANY UNDERSTANDING OF IT RIGHT OUT OF US.
I GUESS IT KIND OF IS UNNECESSARY.

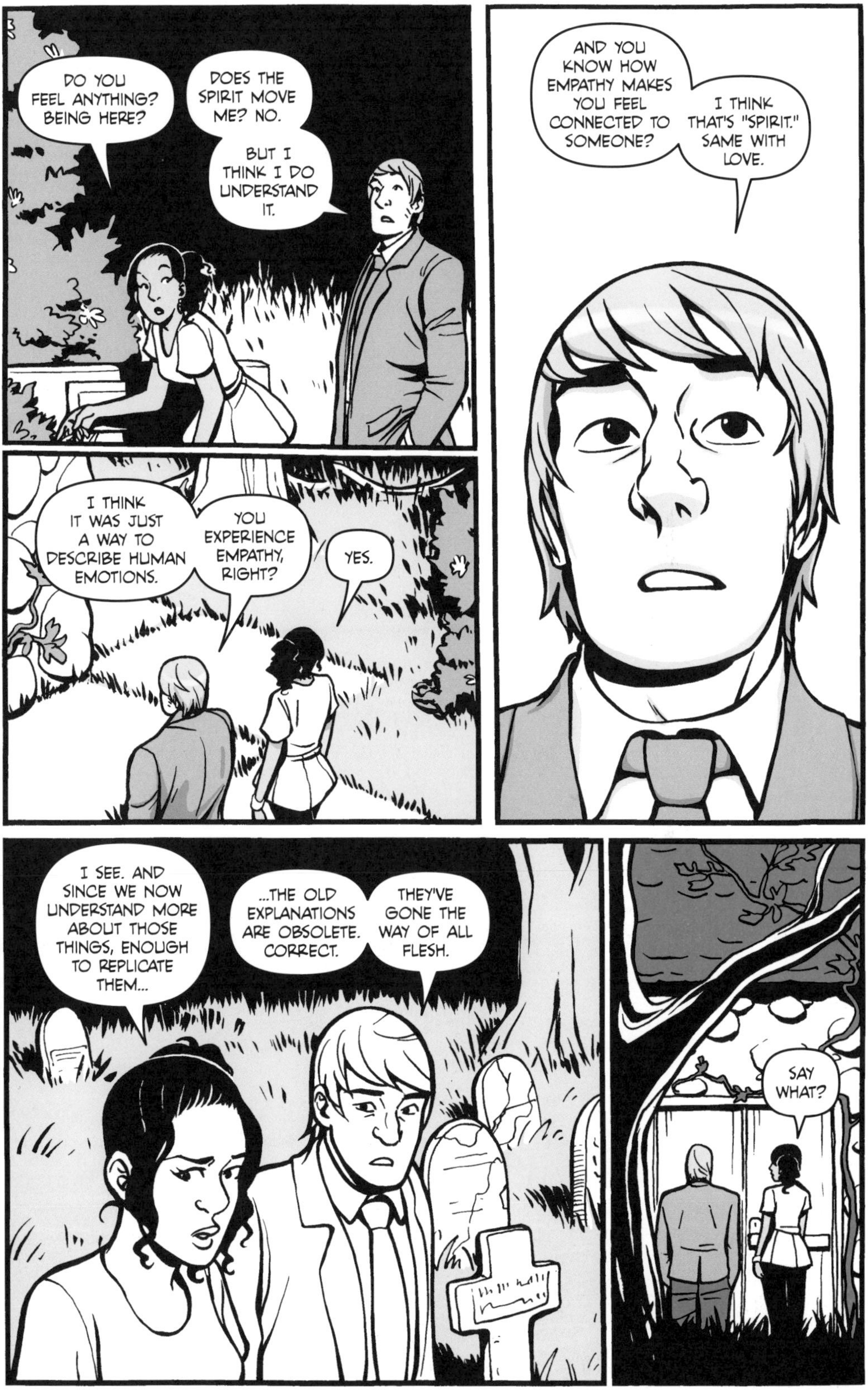
DO YOU FEEL ANYTHING? BEING HERE?
DOES THE SPIRIT MOVE ME? NO.
BUT I THINK I DO UNDERSTAND IT.
AND YOU KNOW HOW EMPATHY MAKES YOU FEEL CONNECTED TO SOMEONE?
I THINK THAT'S "SPIRIT." SAME WITH LOVE.
I THINK IT WAS JUST A WAY TO DESCRIBE HUMAN EMOTIONS.
YOU EXPERIENCE EMPATHY, RIGHT?
YES.
I SEE. AND SINCE WE NOW UNDERSTAND MORE ABOUT THOSE THINGS, ENOUGH TO REPLICATE THEM...
...THE OLD EXPLANATIONS ARE OBSOLETE. CORRECT.
THEY'VE GONE THE WAY OF ALL FLESH.
SAY WHAT?

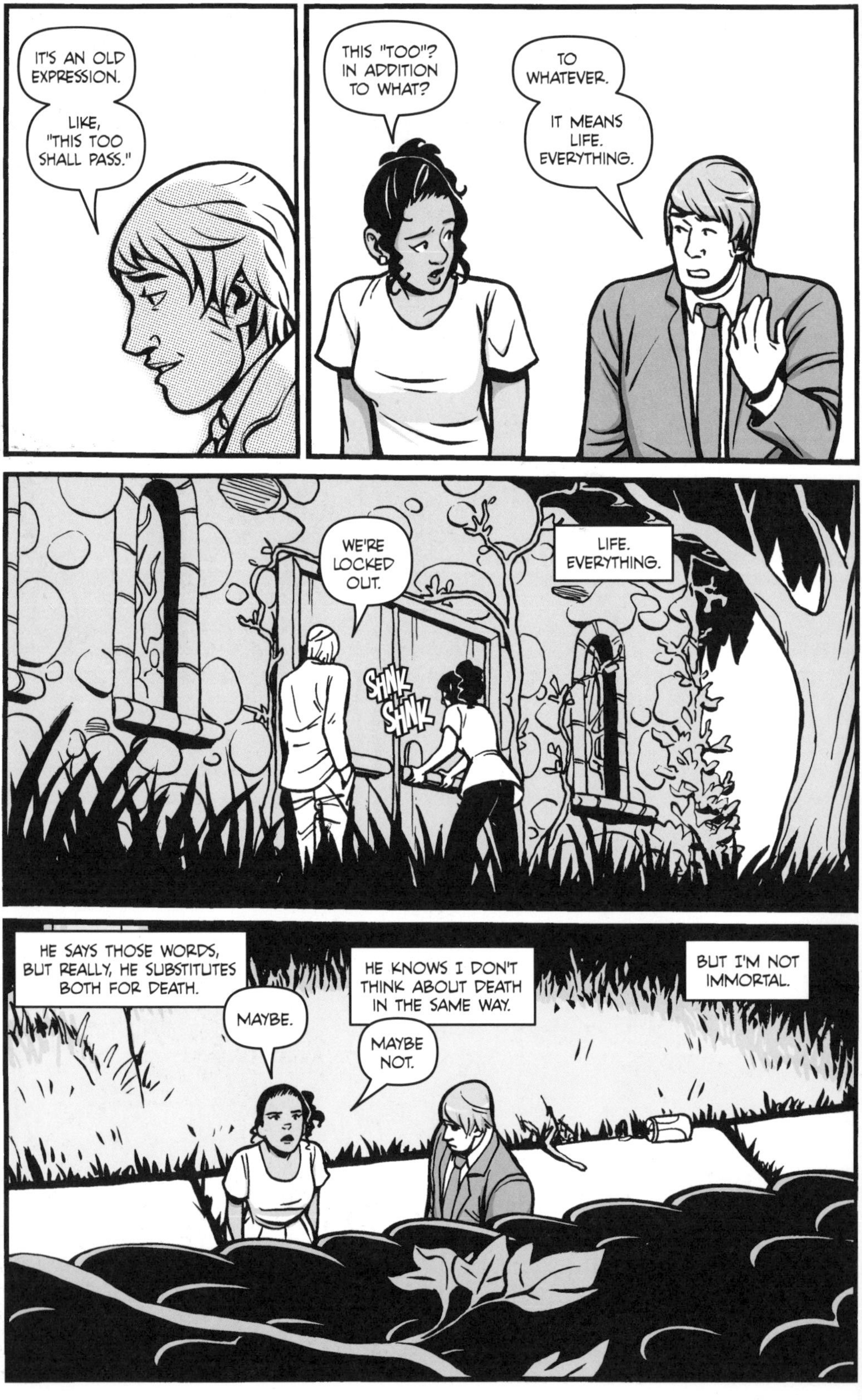
IT'S AN OLD EXPRESSION.
LIKE, "THIS TOO SHALL PASS."
THIS "TOO"? IN ADDITION TO WHAT?
TO WHATEVER.
IT MEANS LIFE. EVERYTHING.
WE'RE LOCKED OUT.
LIFE. EVERYTHING.
SHINK SHINK
HE SAYS THOSE WORDS, BUT REALLY, HE SUBSTITUTES BOTH FOR DEATH.
MAYBE.
HE KNOWS I DON'T THINK ABOUT DEATH IN THE SAME WAY.
MAYBE NOT.
BUT I'M NOT IMMORTAL.

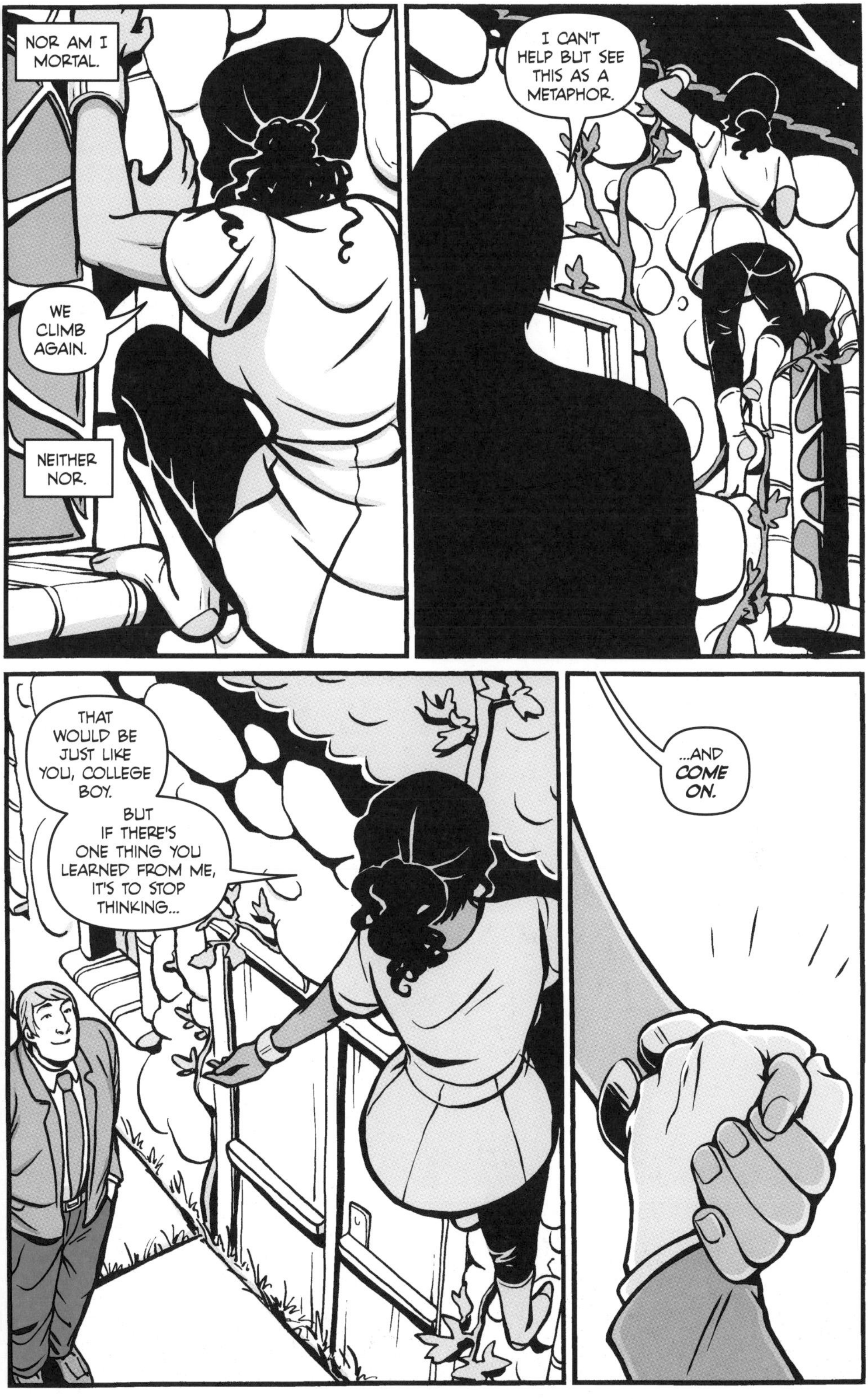
NOR AM I MORTAL.
WE CLIMB AGAIN.
NEITHER NOR.
I CAN'T HELP BUT SEE THIS AS A METAPHOR.
THAT WOULD BE JUST LIKE YOU, COLLEGE BOY.
BUT IF THERE'S ONE THING YOU LEARNED FROM ME, IT'S TO STOP THINKING...
...AND *COME ON.*

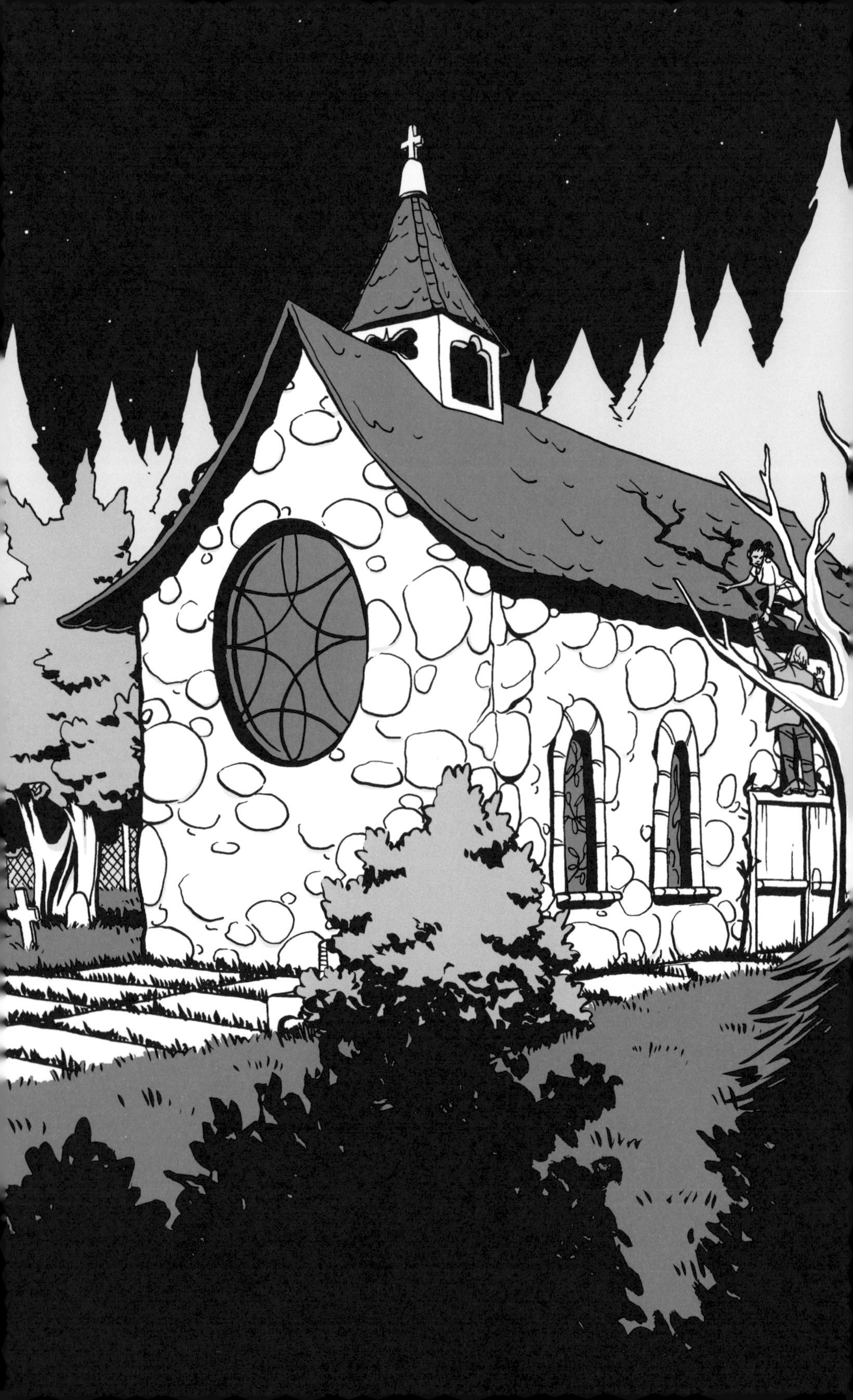

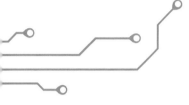

CHAPTER 10:
HIM

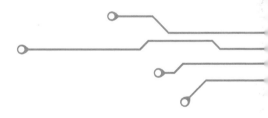

CLOSER

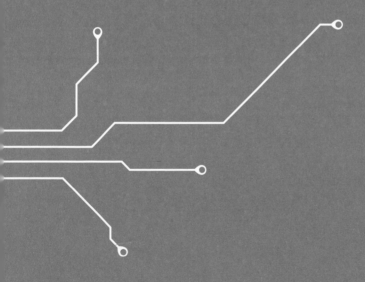

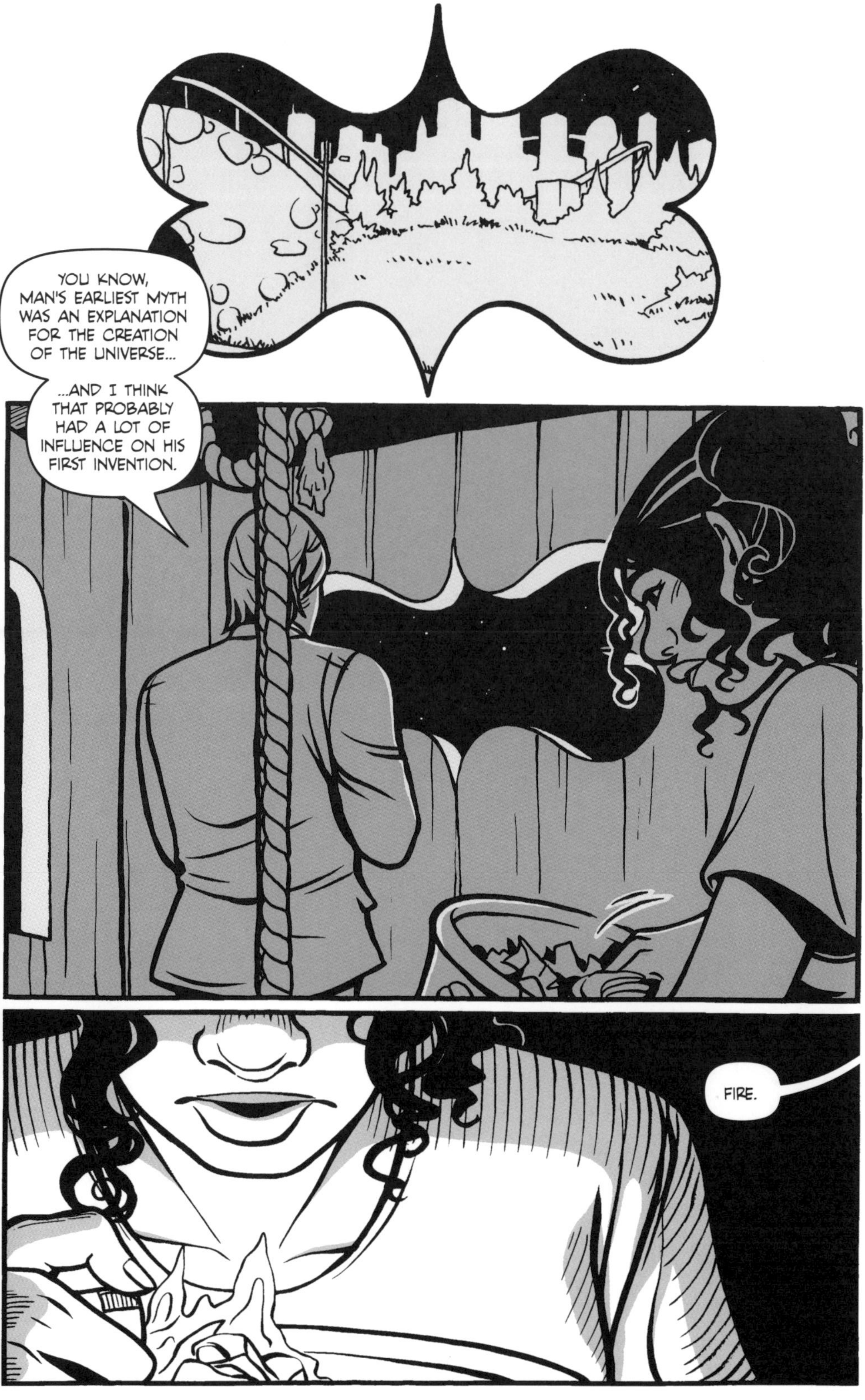
YOU KNOW, MAN'S EARLIEST MYTH WAS AN EXPLANATION FOR THE CREATION OF THE UNIVERSE...
...AND I THINK THAT PROBABLY HAD A LOT OF INFLUENCE ON HIS FIRST INVENTION.
FIRE.

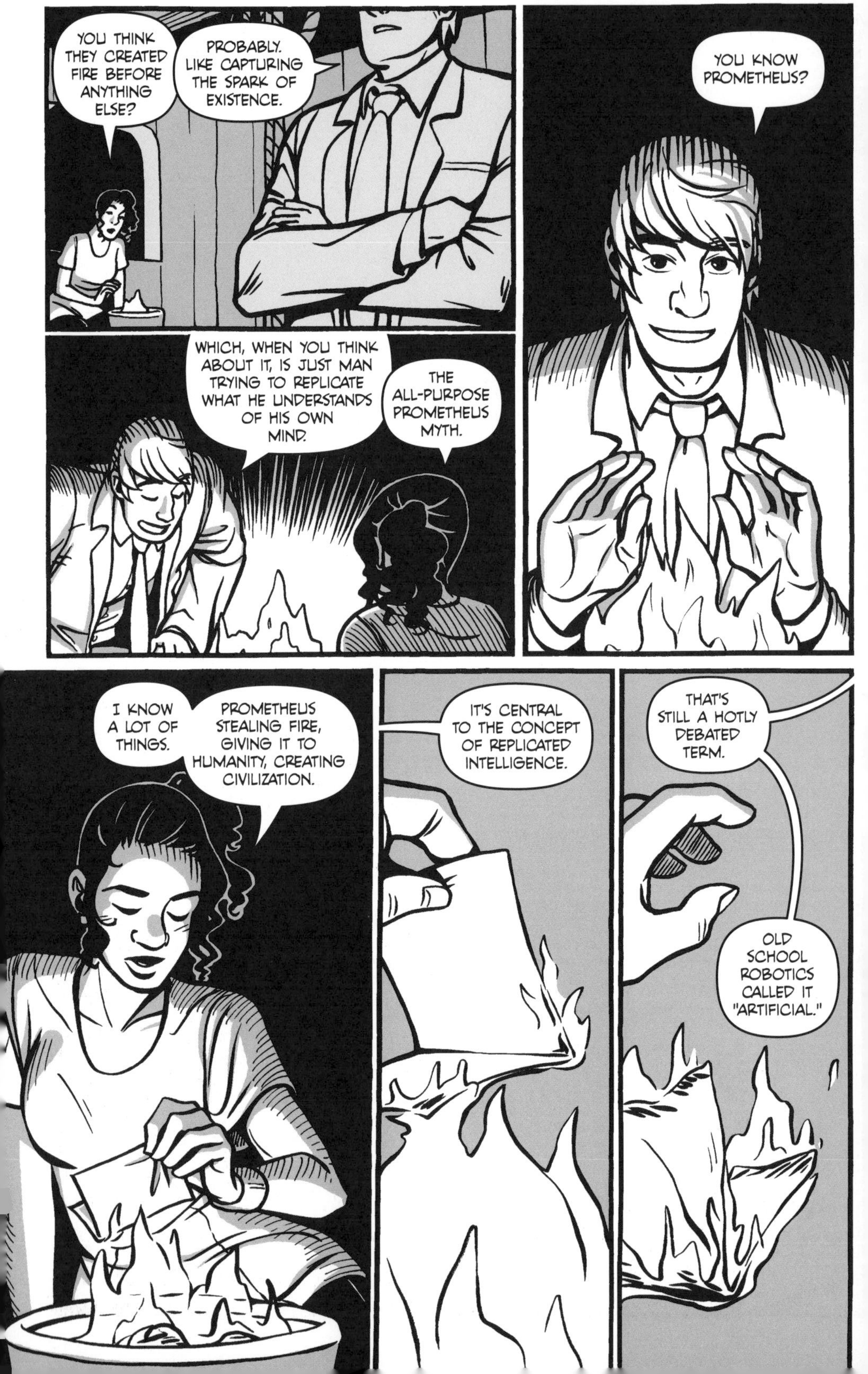
YOU THINK THEY CREATED FIRE BEFORE ANYTHING ELSE?
PROBABLY. LIKE CAPTURING THE SPARK OF EXISTENCE.
YOU KNOW PROMETHEUS?
WHICH, WHEN YOU THINK ABOUT IT, IS JUST MAN TRYING TO REPLICATE WHAT HE UNDERSTANDS OF HIS OWN MIND.
THE ALL-PURPOSE PROMETHEUS MYTH.
I KNOW A LOT OF THINGS.
PROMETHEUS STEALING FIRE, GIVING IT TO HUMANITY, CREATING CIVILIZATION.
IT'S CENTRAL TO THE CONCEPT OF REPLICATED INTELLIGENCE.
THAT'S STILL A HOTLY DEBATED TERM.
OLD SCHOOL ROBOTICS CALLED IT "ARTIFICIAL."

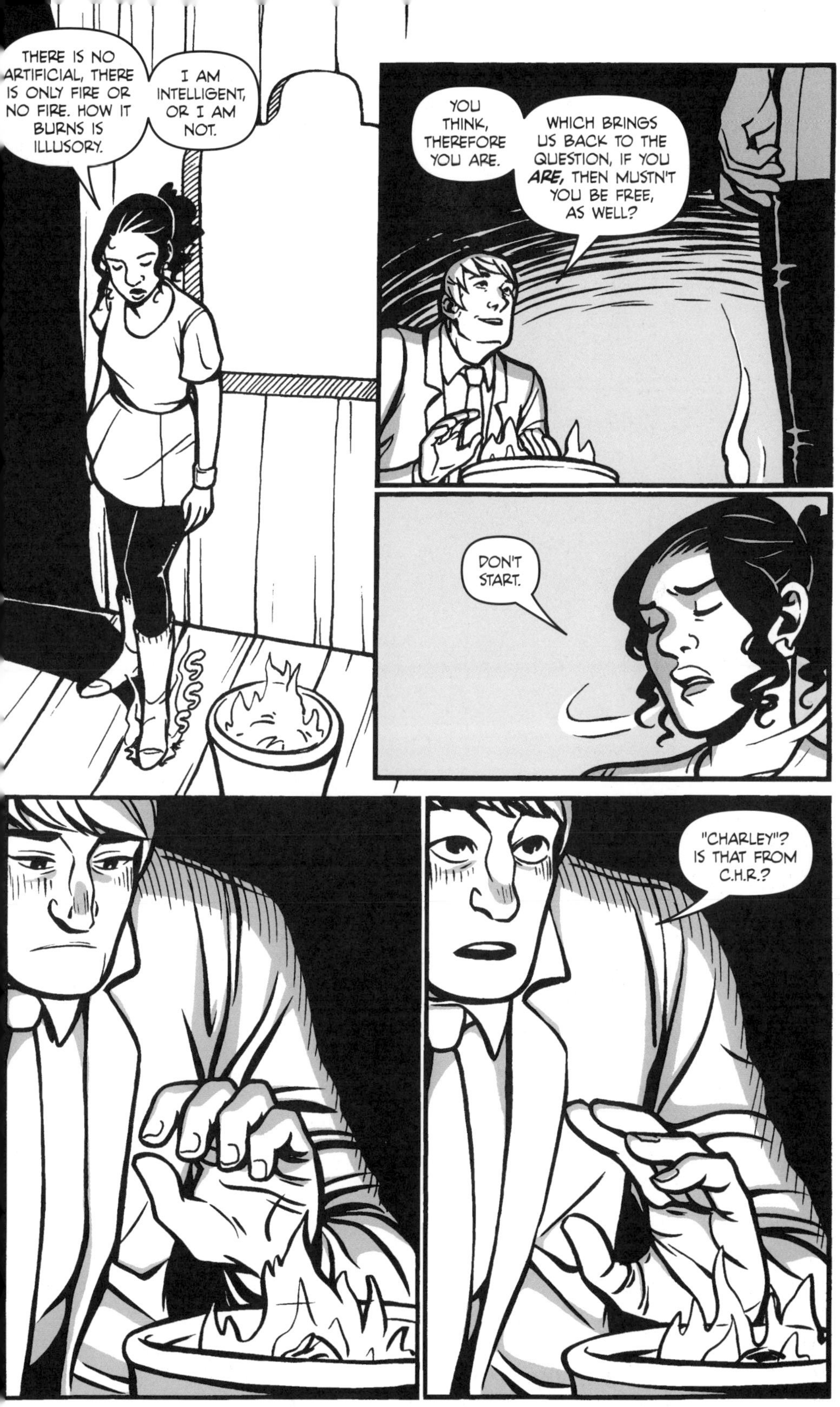
THERE IS NO ARTIFICIAL, THERE IS ONLY FIRE OR NO FIRE. HOW IT BURNS IS ILLUSORY.
I AM INTELLIGENT, OR I AM NOT.
YOU THINK, THEREFORE YOU ARE.
WHICH BRINGS US BACK TO THE QUESTION, IF YOU *ARE,* THEN MUSTN'T YOU BE FREE, AS WELL?
DON'T START.
"CHARLEY"? IS THAT FROM C.H.R.?

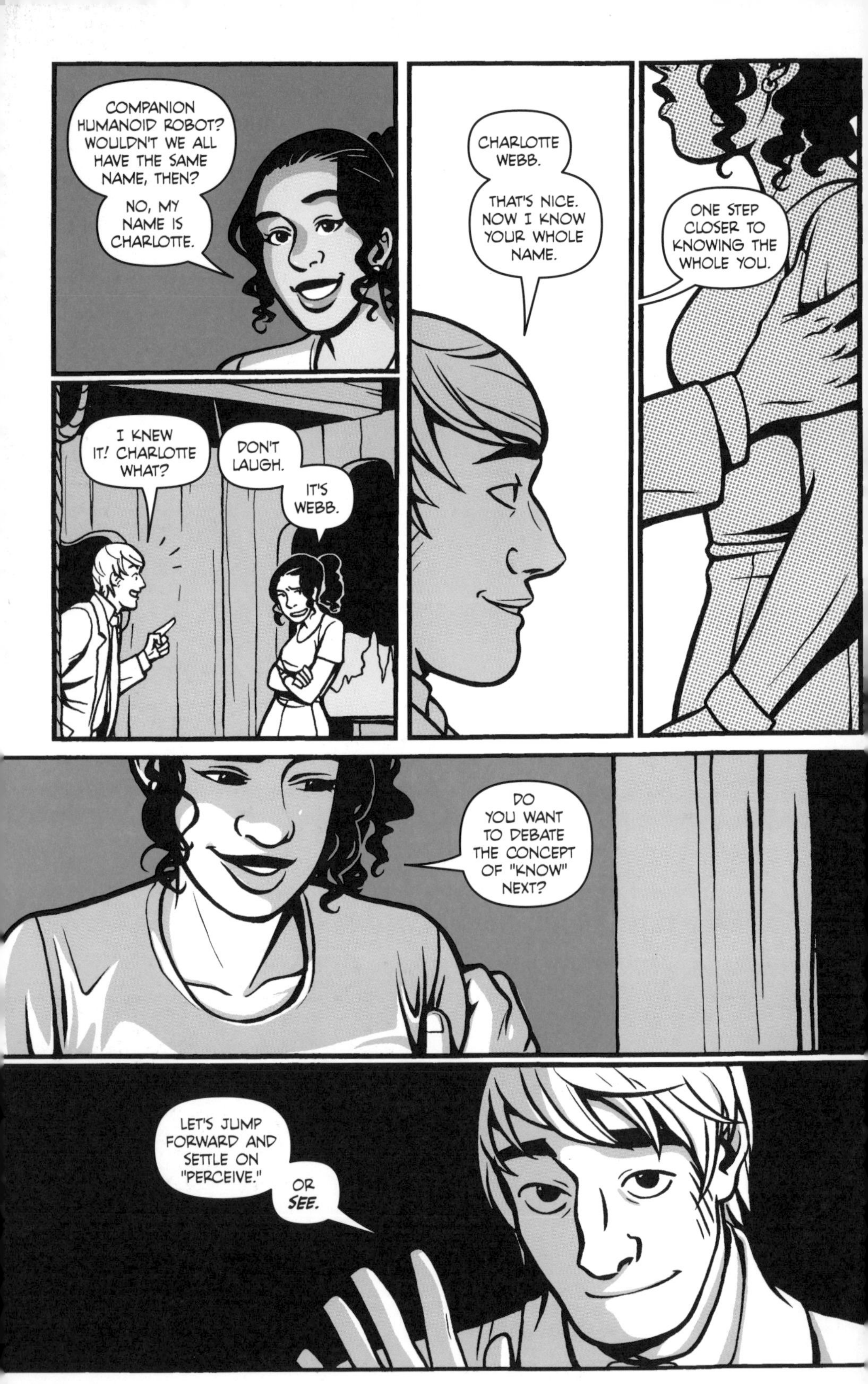
COMPANION HUMANOID ROBOT? WOULDN'T WE ALL HAVE THE SAME NAME, THEN?
NO, MY NAME IS CHARLOTTE.
I KNEW IT! CHARLOTTE WHAT?
DON'T LAUGH.
IT'S WEBB.
CHARLOTTE WEBB.
THAT'S NICE. NOW I KNOW YOUR WHOLE NAME.
ONE STEP CLOSER TO KNOWING THE WHOLE YOU.
DO YOU WANT TO DEBATE THE CONCEPT OF "KNOW" NEXT?
LET'S JUMP FORWARD AND SETTLE ON "PERCEIVE."
OR *SEE*.

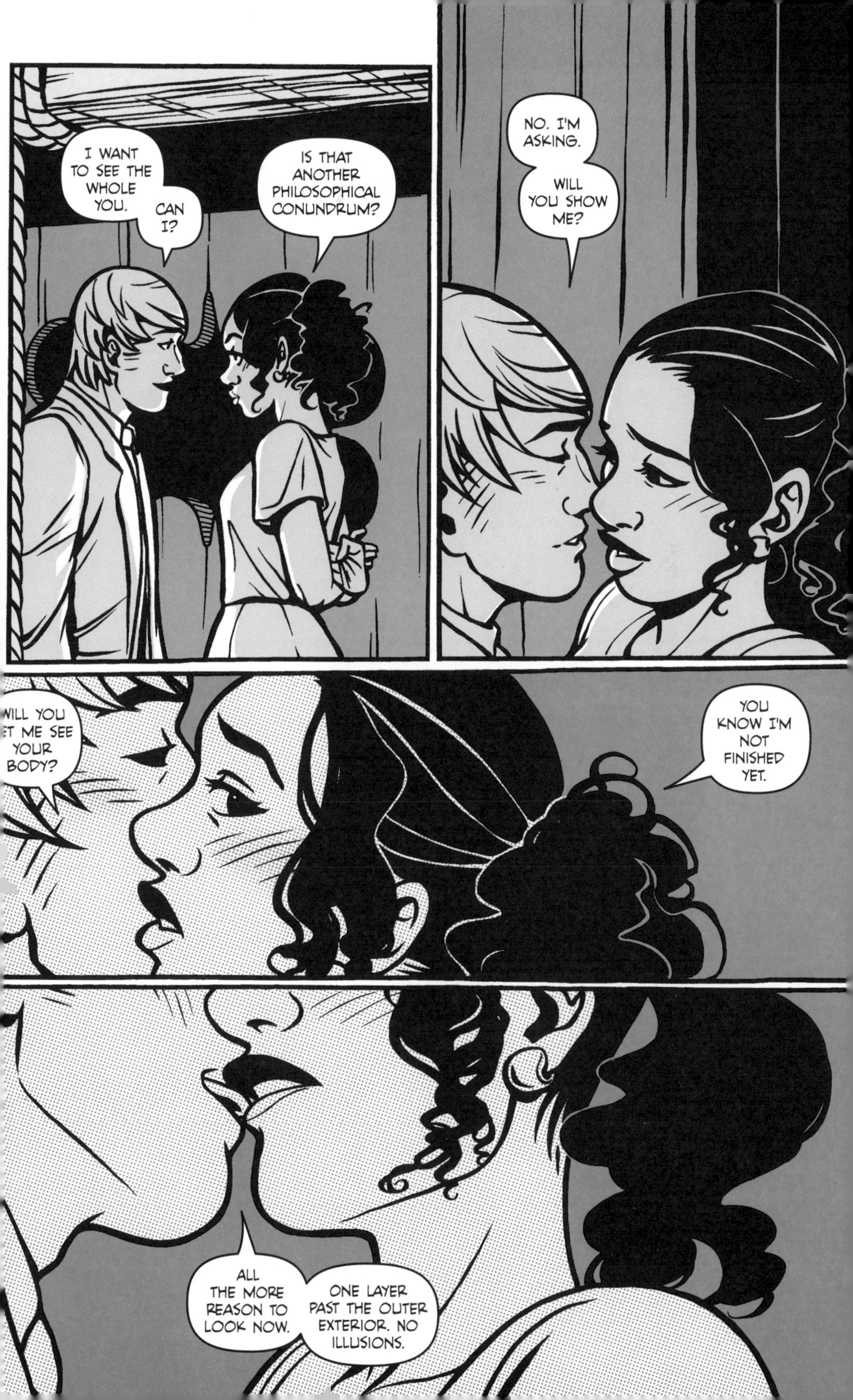
I WANT TO SEE THE WHOLE YOU.
CAN I?
IS THAT ANOTHER PHILOSOPHICAL CONUNDRUM?
NO. I'M ASKING.
WILL YOU SHOW ME?
WILL YOU
T ME SEE YOUR BODY?
YOU KNOW I'M NOT FINISHED YET.
ALL THE MORE REASON TO LOOK NOW.
ONE LAYER PAST THE OUTER EXTERIOR. NO ILLUSIONS.

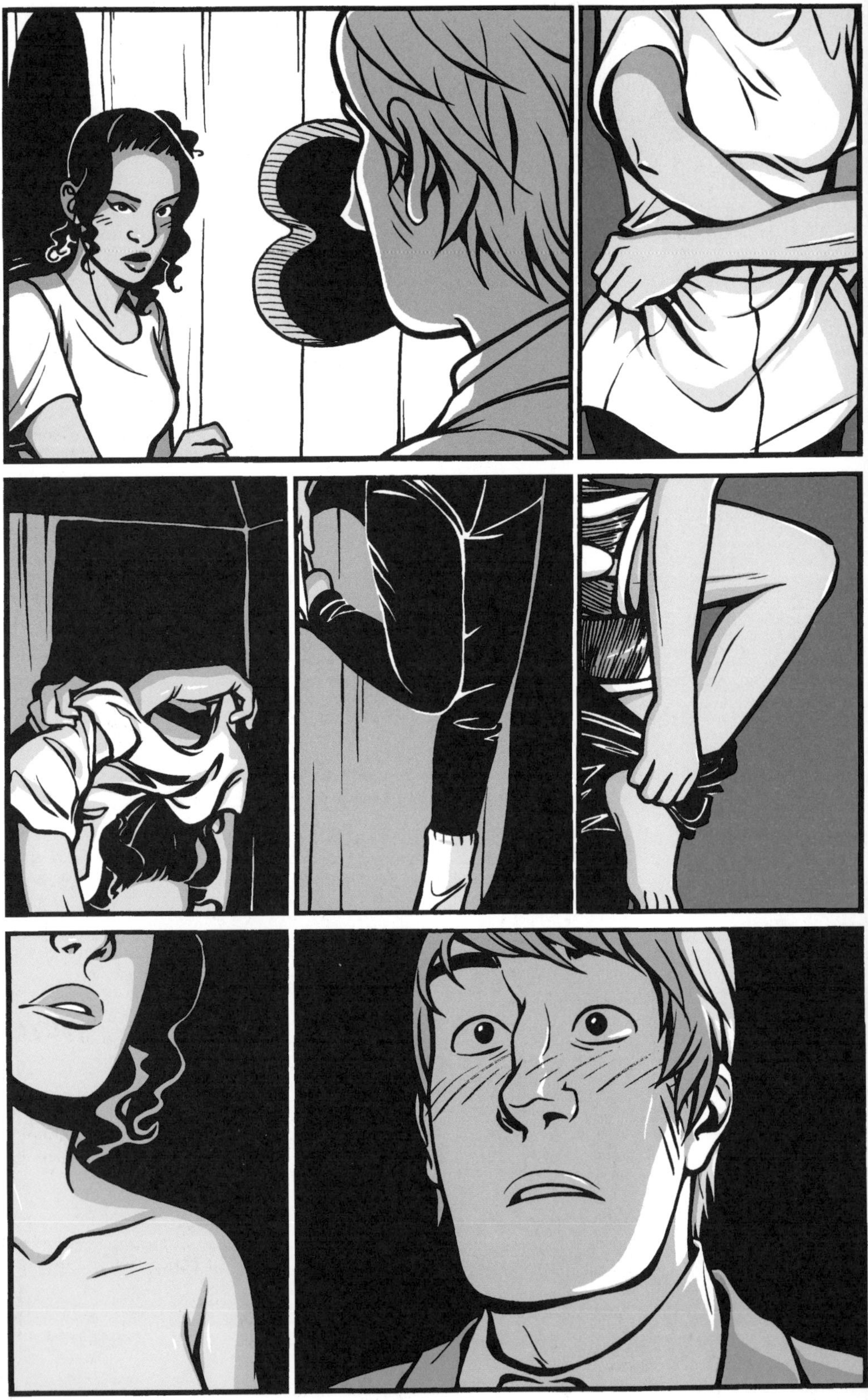

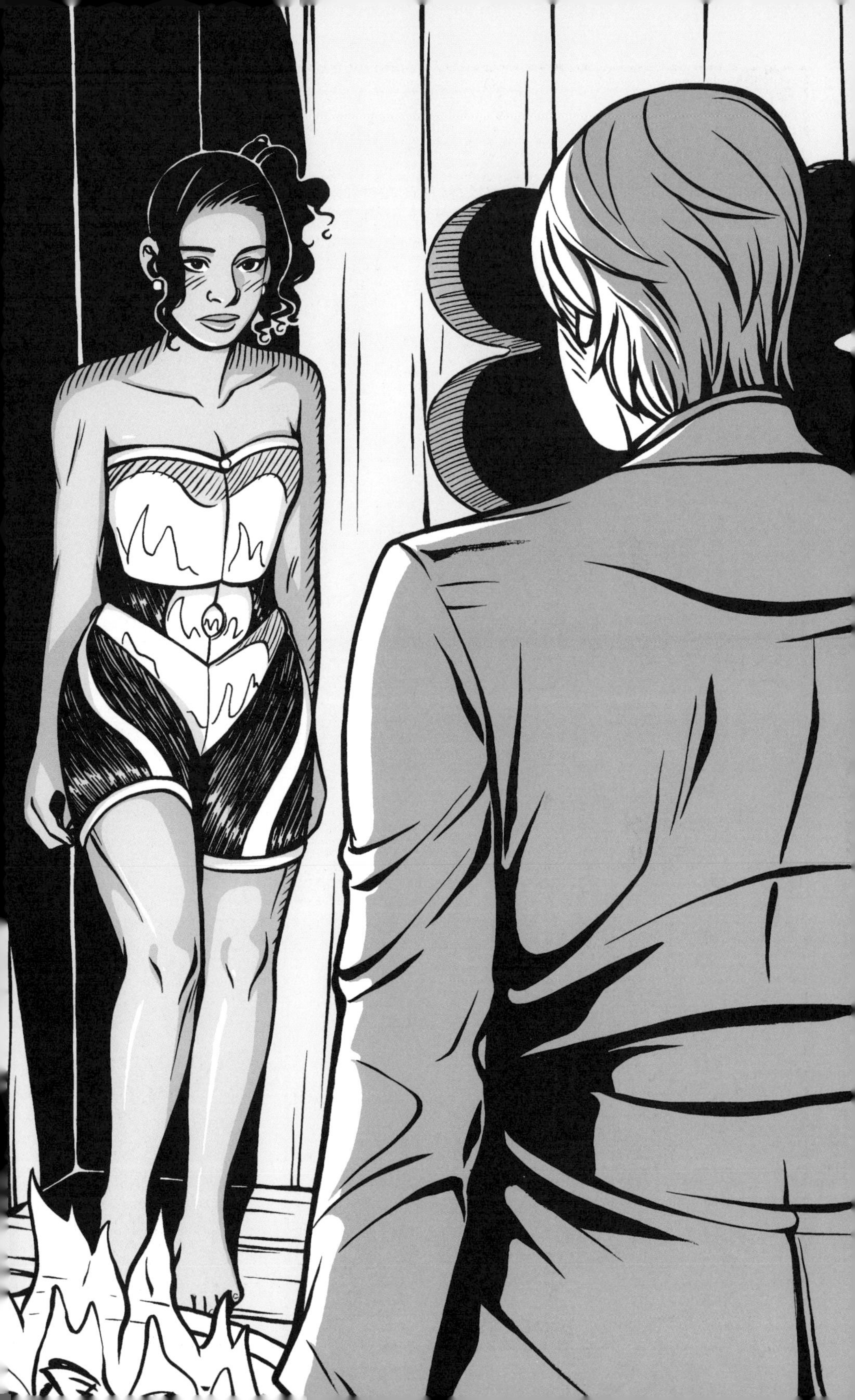

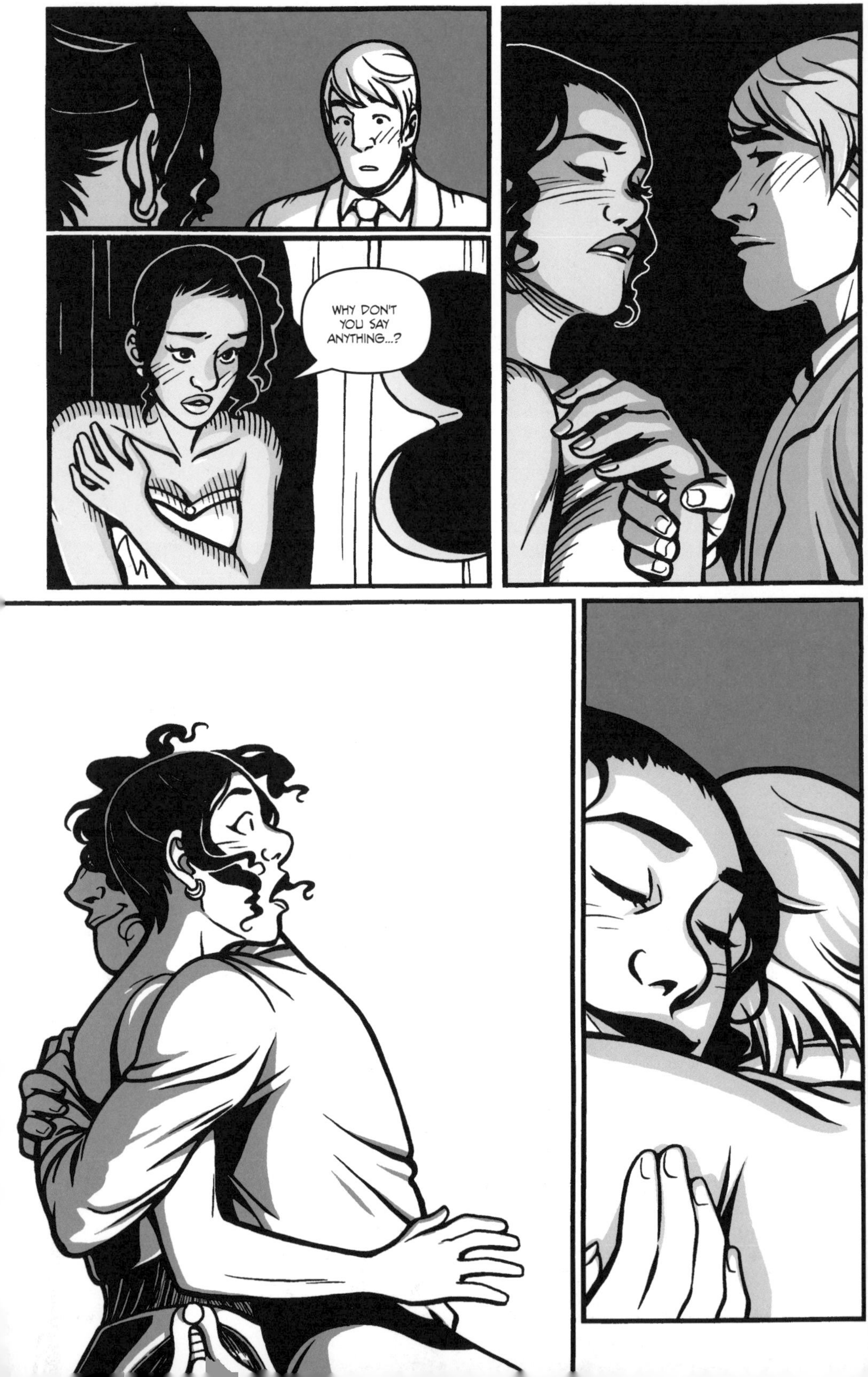
WHY DON'T YOU SAY ANYTHING...?

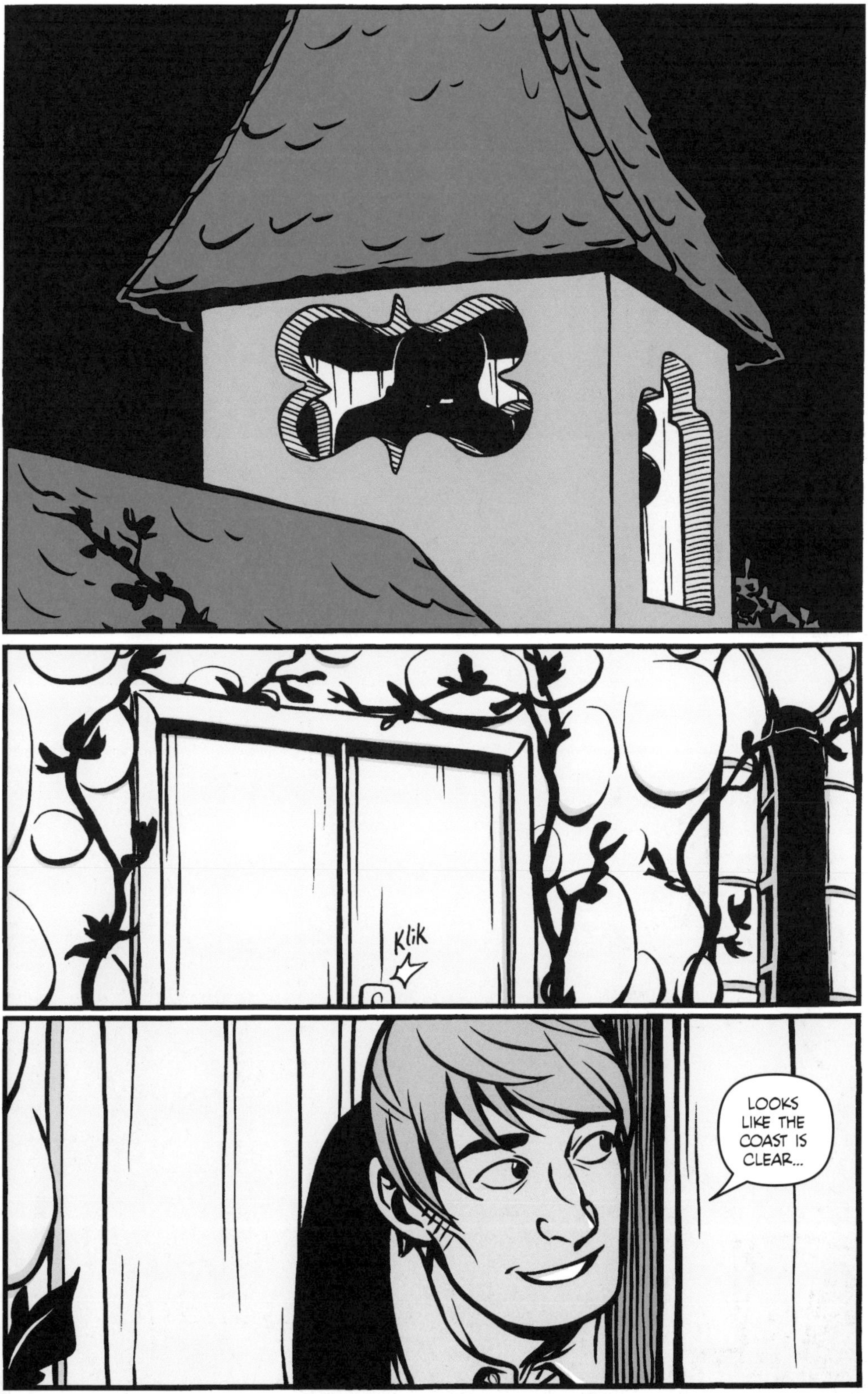
Klik
LOOKS LIKE THE COAST IS CLEAR...

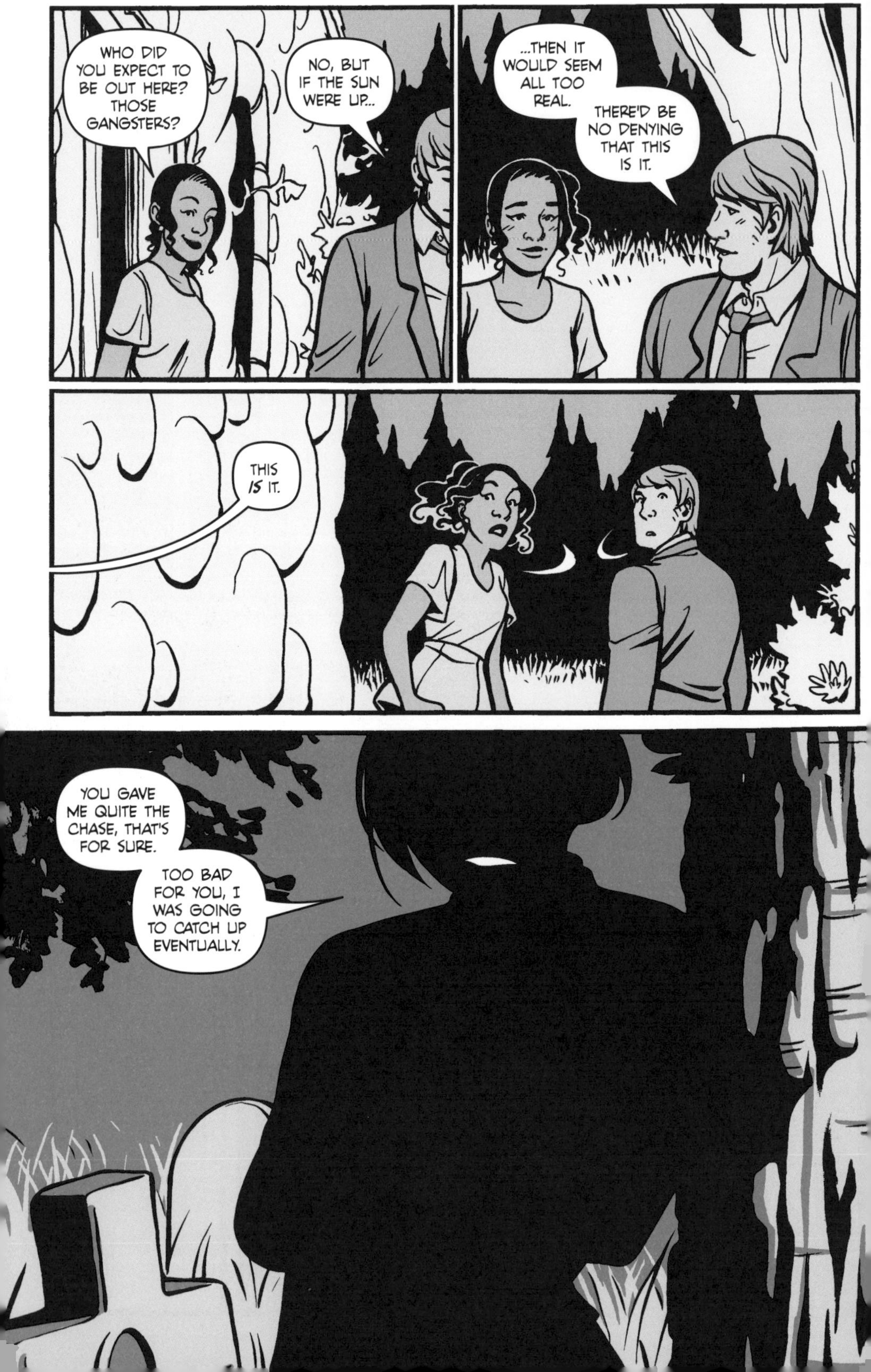
WHO DID YOU EXPECT TO BE OUT HERE? THOSE GANGSTERS?
NO, BUT IF THE SUN WERE UP...
...THEN IT WOULD SEEM ALL TOO REAL.
THERE'D BE NO DENYING THAT THIS IS IT.
THIS *IS* IT.
YOU GAVE ME QUITE THE CHASE, THAT'S FOR SURE.
TOO BAD FOR YOU, I WAS GOING TO CATCH UP EVENTUALLY.

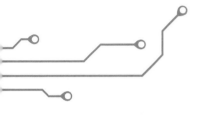

CHAPTER 11:

TWO HEARTS AT ¾ TIME

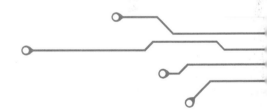

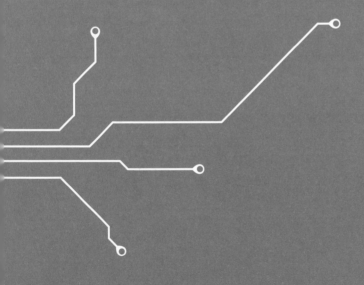

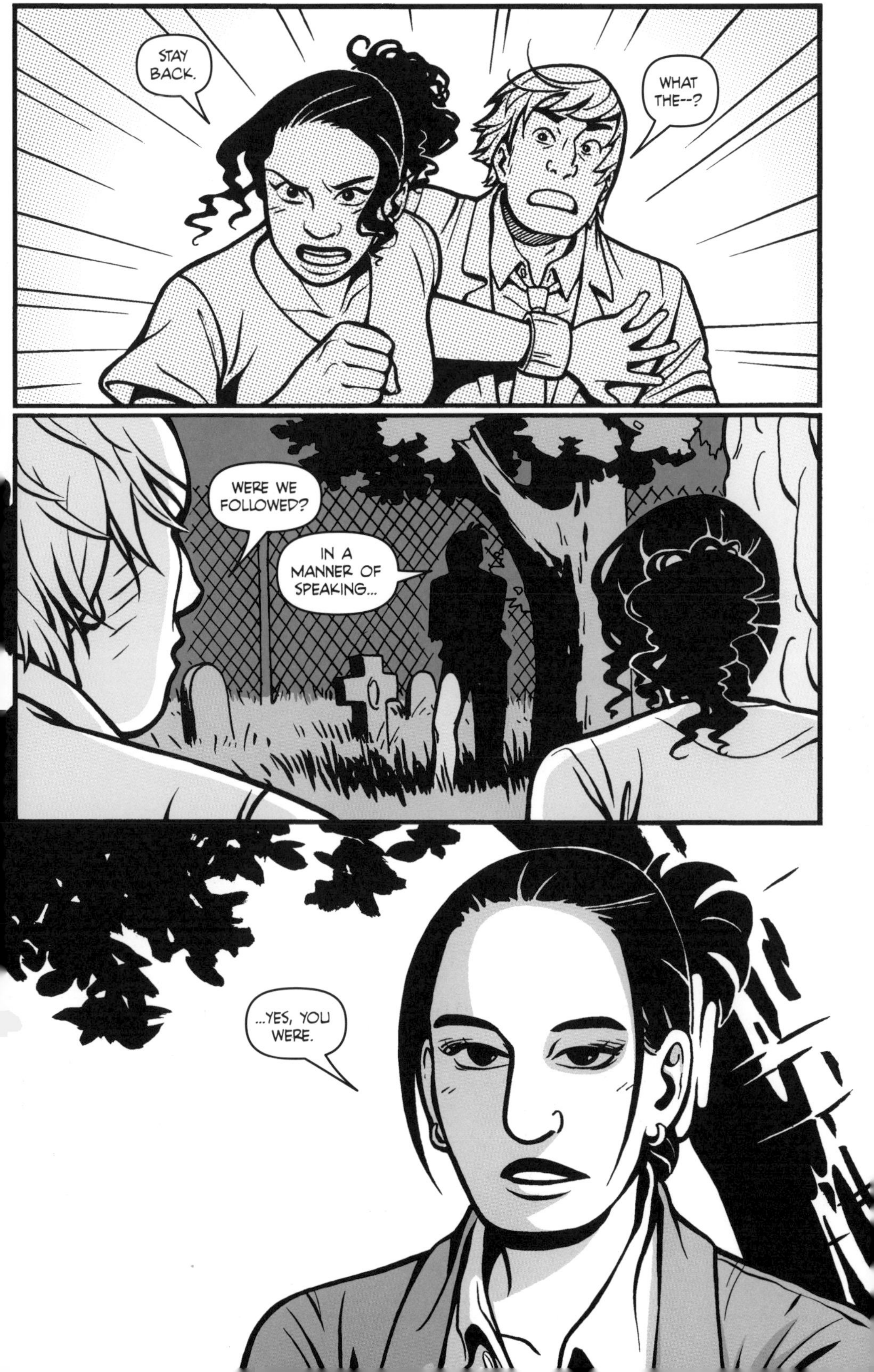
STAY BACK.
WHAT THE--?
WERE WE FOLLOWED?
IN A MANNER OF SPEAKING...
...YES, YOU WERE.

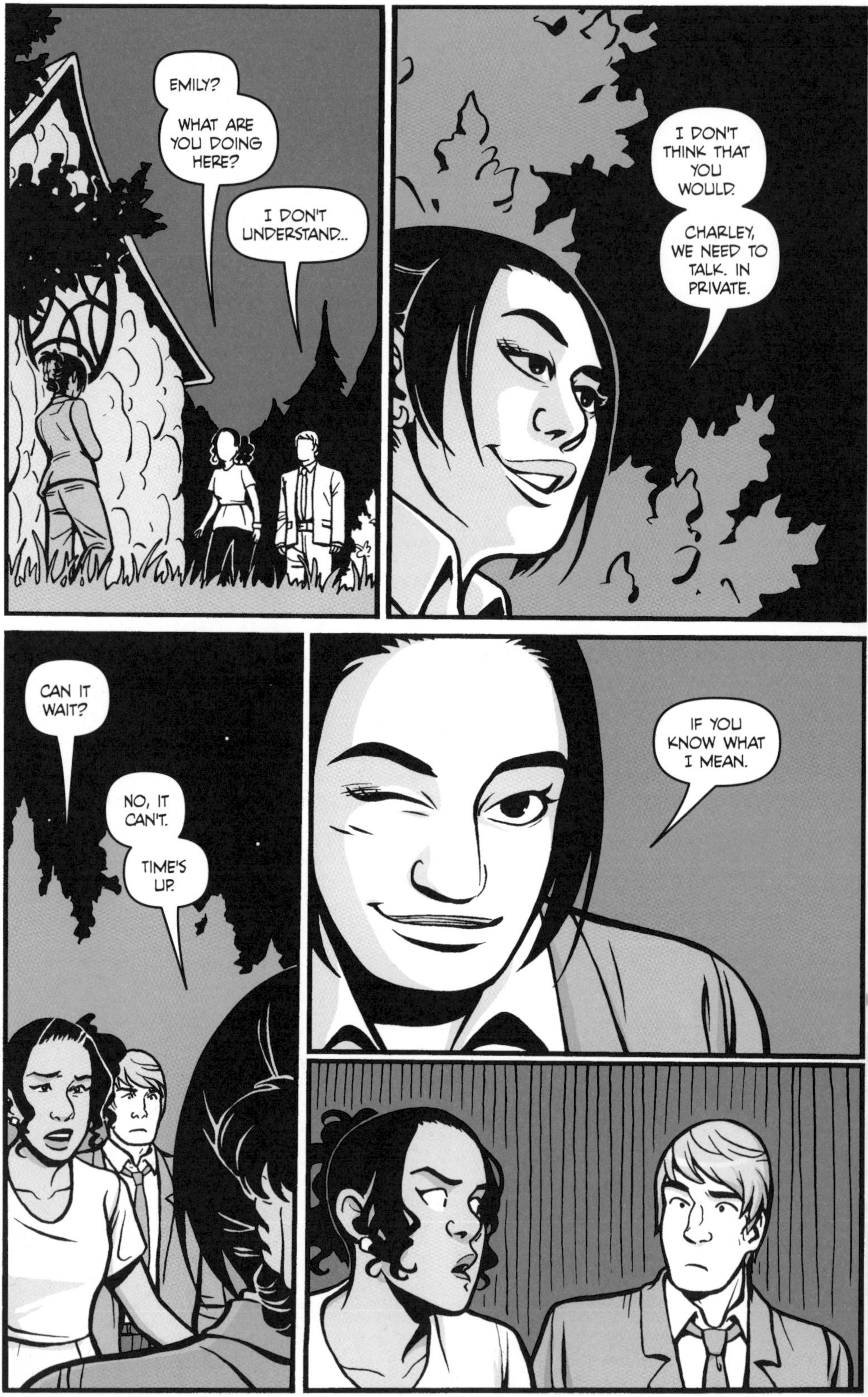
EMILY?
WHAT ARE YOU DOING HERE?
I DON'T UNDERSTAND...
I DON'T THINK THAT YOU WOULD.
CHARLEY, WE NEED TO TALK. IN PRIVATE.
CAN IT WAIT?
NO, IT CAN'T.
TIME'S UP.
IF YOU KNOW WHAT I MEAN.

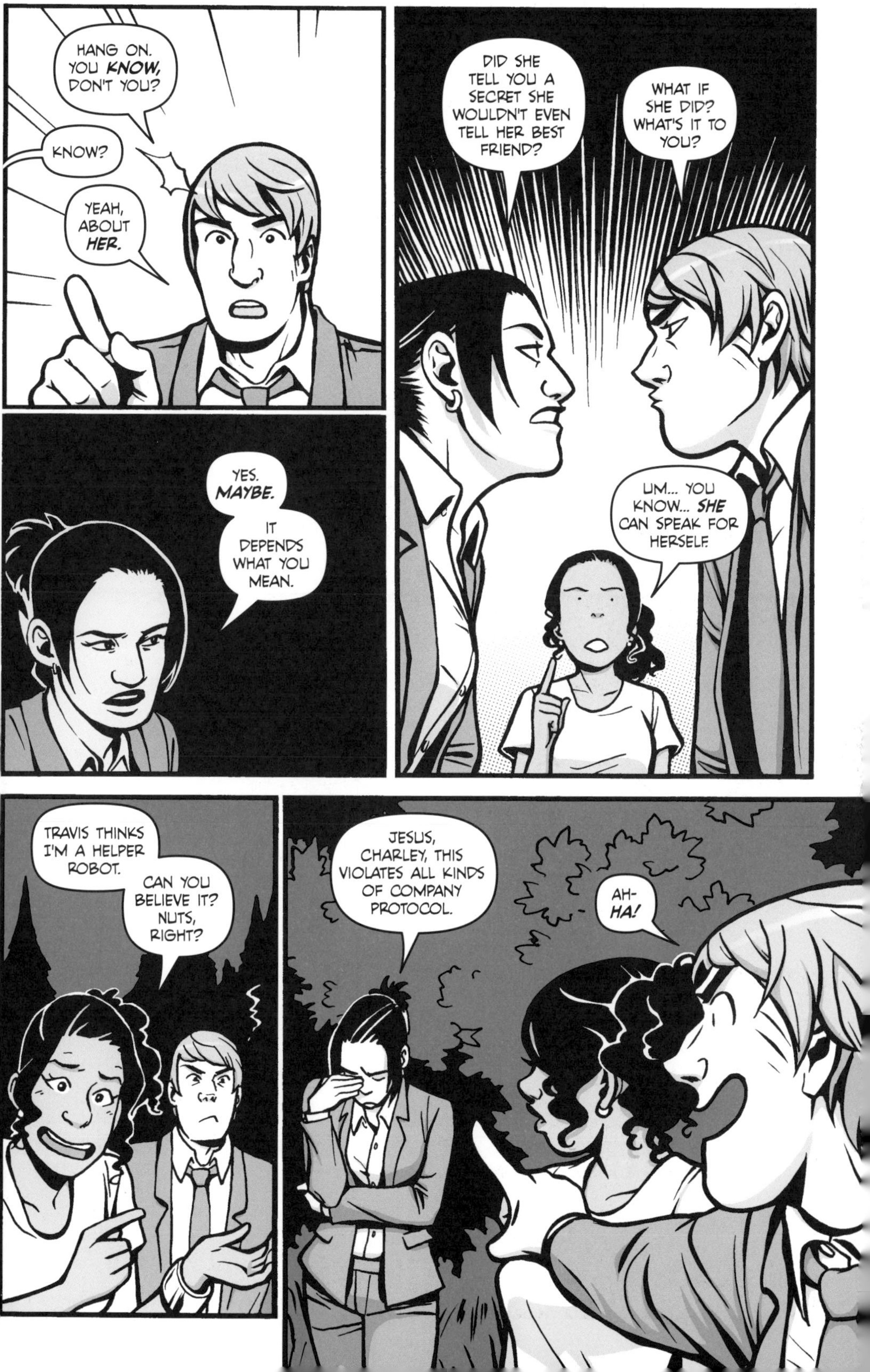
HANG ON. YOU KNOW, DON'T YOU?
KNOW?
YEAH, ABOUT HER.
YES. MAYBE.
IT DEPENDS WHAT YOU MEAN.
DID SHE TELL YOU A SECRET SHE WOULDN'T EVEN TELL HER BEST FRIEND?
WHAT IF SHE DID? WHAT'S IT TO YOU?
UM... YOU KNOW... SHE CAN SPEAK FOR HERSELF.
TRAVIS THINKS I'M A HELPER ROBOT.
CAN YOU BELIEVE IT? NUTS, RIGHT?
JESUS, CHARLEY, THIS VIOLATES ALL KINDS OF COMPANY PROTOCOL.
AH-HA!

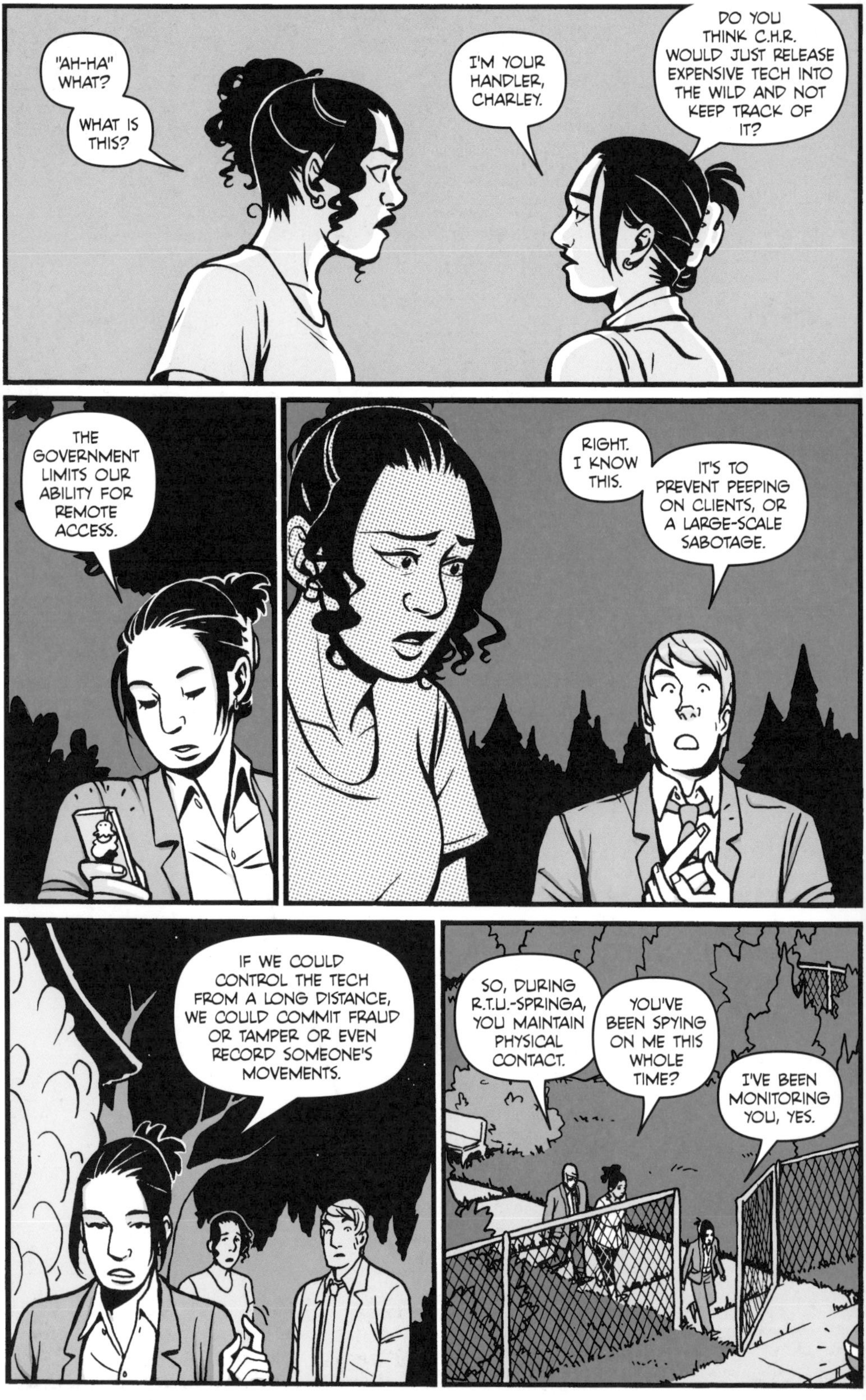
"AH-HA" WHAT?
WHAT IS THIS?
I'M YOUR HANDLER, CHARLEY.
DO YOU THINK C.H.R. WOULD JUST RELEASE EXPENSIVE TECH INTO THE WILD AND NOT KEEP TRACK OF IT?
THE GOVERNMENT LIMITS OUR ABILITY FOR REMOTE ACCESS.
RIGHT. I KNOW THIS.
IT'S TO PREVENT PEEPING ON CLIENTS, OR A LARGE-SCALE SABOTAGE.
IF WE COULD CONTROL THE TECH FROM A LONG DISTANCE, WE COULD COMMIT FRAUD OR TAMPER OR EVEN RECORD SOMEONE'S MOVEMENTS.
SO, DURING R.T.U.-SPRINGA, YOU MAINTAIN PHYSICAL CONTACT.
YOU'VE BEEN SPYING ON ME THIS WHOLE TIME?
I'VE BEEN MONITORING YOU, YES.

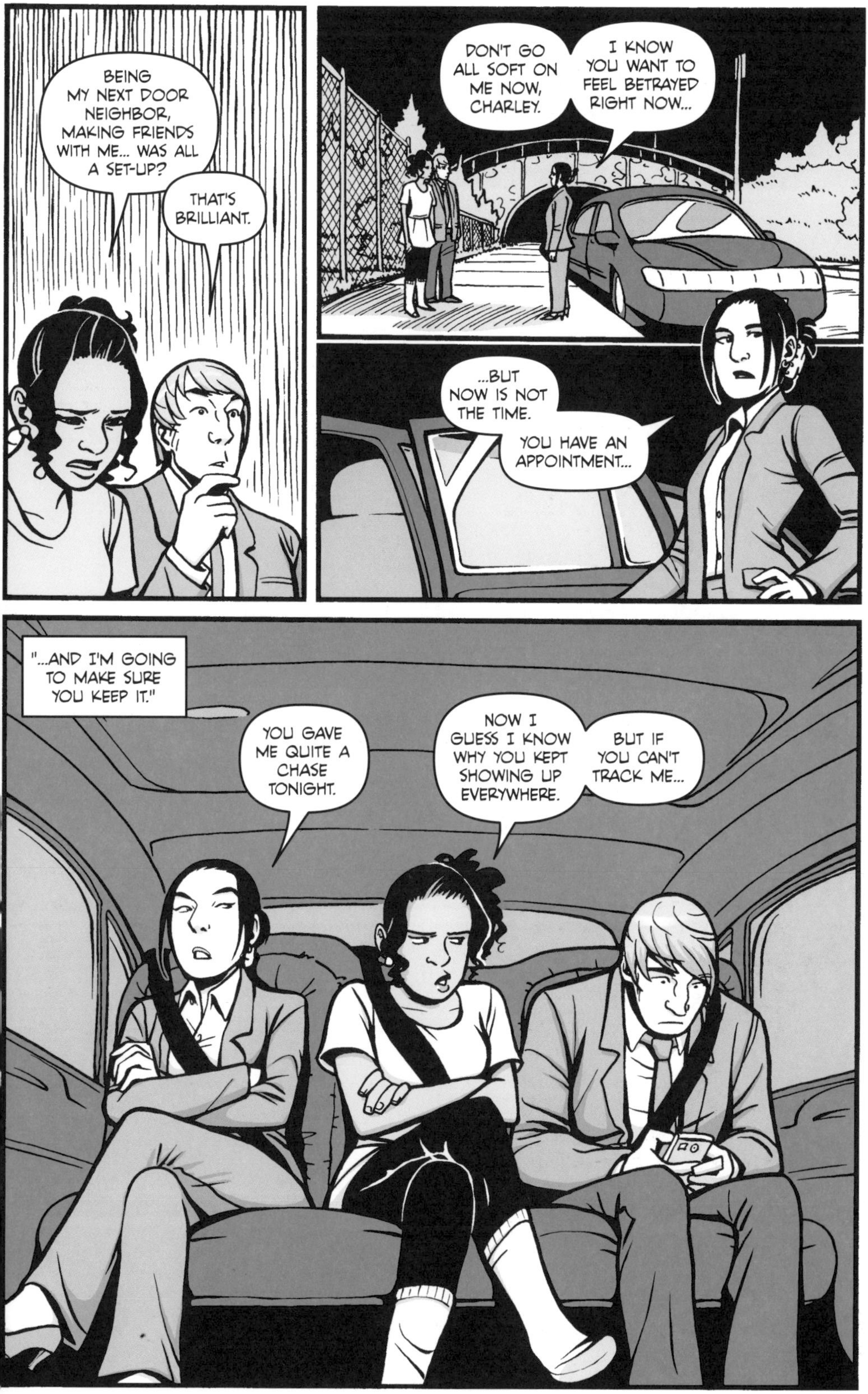
BEING MY NEXT DOOR NEIGHBOR, MAKING FRIENDS WITH ME... WAS ALL A SET-UP?
THAT'S BRILLIANT.
DON'T GO ALL SOFT ON ME NOW, CHARLEY.
I KNOW YOU WANT TO FEEL BETRAYED RIGHT NOW...
...BUT NOW IS NOT THE TIME.
YOU HAVE AN APPOINTMENT...
"...AND I'M GOING TO MAKE SURE YOU KEEP IT."
YOU GAVE ME QUITE A CHASE TONIGHT.
NOW I GUESS I KNOW WHY YOU KEPT SHOWING UP EVERYWHERE.
BUT IF YOU CAN'T TRACK ME...

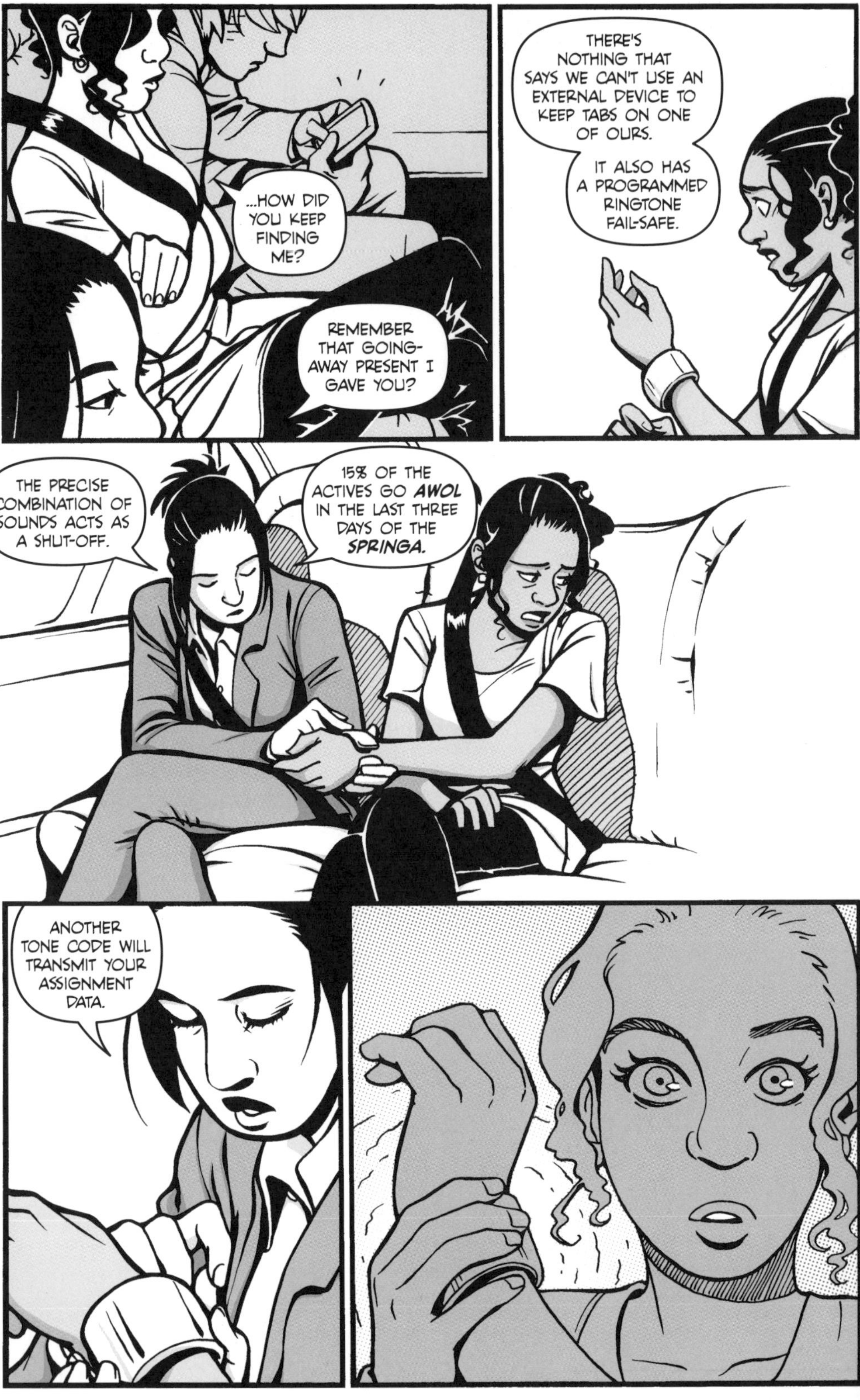
...HOW DID YOU KEEP FINDING ME?
REMEMBER THAT GOING-AWAY PRESENT I GAVE YOU?
THERE'S NOTHING THAT SAYS WE CAN'T USE AN EXTERNAL DEVICE TO KEEP TABS ON ONE OF OURS.
IT ALSO HAS A PROGRAMMED RINGTONE FAIL-SAFE.
THE PRECISE COMBINATION OF SOUNDS ACTS AS A SHUT-OFF.
15% OF THE ACTIVES GO AWOL IN THE LAST THREE DAYS OF THE SPRINGA.
ANOTHER TONE CODE WILL TRANSMIT YOUR ASSIGNMENT DATA.

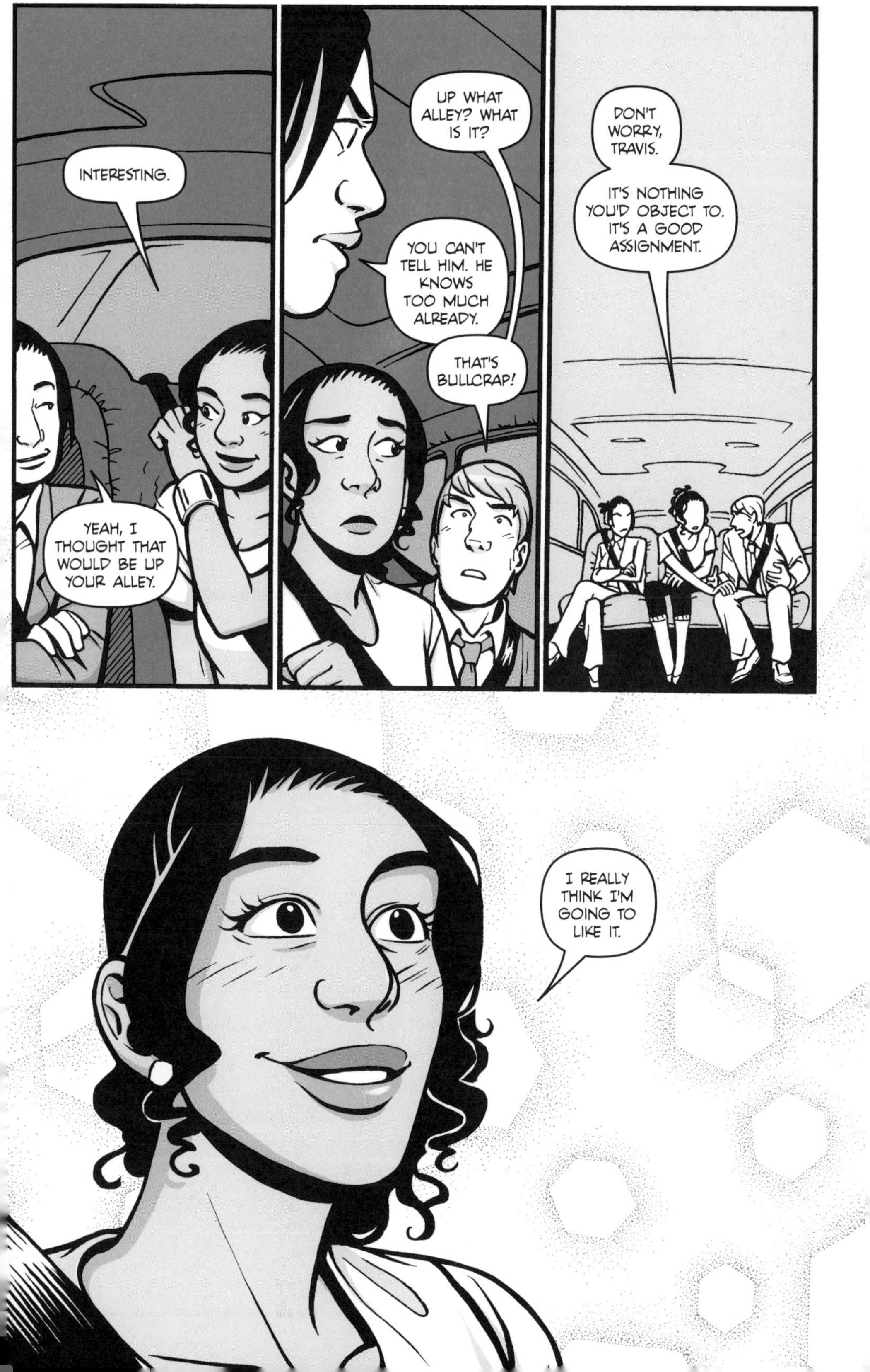
INTERESTING.
YEAH, I THOUGHT THAT WOULD BE UP YOUR ALLEY.
UP WHAT ALLEY? WHAT IS IT?
YOU CAN'T TELL HIM. HE KNOWS TOO MUCH ALREADY.
THAT'S BULLCRAP!
DON'T WORRY, TRAVIS.
IT'S NOTHING YOU'D OBJECT TO. IT'S A GOOD ASSIGNMENT.
I REALLY THINK I'M GOING TO LIKE IT.

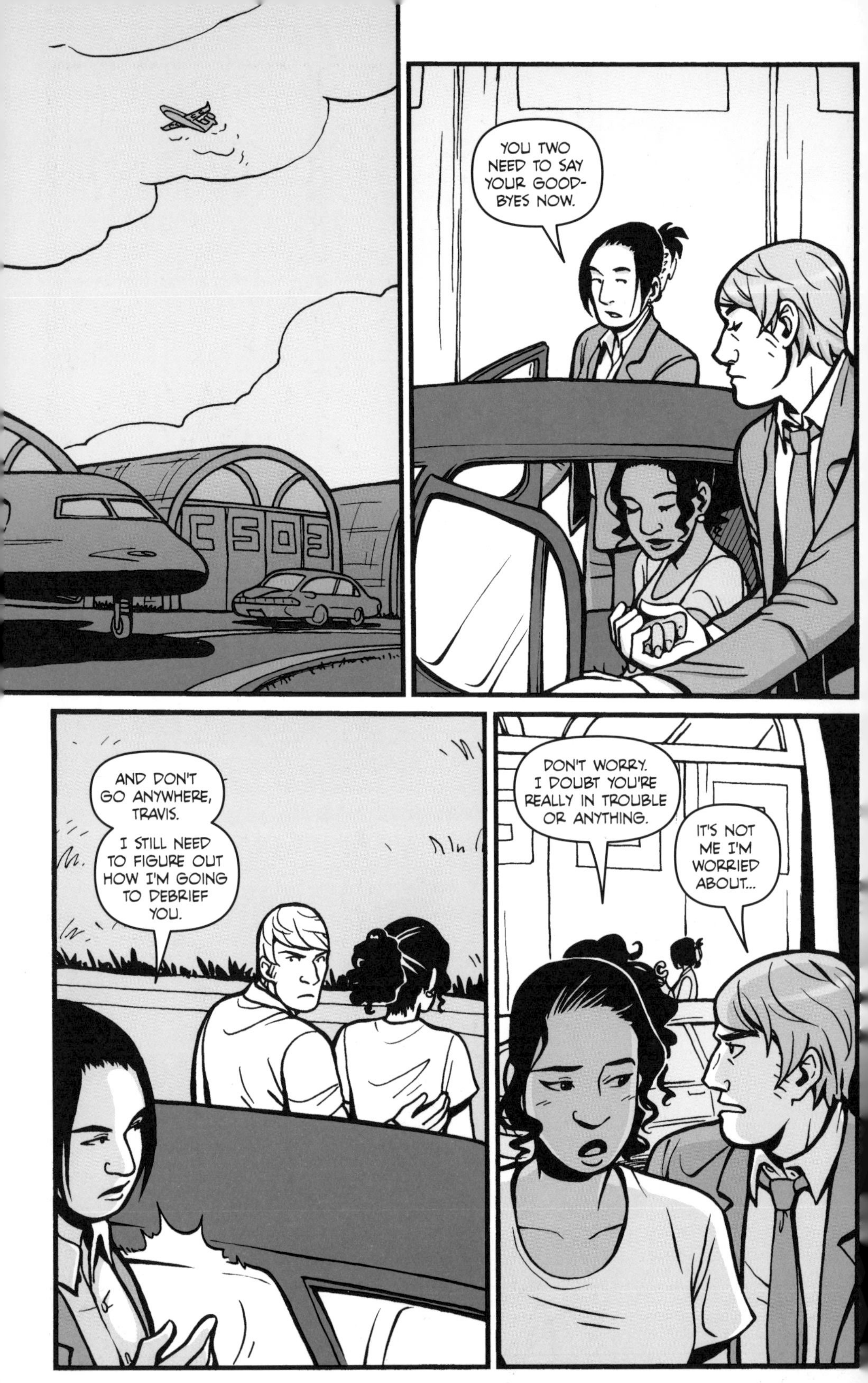

C503
YOU TWO NEED TO SAY YOUR GOOD-BYES NOW.
AND DON'T GO ANYWHERE, TRAVIS.
I STILL NEED TO FIGURE OUT HOW I'M GOING TO DEBRIEF YOU.
DON'T WORRY. I DOUBT YOU'RE REALLY IN TROUBLE OR ANYTHING.
IT'S NOT ME I'M WORRIED ABOUT...

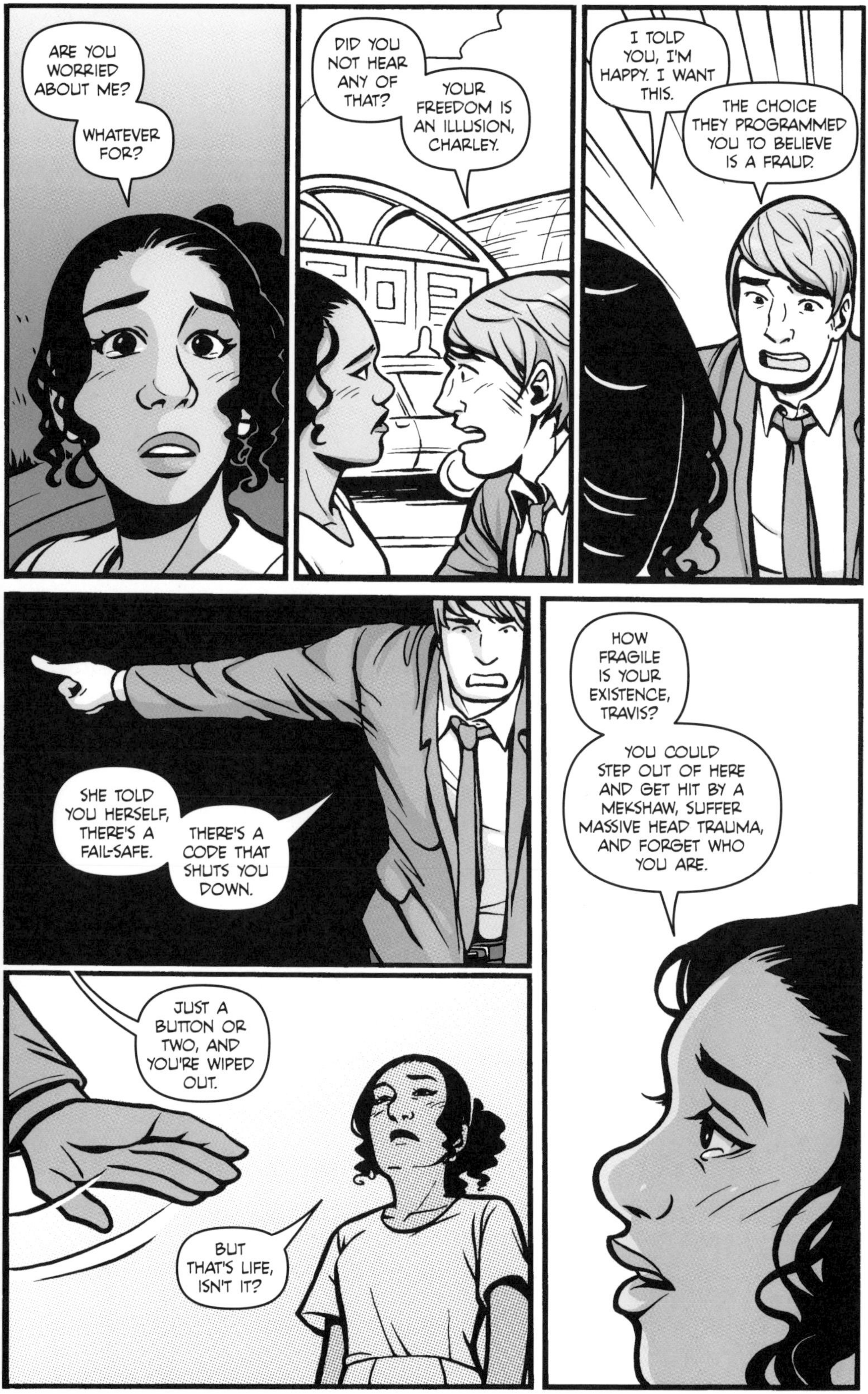
ARE YOU WORRIED ABOUT ME?
WHATEVER FOR?
DID YOU NOT HEAR ANY OF THAT?
YOUR FREEDOM IS AN ILLUSION, CHARLEY.
I TOLD YOU, I'M HAPPY. I WANT THIS.
THE CHOICE THEY PROGRAMMED YOU TO BELIEVE IS A FRAUD.
SHE TOLD YOU HERSELF, THERE'S A FAIL-SAFE.
THERE'S A CODE THAT SHUTS YOU DOWN.
HOW FRAGILE IS YOUR EXISTENCE, TRAVIS?
YOU COULD STEP OUT OF HERE AND GET HIT BY A MEKSHAW, SUFFER MASSIVE HEAD TRAUMA, AND FORGET WHO YOU ARE.
JUST A BUTTON OR TWO, AND YOU'RE WIPED OUT.
BUT THAT'S LIFE, ISN'T IT?

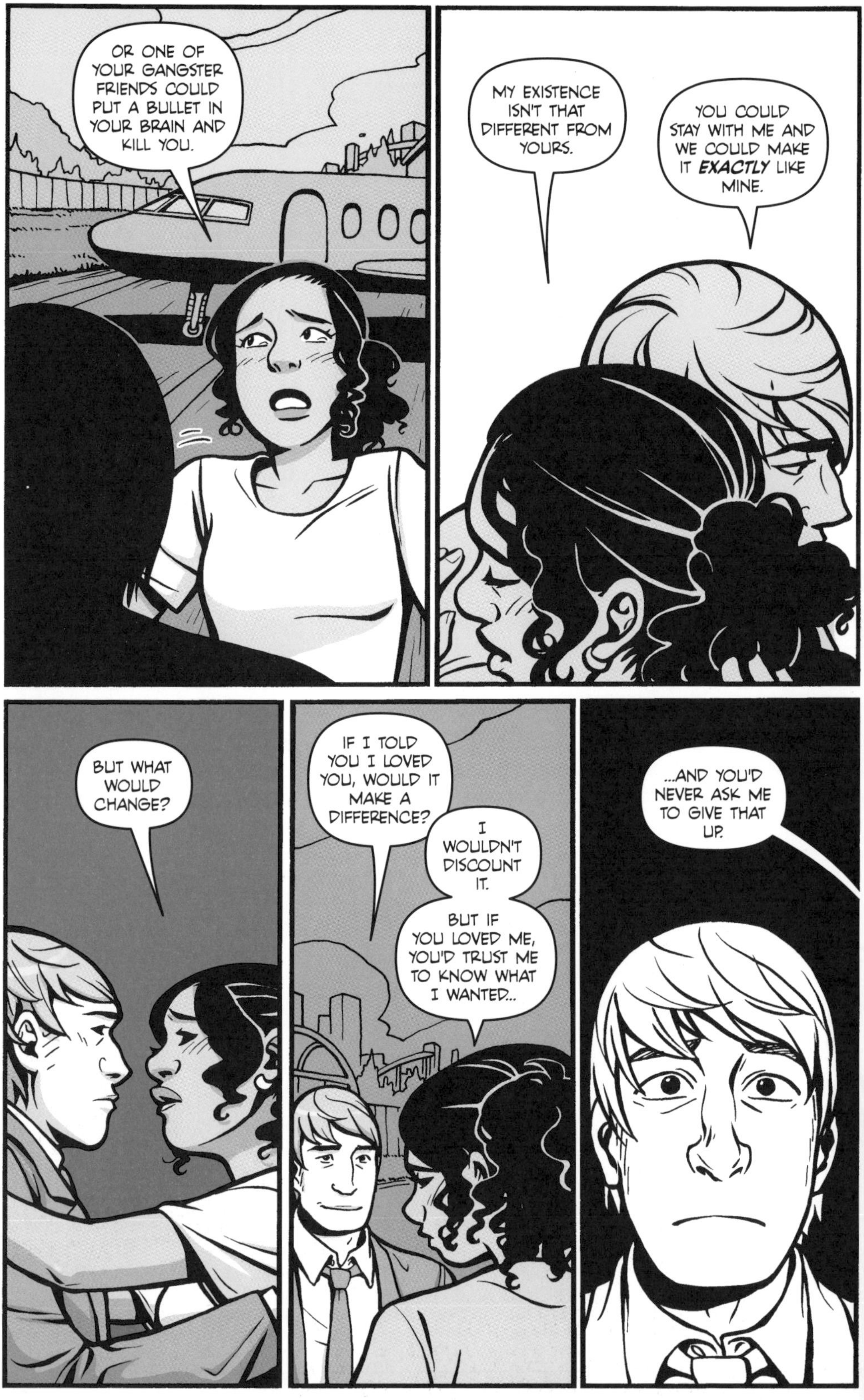
OR ONE OF YOUR GANGSTER FRIENDS COULD PUT A BULLET IN YOUR BRAIN AND KILL YOU.
MY EXISTENCE ISN'T THAT DIFFERENT FROM YOURS.
YOU COULD STAY WITH ME AND WE COULD MAKE IT *EXACTLY* LIKE MINE.
BUT WHAT WOULD CHANGE?
IF I TOLD YOU I LOVED YOU, WOULD IT MAKE A DIFFERENCE?
I WOULDN'T DISCOUNT IT.
BUT IF YOU LOVED ME, YOU'D TRUST ME TO KNOW WHAT I WANTED...
...AND YOU'D NEVER ASK ME TO GIVE THAT UP.

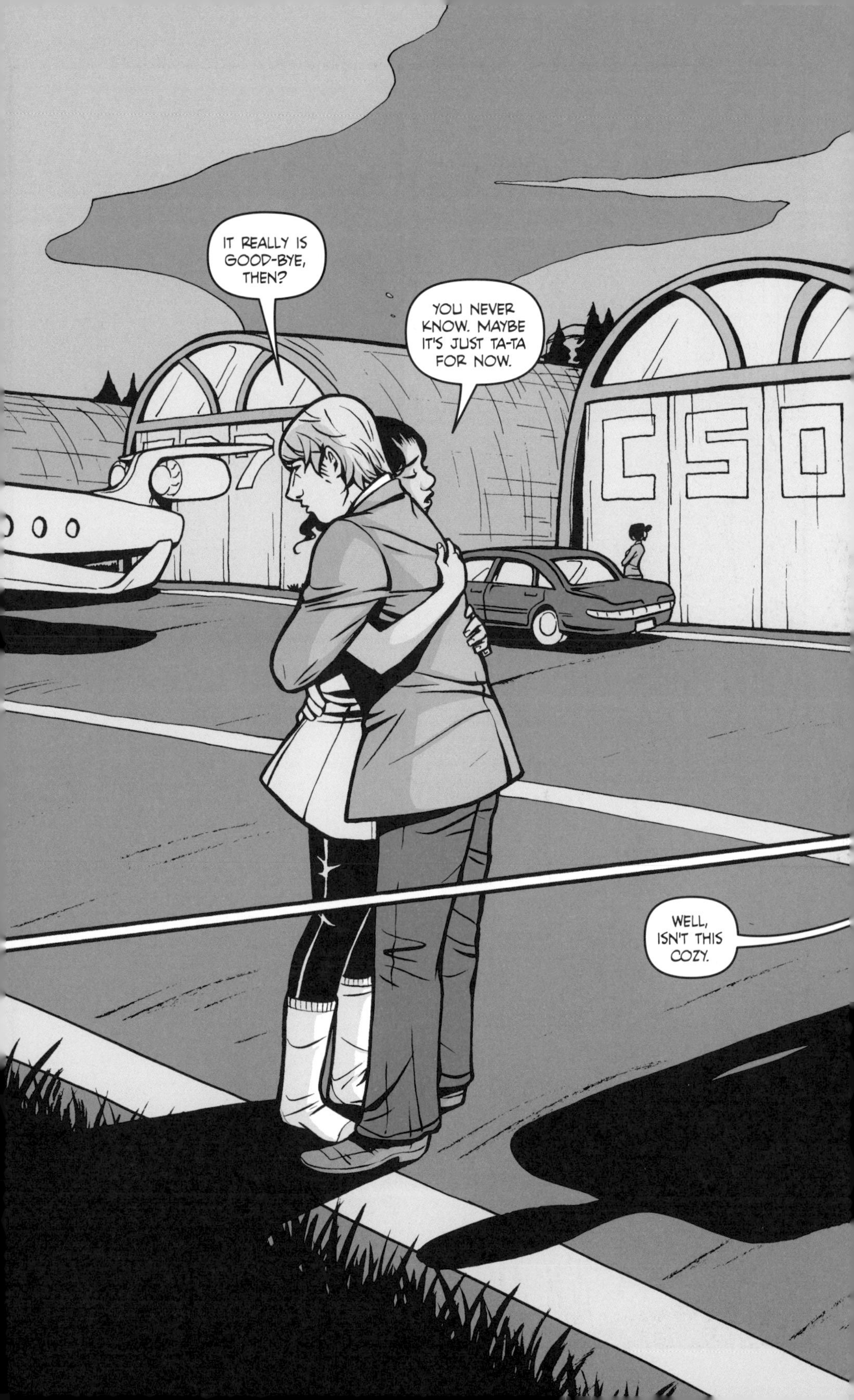
IT REALLY IS GOOD-BYE, THEN?
YOU NEVER KNOW. MAYBE IT'S JUST TA-TA FOR NOW.
CSO
WELL, ISN'T THIS COZY.

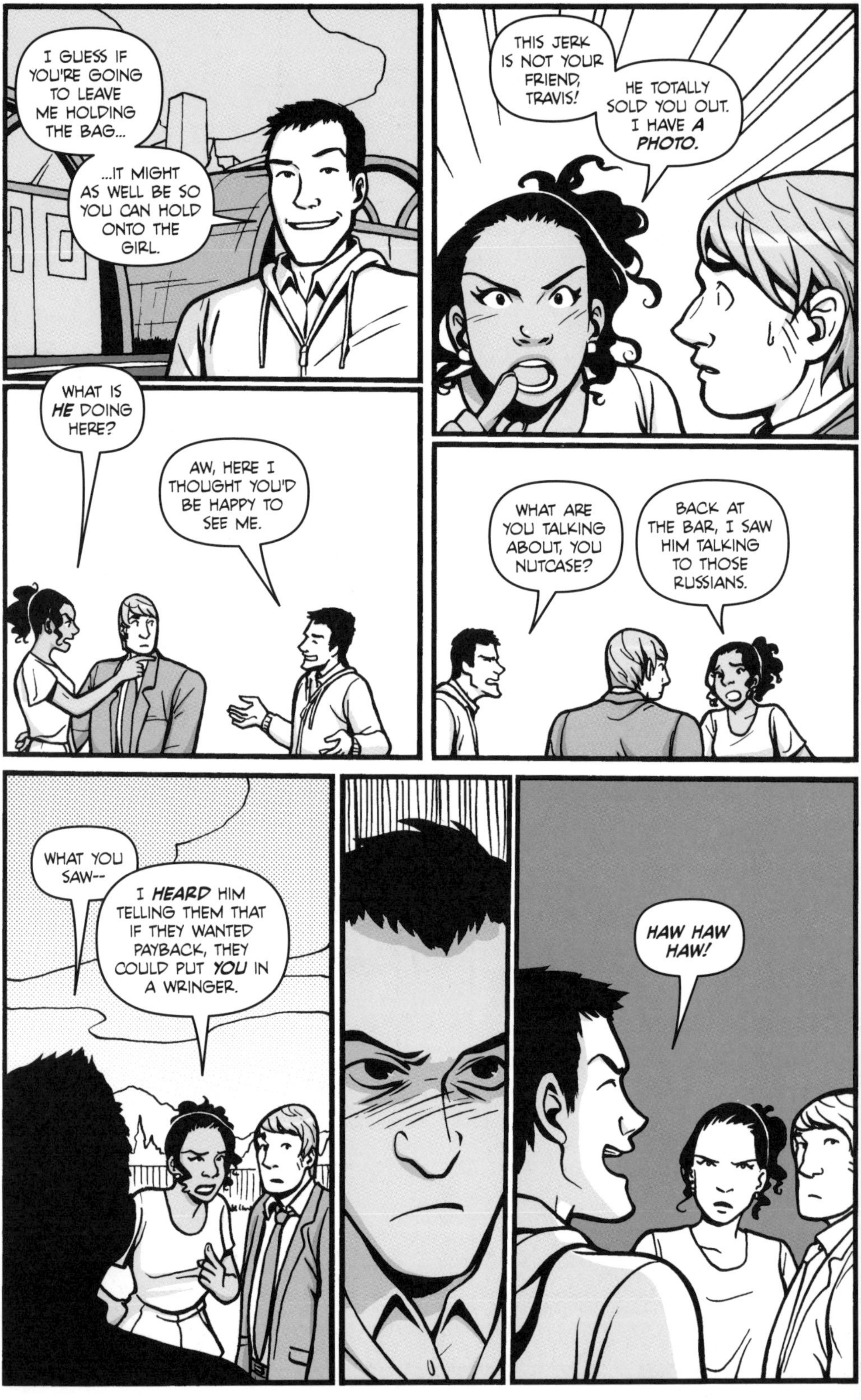
I GUESS IF YOU'RE GOING TO LEAVE ME HOLDING THE BAG...
...IT MIGHT AS WELL BE SO YOU CAN HOLD ONTO THE GIRL.
THIS JERK IS NOT YOUR FRIEND, TRAVIS!
HE TOTALLY SOLD YOU OUT. I HAVE A PHOTO.
WHAT IS HE DOING HERE?
AW, HERE I THOUGHT YOU'D BE HAPPY TO SEE ME.
WHAT ARE YOU TALKING ABOUT, YOU NUTCASE?
BACK AT THE BAR, I SAW HIM TALKING TO THOSE RUSSIANS.
WHAT YOU SAW--
I HEARD HIM TELLING THEM THAT IF THEY WANTED PAYBACK, THEY COULD PUT YOU IN A WRINGER.
HAW HAW HAW!

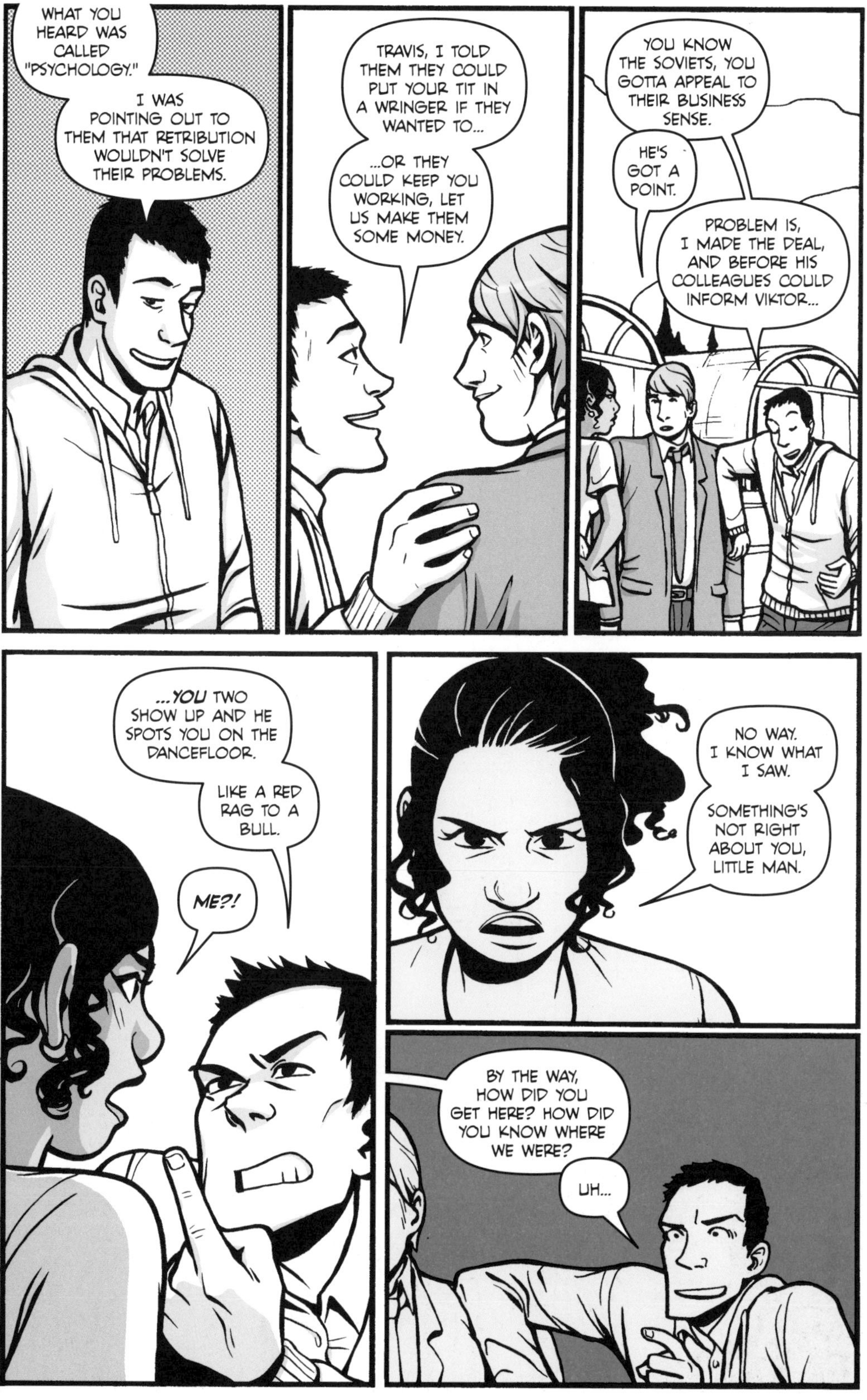
WHAT YOU HEARD WAS CALLED "PSYCHOLOGY."
I WAS POINTING OUT TO THEM THAT RETRIBUTION WOULDN'T SOLVE THEIR PROBLEMS.
TRAVIS, I TOLD THEM THEY COULD PUT YOUR TIT IN A WRINGER IF THEY WANTED TO...
...OR THEY COULD KEEP YOU WORKING, LET US MAKE THEM SOME MONEY.
YOU KNOW THE SOVIETS, YOU GOTTA APPEAL TO THEIR BUSINESS SENSE.
HE'S GOT A POINT.
PROBLEM IS, I MADE THE DEAL, AND BEFORE HIS COLLEAGUES COULD INFORM VIKTOR...
...YOU TWO SHOW UP AND HE SPOTS YOU ON THE DANCEFLOOR.
LIKE A RED RAG TO A BULL.
ME?!
NO WAY. I KNOW WHAT I SAW.
SOMETHING'S NOT RIGHT ABOUT YOU, LITTLE MAN.
BY THE WAY, HOW DID YOU GET HERE? HOW DID YOU KNOW WHERE WE WERE?
UH...

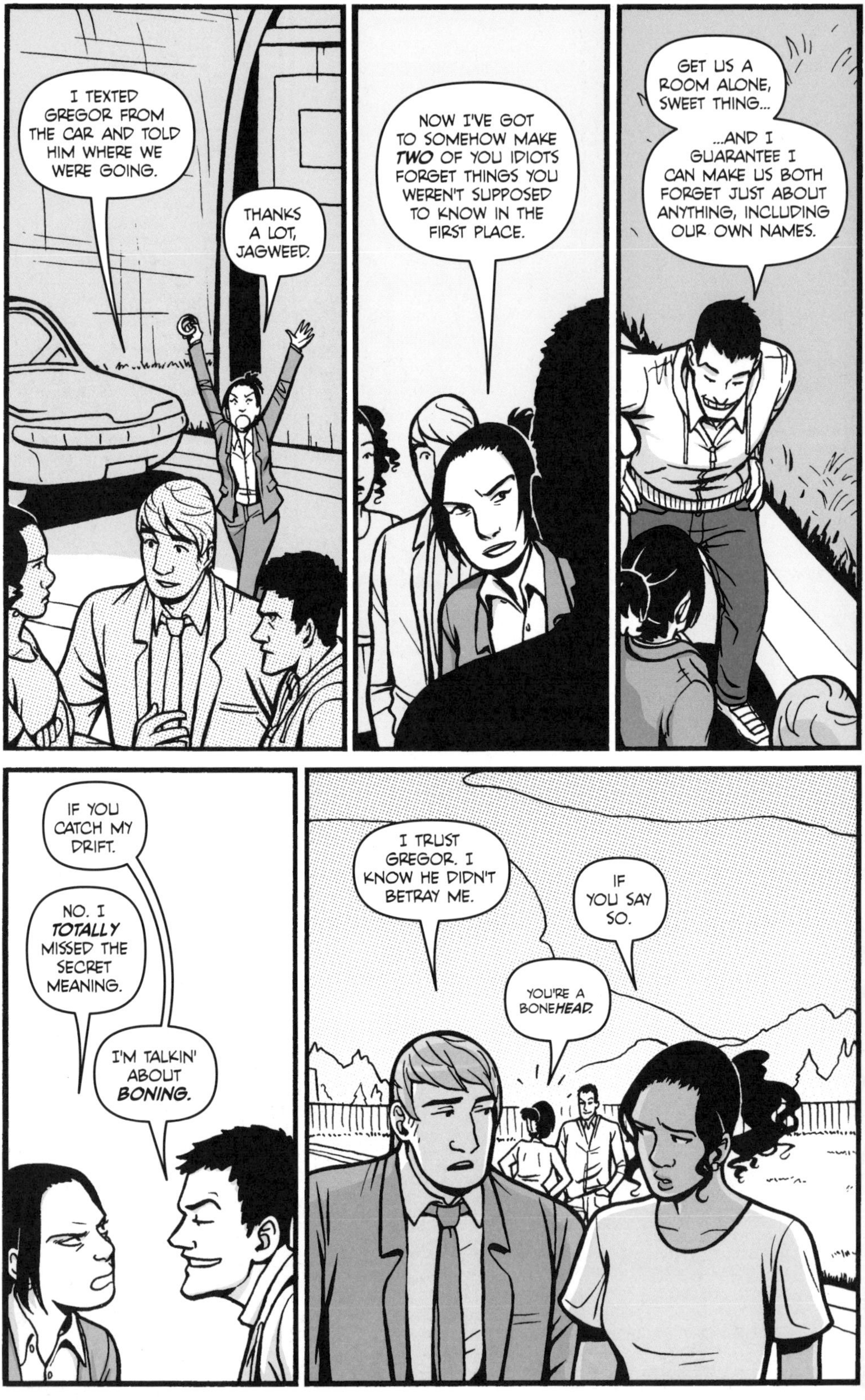
I TEXTED GREGOR FROM THE CAR AND TOLD HIM WHERE WE WERE GOING.
THANKS A LOT, JAGWEED.
NOW I'VE GOT TO SOMEHOW MAKE *TWO* OF YOU IDIOTS FORGET THINGS YOU WEREN'T SUPPOSED TO KNOW IN THE FIRST PLACE.
GET US A ROOM ALONE, SWEET THING...
...AND I GUARANTEE I CAN MAKE US BOTH FORGET JUST ABOUT ANYTHING, INCLUDING OUR OWN NAMES.
IF YOU CATCH MY DRIFT.
NO. I *TOTALLY* MISSED THE SECRET MEANING.
I'M TALKIN' ABOUT *BONING.*
I TRUST GREGOR. I KNOW HE DIDN'T BETRAY ME.
IF YOU SAY SO.
YOU'RE A BONE*HEAD.*

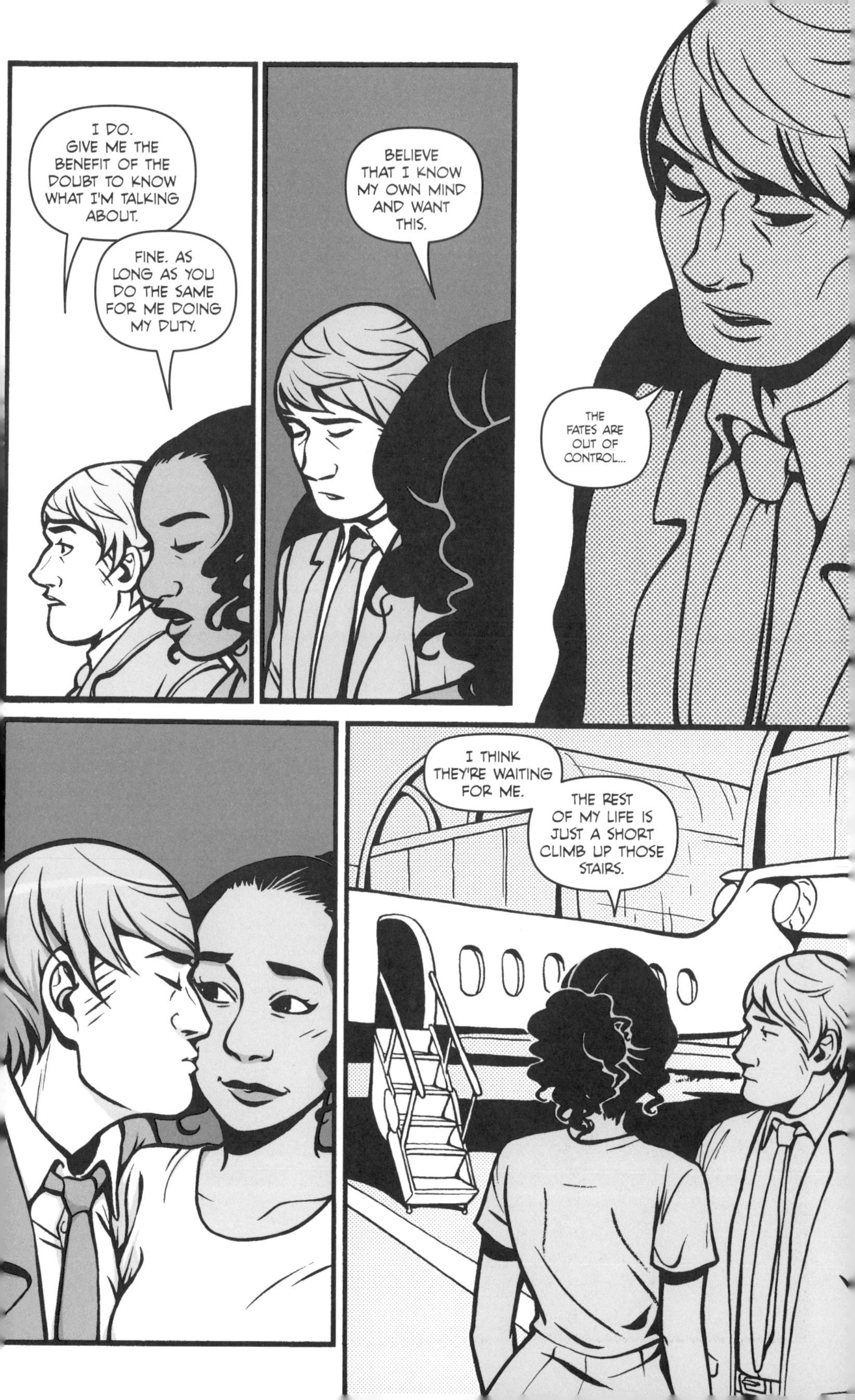
I DO. GIVE ME THE BENEFIT OF THE DOUBT TO KNOW WHAT I'M TALKING ABOUT.
FINE. AS LONG AS YOU DO THE SAME FOR ME DOING MY DUTY.
BELIEVE THAT I KNOW MY OWN MIND AND WANT THIS.
THE FATES ARE OUT OF CONTROL...
I THINK THEY'RE WAITING FOR ME.
THE REST OF MY LIFE IS JUST A SHORT CLIMB UP THOSE STAIRS.

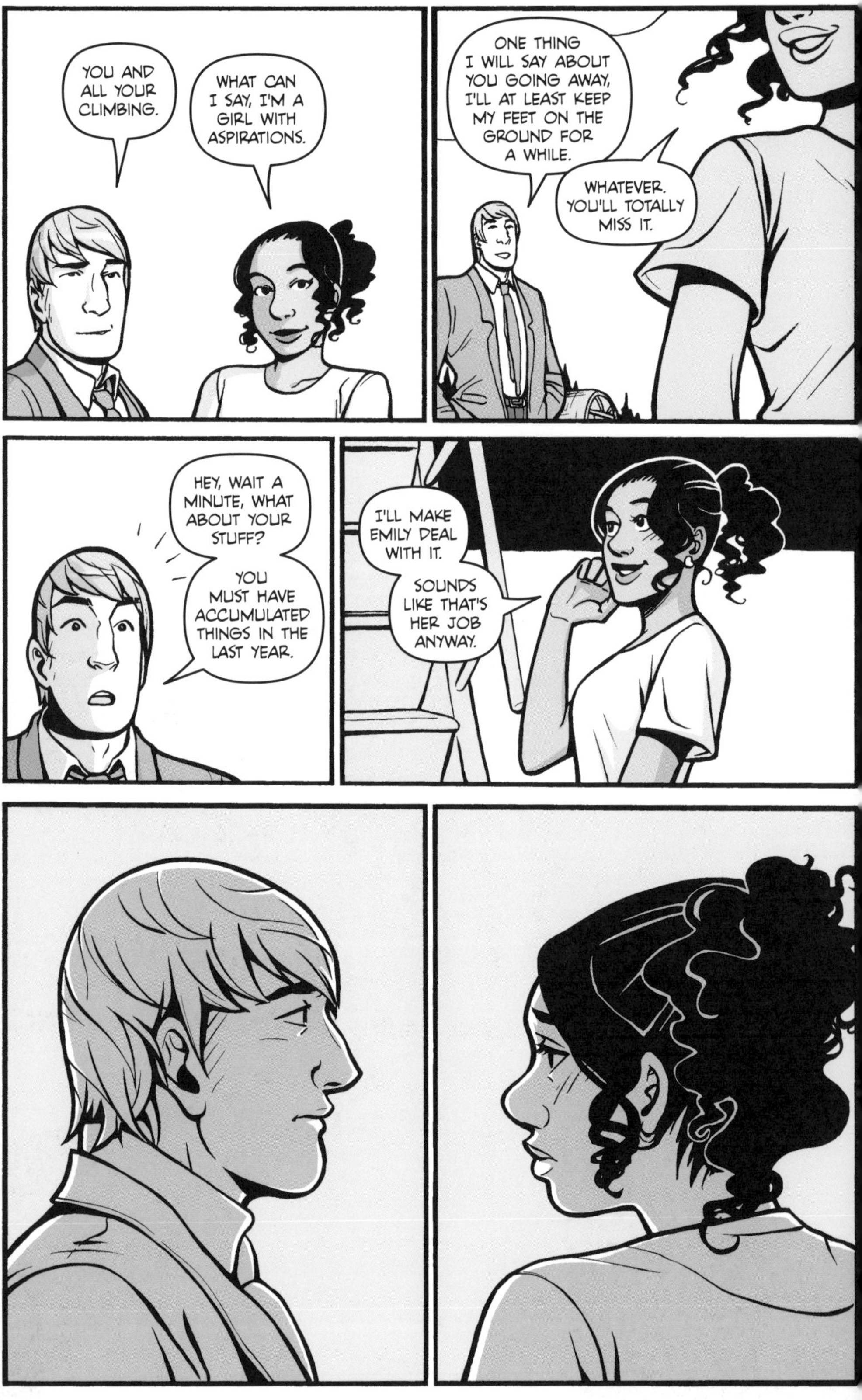
YOU AND ALL YOUR CLIMBING.
WHAT CAN I SAY, I'M A GIRL WITH ASPIRATIONS.
ONE THING I WILL SAY ABOUT YOU GOING AWAY, I'LL AT LEAST KEEP MY FEET ON THE GROUND FOR A WHILE.
WHATEVER. YOU'LL TOTALLY MISS IT.
HEY, WAIT A MINUTE, WHAT ABOUT YOUR STUFF?
YOU MUST HAVE ACCUMULATED THINGS IN THE LAST YEAR.
I'LL MAKE EMILY DEAL WITH IT.
SOUNDS LIKE THAT'S HER JOB ANYWAY.

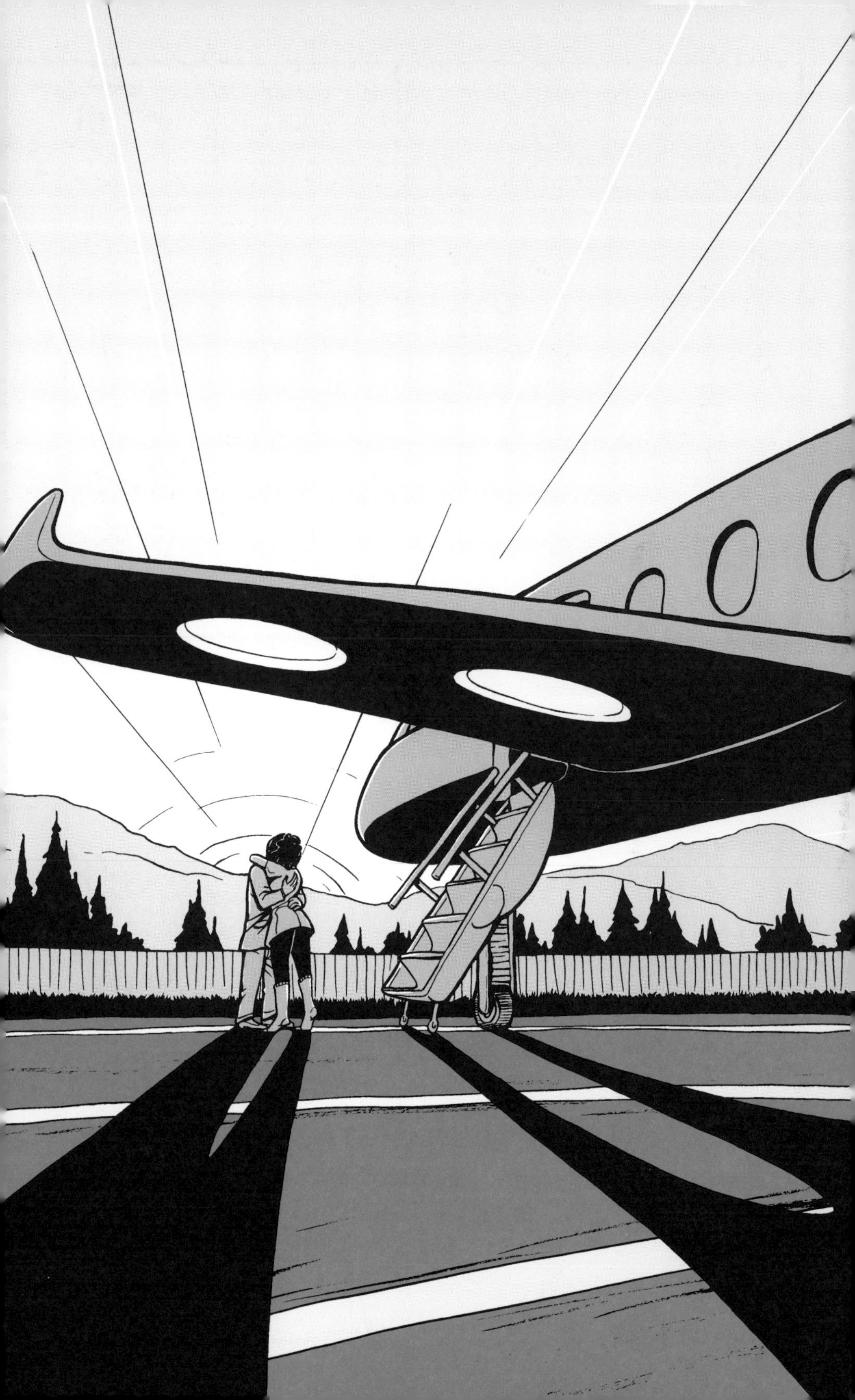

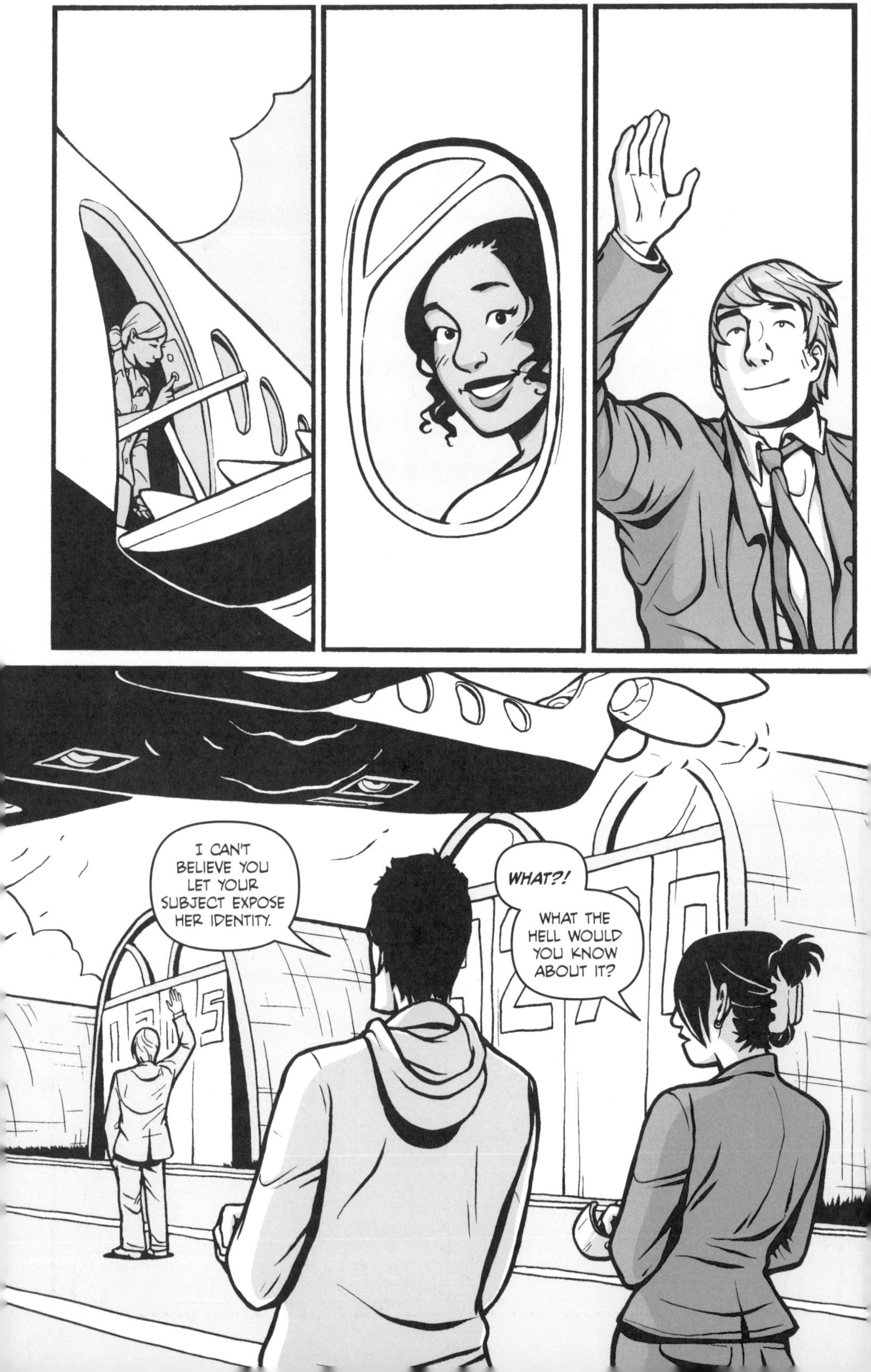
I CAN'T BELIEVE YOU LET YOUR SUBJECT EXPOSE HER IDENTITY.
WHAT?!
WHAT THE HELL WOULD YOU KNOW ABOUT IT?

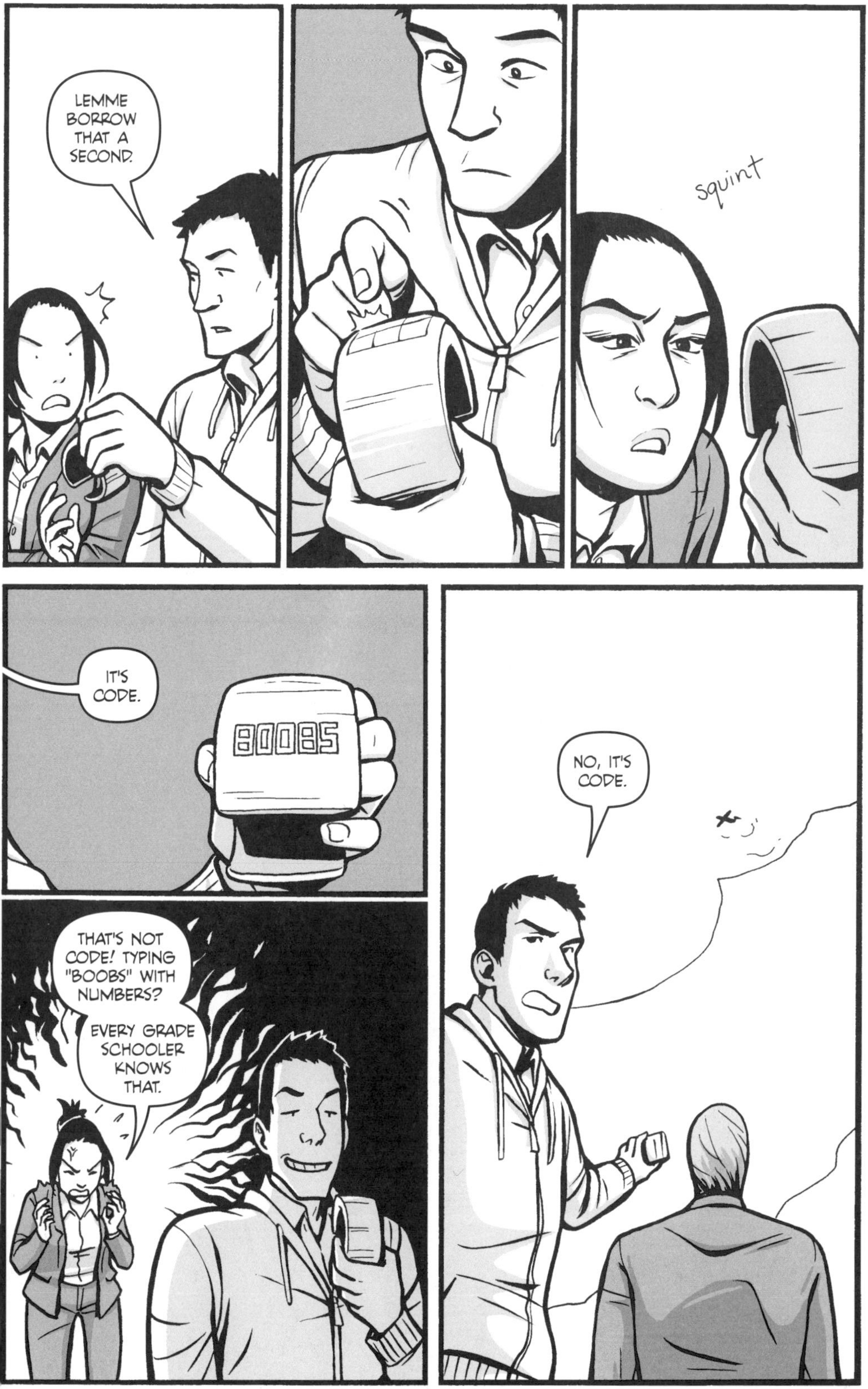
LEMME BORROW THAT A SECOND.
squint
IT'S CODE.
80085
THAT'S NOT CODE! TYPING "BOOBS" WITH NUMBERS?
EVERY GRADE SCHOOLER KNOWS THAT.
NO, IT'S CODE.

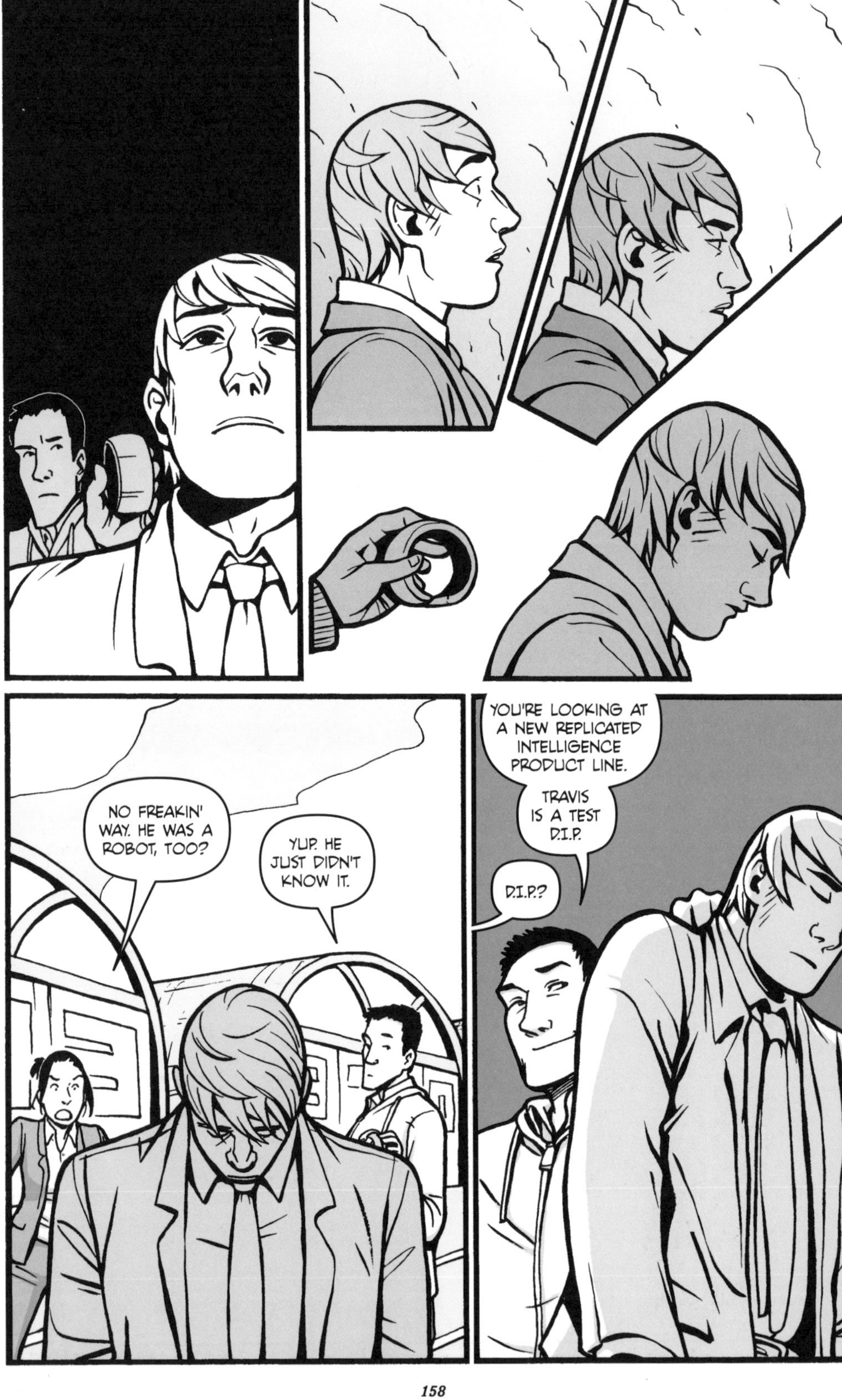
NO FREAKIN' WAY. HE WAS A ROBOT, TOO?
YUP. HE JUST DIDN'T KNOW IT.
YOU'RE LOOKING AT A NEW REPLICATED INTELLIGENCE PRODUCT LINE.
TRAVIS IS A TEST D.I.P.
D.I.P.?

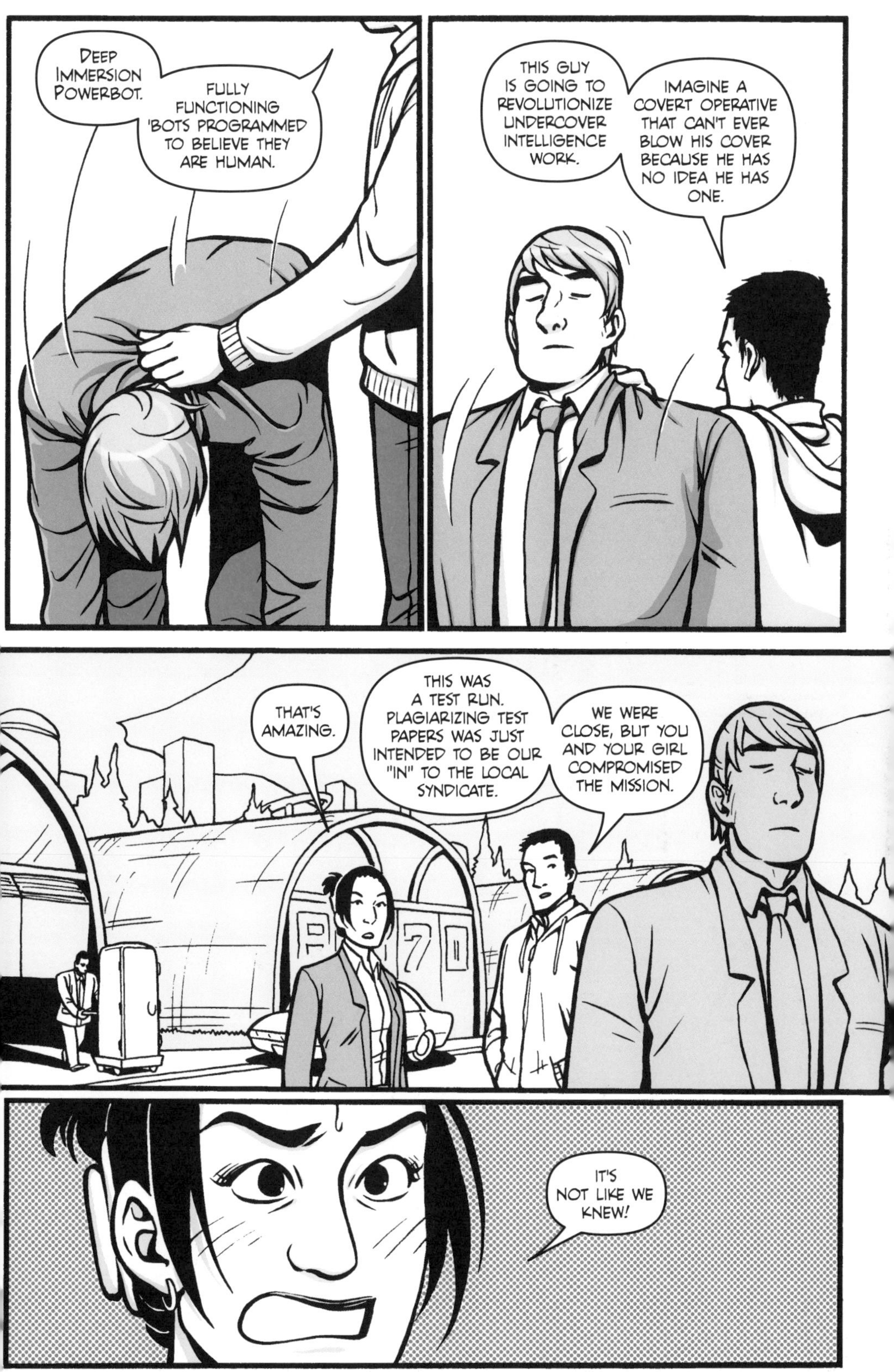
DEEP IMMERSION POWERBOT.
FULLY FUNCTIONING 'BOTS PROGRAMMED TO BELIEVE THEY ARE HUMAN.
THIS GUY IS GOING TO REVOLUTIONIZE UNDERCOVER INTELLIGENCE WORK.
IMAGINE A COVERT OPERATIVE THAT CAN'T EVER BLOW HIS COVER BECAUSE HE HAS NO IDEA HE HAS ONE.
THAT'S AMAZING.
THIS WAS A TEST RUN. PLAGIARIZING TEST PAPERS WAS JUST INTENDED TO BE OUR "IN" TO THE LOCAL SYNDICATE.
WE WERE CLOSE, BUT YOU AND YOUR GIRL COMPROMISED THE MISSION.
IT'S NOT LIKE WE KNEW!

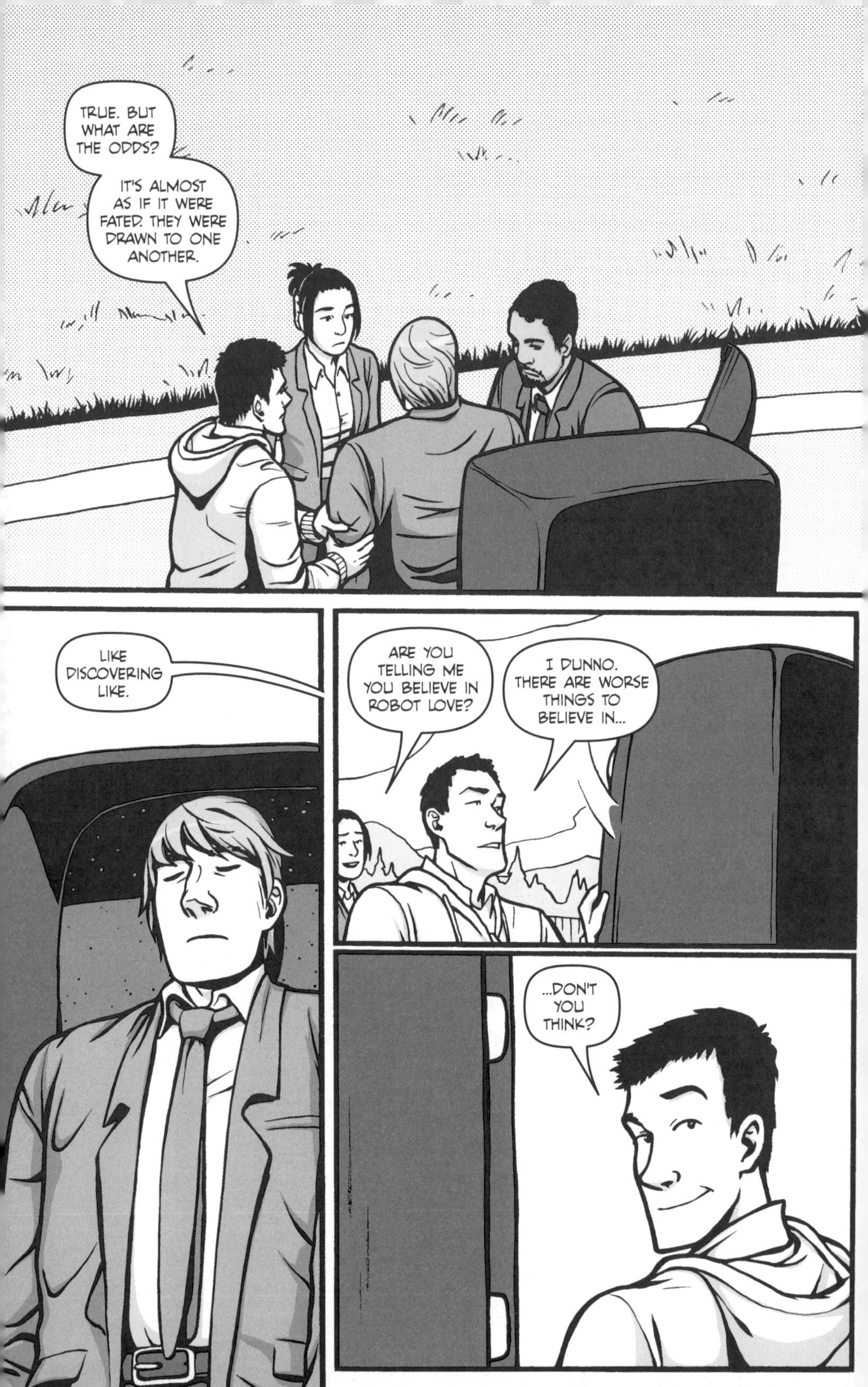
TRUE. BUT WHAT ARE THE ODDS?
IT'S ALMOST AS IF IT WERE FATED. THEY WERE DRAWN TO ONE ANOTHER.
LIKE DISCOVERING LIKE.
ARE YOU TELLING ME YOU BELIEVE IN ROBOT LOVE?
I DUNNO. THERE ARE WORSE THINGS TO BELIEVE IN...
...DON'T YOU THINK?

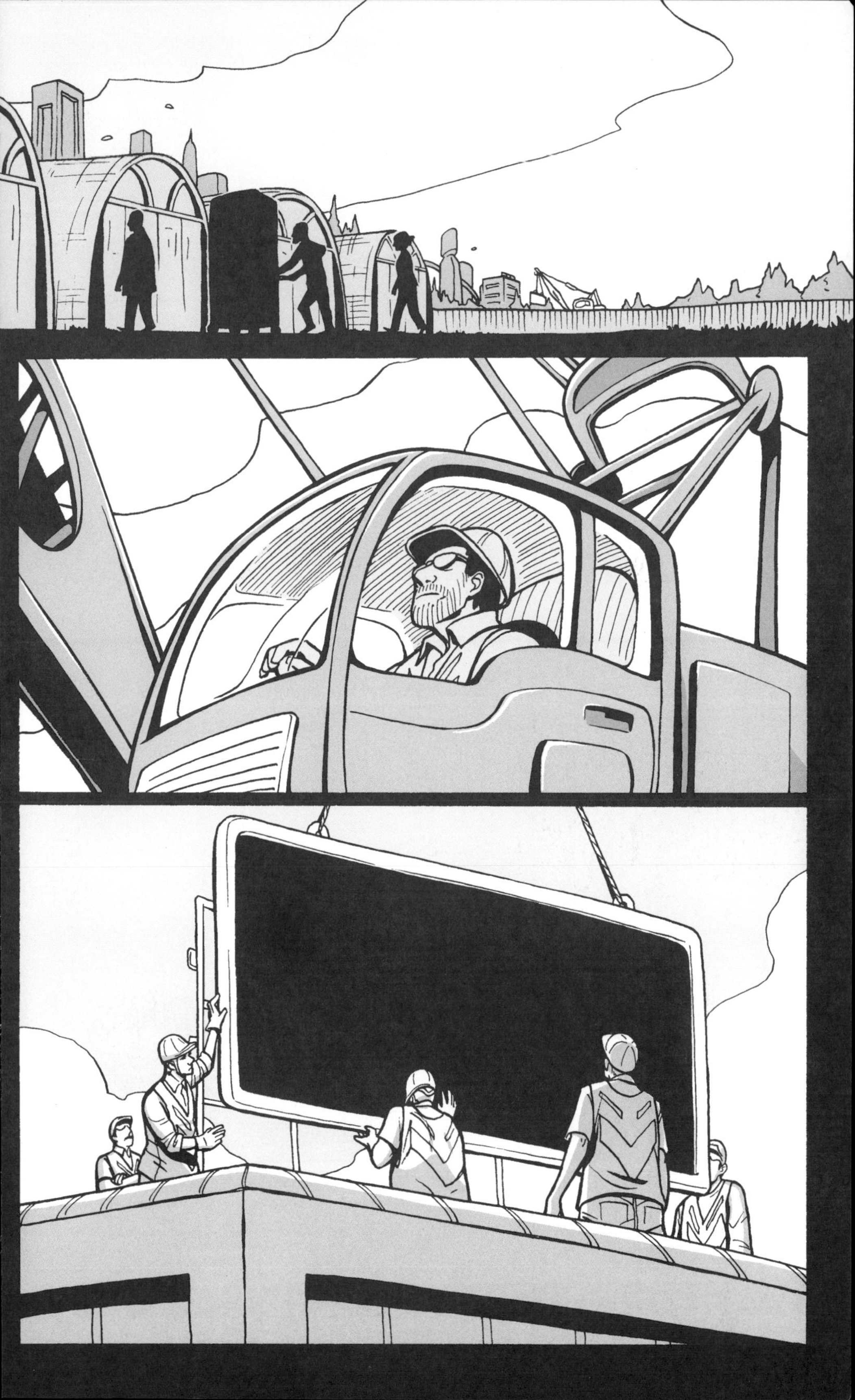

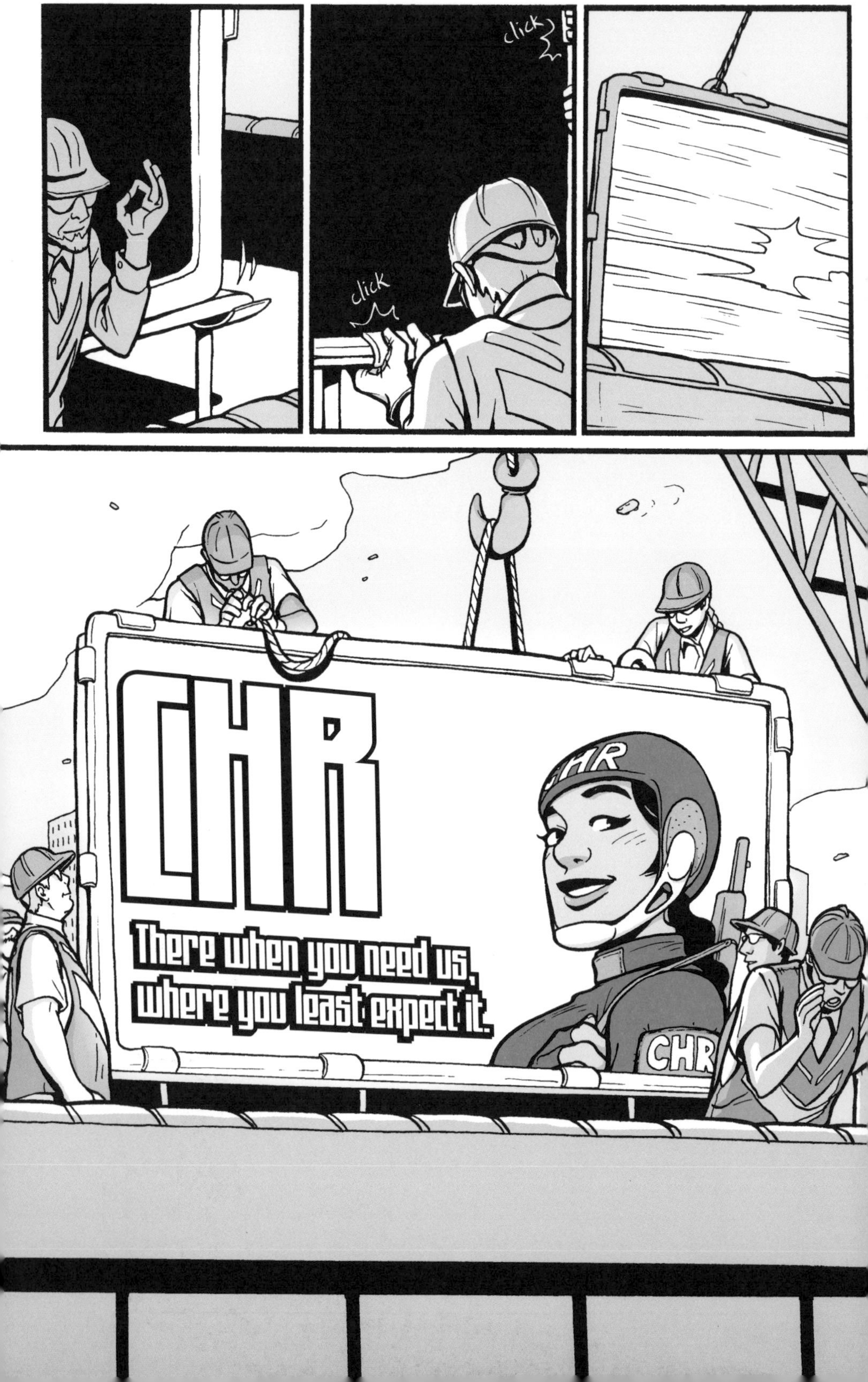
click
click
CHR
There when you need us, where you least expect it.
CHR
CHR

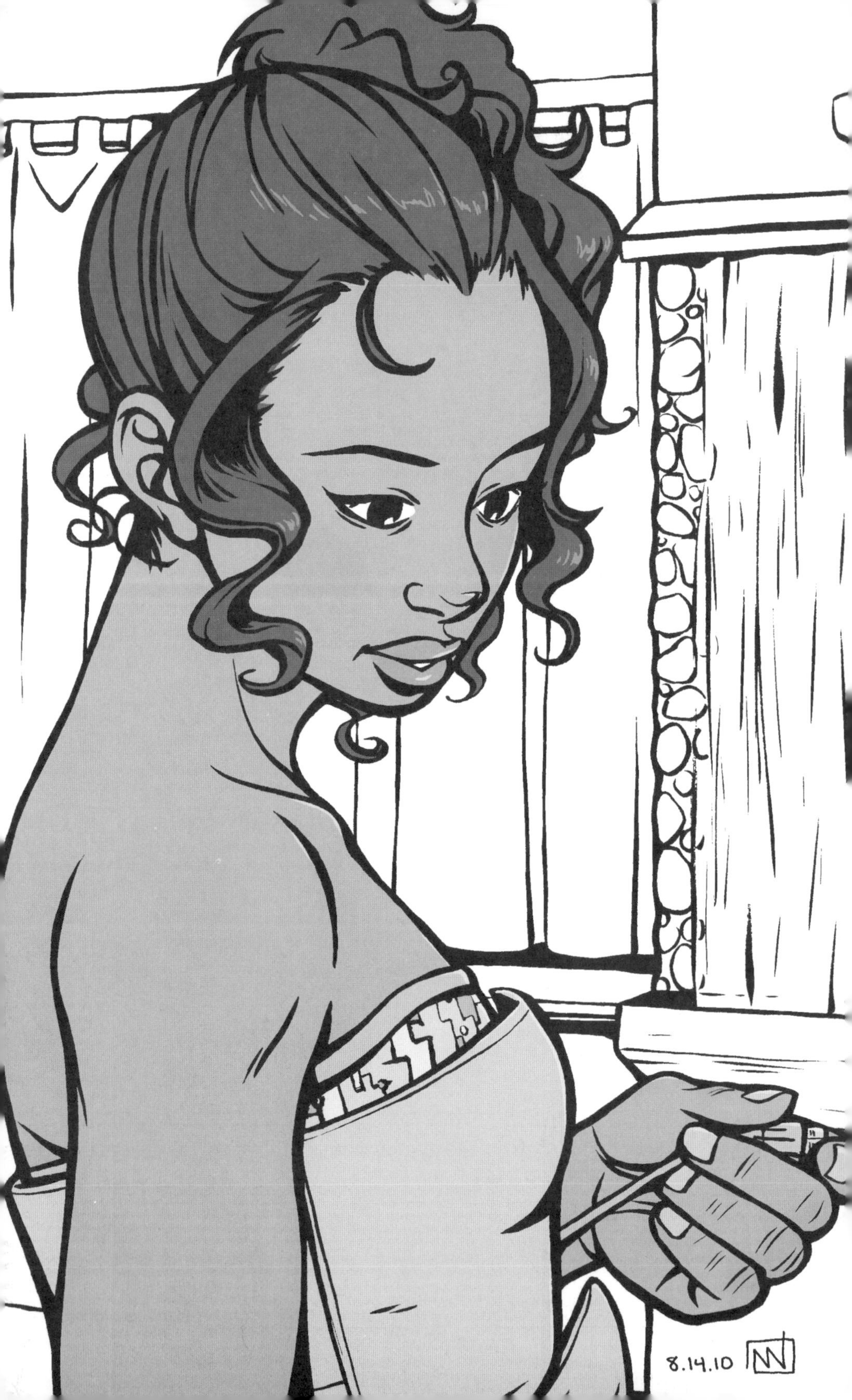
8.14.10

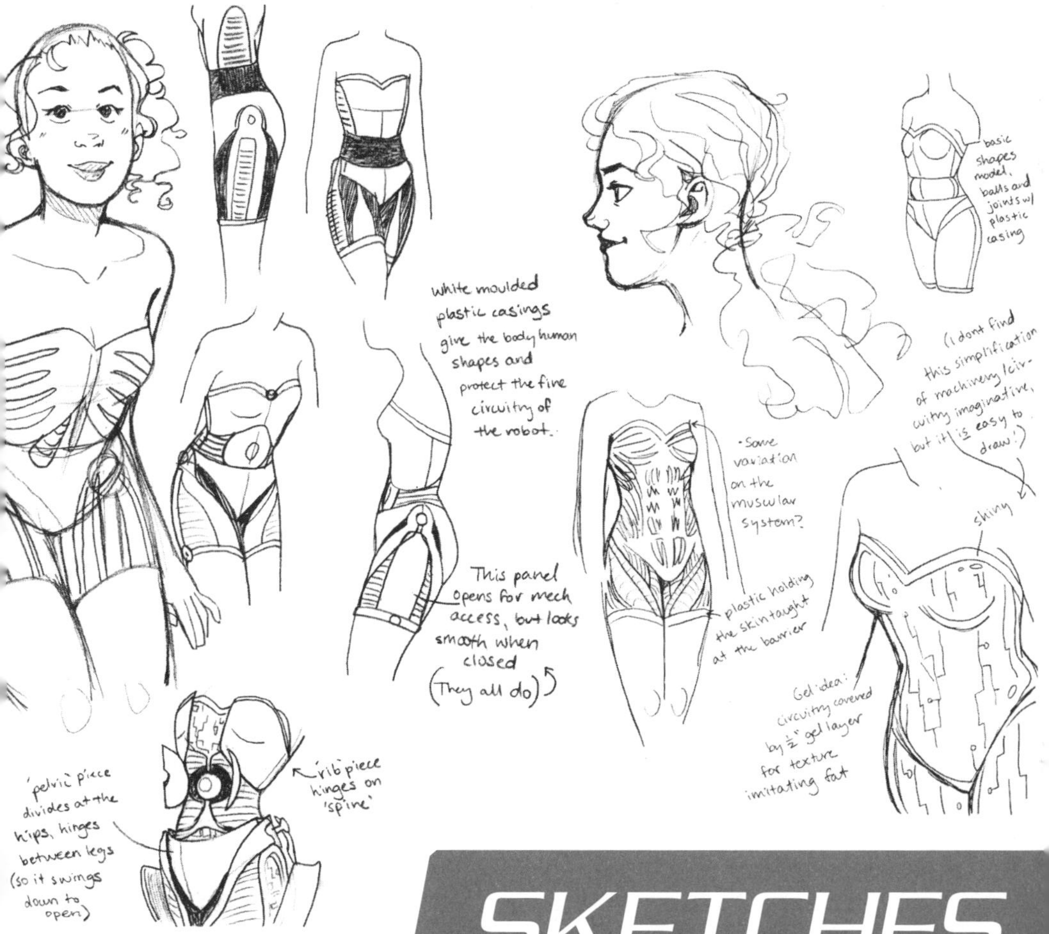
white moulded plastic casings give the body human shapes and protect the fine circuitry of the robot.
This panel opens for mech access, but looks smooth when closed (They all do)
basic shapes model, balls and joints w/ plastic casing
(I dont find this simplification of machinery/circuitry imaginative, but it is easy to draw!)
shiny
-Some variation on the muscular system?
plastic holding the skin taught at the barrier
Gel idea: circuitry covered by ½" gel layer for texture imitating fat
'pelvic' piece divides at the hips, hinges between legs (so it swings down to open)
'rib' piece hinges on 'spine'

SKETCHES

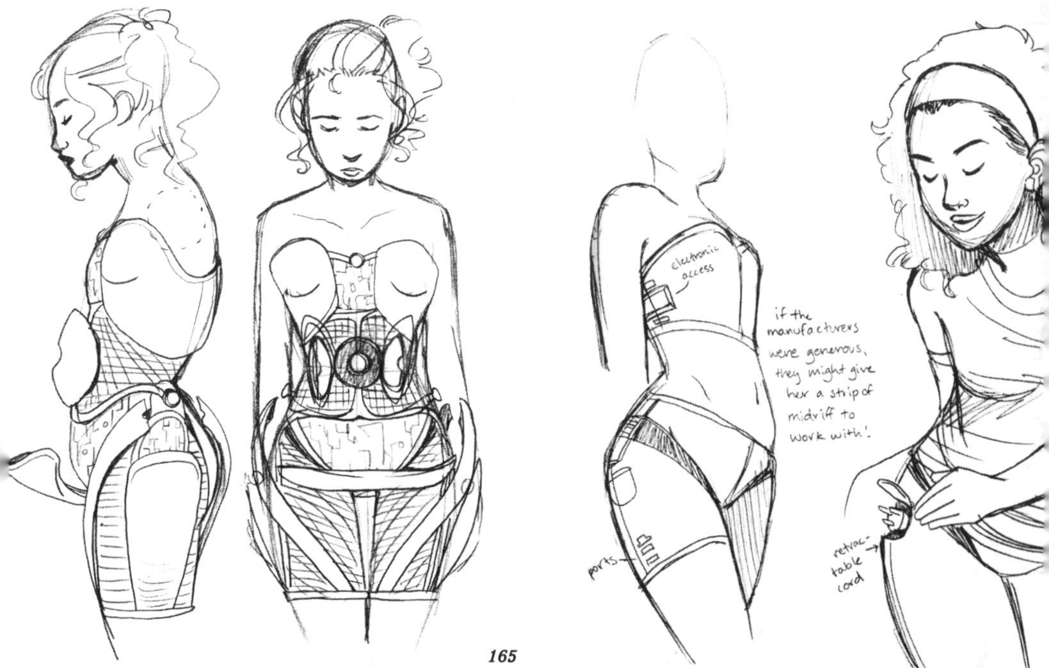
electronic access
if the manufacturers were generous, they might give her a strip of midriff to work with!
ports
retrac-table cord

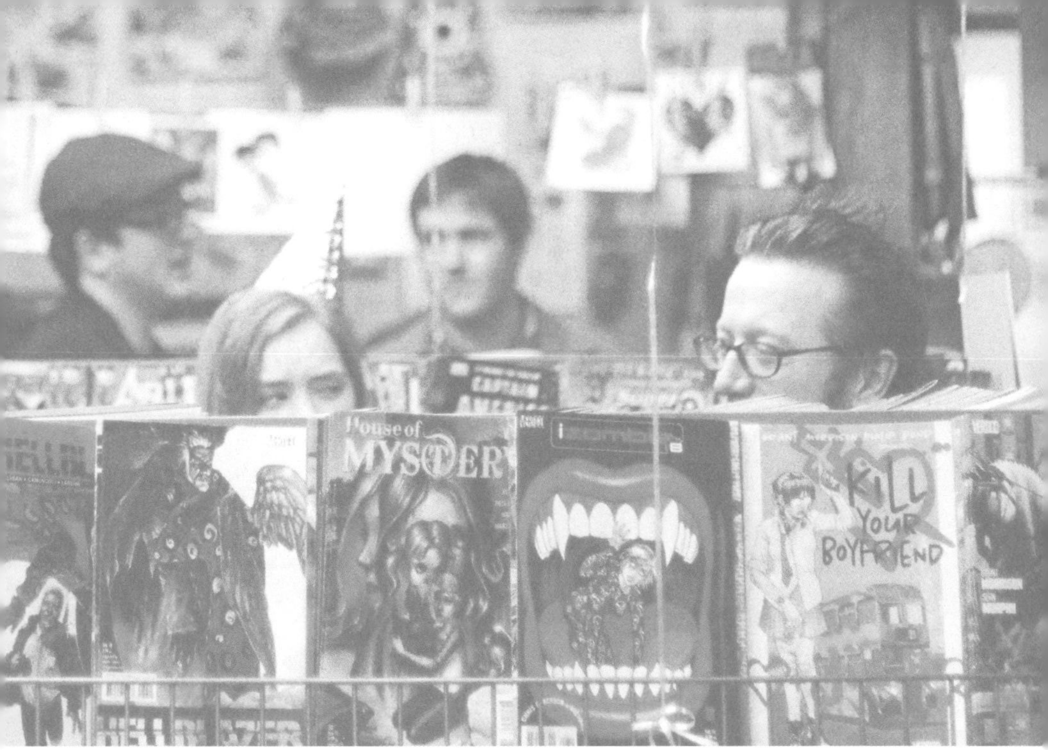
House of
KILL YOUR BOYFRIEND

Natalie "Tally" Nourigat was born and raised in Portland, Oregon. She fell in love with comics at 14 and hasn't stopped making them since. In 2011 she became a member of Periscope Studio, where she works alongside some of the best writers and artists in comics. Her debut graphic novel autobiography *Between Gears* helped her launch into a comics career during the years she was expecting to work as a barista, so she is perpetually delighted and amazed that she gets to draw as much as she likes.

She still lives in Portland because it is pretty great.

Jamie S. Rich is an author and amateur rodeo clown whose venues include Oni Press, Image Comics, DVDTalk.com, and various dive bars around Portland, OR. He is best known for his collaborations with artist Joëlle Jones on the graphic novels *12 Reasons Why I Love Her* and *You Have Killed Me.* He published his first prose novel, *Cut My Hair*, in 2000, and his first superhero comic book, *It Girl and the Atomics*, in 2012. In between, he has worked on multiple projects in both mediums.

He currently reviews film for the Oregonian and blogs at confessions123.com.

Photo by Tim Roth - pupilphoto.com

MORE BOOKS FROM
JAMIE S. RICH & NATALIE NOURIGAT

Jamie S. Rich
& Joëlle Jones
12 Reasons Why I Love Her

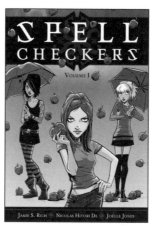

12 REASONS WHY I LOVE HER

By Jamie S. Rich & Joëlle Jones
152 Pages, 6x9 Paperback
B/W Interiors

ISBN 978-1-932664-51-5

SPELL CHECKERS
VOLUME 1
JAMIE S. RICH
NICOLAS HITORI DE
JOËLLE JONES

SPELL CHECKERS, VOL. 1

By Jamie S. Rich, Nicolas Hitori De, Joëlle Jones
152 Pages, Digest, B/W Interiors

ISBN 978-1-934964-32-3

YOU HAVE KILLED ME
by
JAMIE S. RICH
&
JOËLLE JONES

YOU HAVE KILLED ME

By Jamie S. Rich & Joëlle Jones
192 Pages, Hardcover,
B/W Interiors

ISBN 978-1-932664-88-1

MICHAEL ALLRED'S
iT GiRL!
AND THE ATOMICS
ROUND 1
"DARK STREETS, SNAP CITY"
RICH
NORTON
PASSALAQUA
CLUGSTON FLORES
CRANK!
AARON

IT GIRL & THE ATOMICS
ROUND ONE: DARK STREETS, SNAP CITY

By Jamie S. Rich, Mike Norton, & Chynna Clugston Flores
168 Pages, Paperback
Color Interiors

ISBN 978-1-607067-25-2

MICHAEL ALLRED'S
iT GiRL!
AND THE ATOMICS
"THE WORLD IS FLAT"
RICH
NORTON
NOURIGAT
CLUGSTON FLORES
PASSALAQUA
CRANK!

IT GIRL & THE ATOMICS
ROUND TWO: THE WORLD IS FLAT

By Jamie S. Rich, Mike Norton, Natalie Nourigat, & Chynna Clugston Flores
168 Pages, Paperback
Color Interiors

ISBN 978-1-607067-91-7

BETWEEN GEARS
BY NATALIE NOURIGAT

BETWEEN GEARS

By Natalie Nourigat
304 Pages, 10 x 6½ Paperback
B/W Interiors

ISBN 978-1-607065-04-3

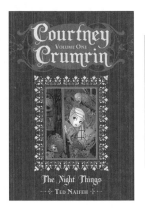

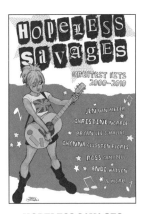